# A
# TORAH
# COMMENTARY
# FOR OUR
# TIMES

## VOLUME II : EXODUS AND LEVITICUS

*HARVEY J. FIELDS*

*Illustrations by*
GIORA CARMI

REFORM JUDAISM PUBLISHING

Central Conference of American Rabbis, New York

For
the members of
THE WILSHIRE BOULEVARD SYNAGOGUE
Los Angeles, California

Library of Congress Cataloging-in-Publication Data
Fields, Harvey J.
A Torah commentary for our times / Harvey J. Fields;
illustrations by Giora Carmi.
    p.  cm.
Includes bibliographical references.
Contents: v. 1. Genesis
ISBN 978-0-88123-252-3 (v. 1)
ISBN 978-0-88123-253-0 (v. 2)
I. Bible O.T. Pentateuch—Commentaries. | 1. Bible O.T.
Pentateuch.|  I. Karmi, Giyora, ill.  II. Title.
BS1225.3.F46 1990
222'.1077—dc20            89–28478
                    CIP
                    AP

# Feldman Library

THE FELDMAN LIBRARY FUND was created in 1974 through a gift from the Milton and Sally Feldman Foundation. The Feldman Library Fund, which provides for the publication by the UAHC of selected outstanding Jewish books and texts, memorializes Sally Feldman, who in her lifetime devoted herself to Jewish youth and Jewish learning. Herself an orphan and brought up in an orphanage, she dedicated her efforts to helping Jewish young people get the educational opportunities she had not enjoyed.

*In loving memory of my beloved wife Sally*
*"She was my life, and she is gone;*
*She was my riches, and I am a pauper."*

*"Many daughters have done valiantly,*
*but thou excellest them all."*

Milton E. Feldman

# Contents

*Acknowledgments* vii

Exploring Torah: Questions and Meanings   1

## THE TORAH PORTIONS OF EXODUS

*Parashat Shemot*   7

   Pharaoh's war against the Jews
   When is civil disobedience justified?
   Moses: fear, courage, self-doubt, or humility?

*Parashat Va'era*   17

   Why so many names for one God?
   The "hardening" of Pharaoh's heart

*Parashat Bo*   25

   Were the Israelites justified in taking gold and silver from the Egyptians?
   Origins of the Pesach celebration

*Parashat Beshalach*   32

   Was Israel's escape from Egypt a "miracle"?
   Why all the complaints against Moses and God?
   Amalek's attack upon the Israelites

*Parashat Yitro*   42

   The burden of leadership
   What happened at Mount Sinai?

*Parashat Mishpatim*   51

   Ethical and ritual mitzvot
   Caring for the stranger

*Parashat Terumah*   61

   The sanctuary in Jewish tradition
   "Exactly as I show you . . . so shall you make it"

*Parashat Tetzaveh*   69

   What is the ner tamid?
   Priestly clothing: fashionable style or significant symbol?

*Parashat Ki Tisa*   77

   Why did they build the golden calf?
   Moses protests on behalf of his people

*Parashat Vayakhel-Pekude*   86

   The Sabbath is for celebration, for rest, not work!
   The obligation of giving charity, tzedakah
   Accountability of public officials


## THE TORAH PORTIONS OF LEVITICUS

*Parashat Vayikra*   97

   The meanings of sacrifice and prayer
   Defining "sin" in Jewish tradition

*Parashat Tzav*   104

   Finding meaning in obsolete traditions
   The holiness of blood

*Parashat Shemini*   111

   What did Nadab and Abihu do wrong?
   Different views on kashrut—the Jewish art of eating

*Parashat Tazria-Metzora*   120

   Biblical medicine, ritual, and ethics
   The sin of slandering others

*Parashat Achare Mot-Kedoshim*   127

   Seeking meaning for the strange ritual of the scapegoat
   Defining "holiness" in Jewish tradition
   Can we love others as ourselves?

*Parashat Emor*   138

   The Jewish festivals: Pesach, Shavuot, and Sukot
   Eye for an eye, tooth for a tooth: about Lex Talionis

*Parashat Behar-Bechukotai*   150

   Lessons from the sabbatical and jubilee years
   The mitzvah of caring for the poor
   Rewards and punishments: the consequences of our choices

*Glossary of Commentaries and Interpreters*   162
*Bibliography*   165

# Acknowledgments

As with Volume I of *A Torah Commentary for Our Times* , Volume II has been enriched through the constant wise advice of teachers, students, and editors. I am particularly grateful to Aron Hirt-Manheimer for his continuing enthusiasm and direction; to Rabbi Howard I. Bogot, Rabbi Shelton Donnell, and Rabbi Steven Z. Leder for carefully reacting to the text. Annette Abramson's meticulous editing and interest in this project are deeply appreciated, as are the understanding and production care of Stuart L. Benick.

I am grateful to the leadership and membership of Wilshire Boulevard Temple who have encouraged my conviction, borrowed from Hillel, that "the more Torah, the more life; the more Torah, the more freedom; the more Torah, the more peace." (*Avot* 2:8) I dedicate this volume to them.

Finally, my wife, Sybil, continues to read and critique my work with devotion; her support and love are a source of inspiration.

*Harvey J. Fields*

# EXPLORING TORAH
## *Questions and Meanings*

Nobel Laureate Isaac Bashevis Singer observes that, whenever he takes the Bible from his book-case, he cannot put it down. "I always find new apsects, new facts, new tensions, new information in it. I sometimes imagine that, while I sleep or walk, some hidden scribe invades my house and puts new passages, new names, new events into this wonderful book." (David Rosenberg, editor, *Congregation: Contemporary Writers Read the Jewish Bible,* Harcourt Brace Jovanovich Publishers, New York, 1987, pp. 7–8)

Singer's view of the Hebrew Bible grows out of a deep knowledge of its contents and an ap-preciation of its literary power and beauty. *A Torah Commentary for Our Times,* Volume I: Genesis, introduces the reader to a vast array of ancient legends about creation, early human life on our planet, and the origins of the Jewish people. The stories of Adam and Eve; Abraham and Sarah; Isaac and Rebekah; Jacob, Leah, and Rachel; and Joseph and his brothers are all more than ordinary narratives. They present distant memories and moral lessons passed on from one generation to the next as tribal pride and history.

For centuries Jews have read the Torah not only like a map, charting the adventures of the Jewish people, but like a guide, revealing the ethical and spiritual purposes for human life. The tales of treachery and jealousy between Cain and Abel, Sarah and Hagar, Jacob and Esau were read, not

only because they were "good stories," but also because the readers found themselves inside the confusion, turmoil, and ambitions of their biblical ancestors.

Noah deciding whether to save himself or to protest against the evil of his time, Abraham rising above his pain to welcome visitors into his home, Rebekah deliberately favoring Jacob over Esau, or Joseph declaring his dreams of superiority over his brothers—all these are examples of choices facing each of us. The characters of Genesis, as we have noted in Volume I of *A Torah Commentary for Our Times,* mirror us. The ancient stories are amazingly contemporary. They seem always fresh, novel, and pertinent to our lives.

### Mining the treasures of Torah

Little wonder that Jewish interpreters throughout the centuries have felt so challenged by the Torah text. According to the Jerusalem Talmud there are forty-nine different ways to decipher the Torah's meanings. (*Sanhedrin* 4:2) With so many diverse approaches to the text promoted, it should not surprise us to find within Jewish tradition a wide variety of points of view among commentators. In our discussions of Genesis we have seen how Rashi may present a differing view from the early rabbis, or how Nachmanides will sharply criticize Rashi or take issue with Maimonides. We have also noted the way in which mystic commentators will find insights into words or phrases of the Torah text; or how modern biblical critics, using new knowledge taken from the study of ancient languages or from recent archeological findings, will introduce explanations unavailable to earlier interpreters. Mining the treasures of Torah is unending.

Clearly, the Torah and our tradition of commenting upon its stories and characters, conflicts and commandments deal with every aspect of human life. Out of the tales of Genesis we extract wisdom about such diverse topics as settling disagreements; hospitality; defining beauty, love, justice, and leadership; dealing with "power"; reconciliation between enemies; and achieving peace. Genesis is largely about individual human beings and their personal struggles to find purpose and fulfillment in life. It is the drama of their relationships with one another and with God that captures our interest and imagination.

In this volume, A Torah Commentary for Our Times, Volume II, we turn to the second and third books of the Torah: Exodus and Leviticus. Here we encounter a very different kind of narrative and literature. Where Genesis is about individuals, Exodus is about the Jewish people. While Genesis unlocks private stories, Exodus moves us onto the huge stage of history, where nations battle for existence and where the Jewish people, beaten and oppressed, seek their liberation from Egypt and their way back to the Promised Land.

In Genesis, the human relationship with God is portrayed as personal and private. Adam, Noah, Abraham, Isaac, Jacob—all meet God alone. In Exodus and in Leviticus, God speaks not only to Moses but constantly to the Jewish people. They stand at Sinai and are given "the Torah." Laws and commandments are formulated for "the people of Israel." They are told to build a sanctuary for worship and are provided, not only with all the architectural details, but also specific directions for offering sacrifices to God.

We will discover inside these pages that Jewish interpreters relish the drama on the larger stage of Israel's history just as they did in exploring the lives of the patriarchs and matriarchs. Moses is portrayed as a young revolutionary defending his people, as a humble shepherd, as a reluctant leader, as a brave spokesman before the powerful Pharaoh, and as a liberator, lawgiver, and short-tempered manager of a complaining and confused people. The first chapters of Exodus are filled with high drama, the "stuff" from which movies are made. For Jewish commentators these first chapters are rich with opportunities for discussing themes of liberation, civil disobedience, stubbornness, leadership, treatment of strangers, and the obligation of tzedakah, or "charity."

## Problems, challenges

Yet they also present unusual problems. While the first chapters of Exodus contain the exciting tale of Israel's liberation from Egypt and experience at Mount Sinai, where they receive the Ten Commandments, the last sections of Exodus and most of the Book of Leviticus contain long chapters filled with details for building the ancient sanctuary. Instructions are given to the priests on how they are to preside over the variety of sacrifices offered by the Israelites to God. Several chapters describe how those with skin infections are to be treated.

At times these chapters read like an architect's plan, sometimes like an interior decorator's notepad, at times like a clothing designer's sketches, occasionally like the grizzly directions in a slaughter-house, and at other times like the prescriptions of a specialist in infectious diseases.

Seeking to understand the significance of these chapters of Exodus and Leviticus, Jewish commentators throughout the ages have asked: "What lessons can you derive from such remote subjects and seemingly irrelevant material?"

The following example illustrates the point: If a person suddenly notices a rash and swelling or discoloration on the skin, the Torah instructs that person to seek out the advice of a priest and to observe seven days of isolation. If the rash is cured, the person is to offer sacrifices on the altars of the sanctuary.

The questions growing out of this example of what may have been leprosy are important: Is this a description of an outdated medical procedure, or does it contain ideas and values of continuing importance? If we no longer diagnose skin diseases the way the ancient priests once did and do not offer sacrifices in the Temple, then why should we continue to read and study such chapters of

Torah? Why not skip them? Indeed, if we take the Torah text seriously, how should patients with infectious diseases be treated? Should they be isolated? What care should be provided?

What emerges from the various discussions by commentators of such subjects as skin disease, construction of the sanctuary, the details of priestly dress, the collection of donations for the sanctuary, and many others is a serious and fascinating confrontation with major questions about our own human motives and ethical behavior. Attention to the construction details of the sanctuary leads commentators to a discussion of the importance of dealing with the seemingly small details of our lives. The subject of collecting donations for the sanctuary provides an opportunity for asking important questions about the accountability of public officials for public funds.

The ritual of spilling blood at the altar allows the opportunity for dealing with the sacredness of life. Dietary rules advanced within Leviticus become a forum for examining the art of eating as a function of holiness, not just a response to hunger.

### Join the adventure

The adventure of Torah study offered by Exodus and Leviticus is often surprising and always challenging. Little wonder that students of Torah have constantly been enriched by exploring the themes encountered in these sacred books of Jewish tradition. In the pages ahead you will join the debate and adventure and, perhaps, discover why Rabbi Meir taught that those who study Torah not only make the world a more caring place but are called lovers of human beings and of God. (*Avot* 6:1)

# THE
# TORAH
# PORTIONS
# OF
# EXODUS

# PARASHAT SHEMOT
## *Exodus 1:1–6:1*

*Parashat Shemot* begins by mentioning the *shemot,* or "names," of Jacob's sons and telling us that after they died a new pharaoh, who did not know Joseph, comes to power. Fearing the Jewish people, the new ruler orders taskmasters to enslave them and drown their male children in the Nile River. Defying that order, one mother places her son in a basket and casts the basket into the river. Pharaoh's daughter who was bathing nearby rescues the child and adopts him as her own. She names him Moses. Some time after Moses has grown up, he sees an Egyptian beating a Jew. Defending the Jew, Moses strikes the Egyptian and kills him. When Pharaoh hears what has happened, he orders Moses put to death. So Moses flees from Egypt. When he arrives in Midian, he is welcomed by Jethro, a local priest, whose daughter, Zipporah, he later marries. While Moses is shepherding Jethro's flock, God speaks to him out of a burning bush, promising that Aaron, his brother, will help him liberate the Israelites from oppression. Moses then returns to Egypt where he and Aaron go to Pharaoh to demand freedom for their people. Pharaoh refuses and imposes hard labor upon the people, who blame Moses for making their situation worse. When Moses complains to God, he is told, "You shall soon see what I will do to Pharaoh: he shall let them go because of a greater might."

## OUR TARGUM

### · 1 ·

The second book of the Torah is called *Shemot,* or "names," since it begins with a list of the names of Jacob's sons. It is also known as Exodus because it relates the history of the Jewish people's liberation from Egyptian slavery.

We are told that, after Joseph's death, the Jewish population in Egypt increases, and a new pharaoh, who does not know Joseph, comes to power. Suspecting the loyalty of the Jewish people, the new pharaoh fears that, if Egypt is attacked, the Jews

will side with his enemy. So he orders the Israelites enslaved and puts them to work building the cities of Pithom and Raamses. Yet, the more the Israelites are oppressed, the more they increase in numbers.

Pharaoh speaks to Shiphrah and Puah, the Jewish midwives, and orders them to kill all male Jewish babies, but they refuse. Pharaoh then orders that all Jewish male babies be drowned in the Nile.

Hoping to save her son, one Jewish mother places him in a basket and floats it in the Nile near the place where Pharaoh's daughter is bathing. When Pharaoh's daughter rescues the child, the woman's daughter rushes forward and asks if she might find a mother to nurse him. Pharaoh's daughter agrees. She treats the child like a son and names him Moses, which means "drew" him out of the water.

· 2 ·

As a young man, Moses sees an Egyptian beating a Jew. When he notices that no one is looking, Moses strikes the Egyptian and kills him. Afterwards, he buries him. The next day he comes upon two Jews fighting. When he tries to stop them, one of them says to him, "Do you mean to kill me as you killed the Egyptian?" Moses realizes that others know what he has done and that he is in danger. When Pharaoh learns that Moses has killed an Egyptian, he orders him put to death.

So Moses flees Egypt. He travels to Midian, which is located in the southern part of the Negev desert. In Midian, Moses is taken in by Jethro, a local priest and shepherd. He marries Jethro's daughter, Zipporah, and they have a son whom Moses names Gershom, meaning "I have been a stranger in a foreign land."

·3·

One day, while caring for Jethro's flock, Moses sees a strange sight: a bush that burns but is not consumed. When Moses approaches the bush, God speaks to him from the flames, telling him to return to Egypt to free the Israelites from bondage. Moses wonders how he will be able to prove to the Israelites that God has sent him.

"When they ask me, 'Who sent you?' what shall I say?" he says to God.

And God tells him, "Say that *Ehyeh-Asher-Ehyeh* [which means 'I will be what I will be'] sent you. The Lord, the God of your people, the God of Abraham, the God of Isaac, and the God of Jacob, has sent me to you."

Because Moses still has his doubts, he asks God, "What if they do not believe me or insist on proof that God has spoken to me?" God then turns Moses' staff into a snake and makes his skin white with leprosy. God tells Moses that, if the Israelites do not believe him after seeing both these signs,

he is to take water from the Nile and pour it on the ground, where it will turn to blood.

Moses still hesitates about taking on the task of freeing the Israelites. He tells God that he is "slow of speech and tongue," meaning that he is no public speaker. God tells him that his brother, Aaron, will be appointed to speak to Pharaoh and to the Israelites.

·4·

Moses returns to Egypt and is met by Aaron. Together, they go to Pharaoh to request that he allow the Israelites to celebrate a festival. Pharaoh refuses and accuses them of troublemaking. He orders the taskmasters to increase the work of the slaves and to beat those who fail to produce. Finding themselves in trouble, the Israelites complain to Moses and Aaron.

Their complaints stir up new doubts in Moses. He turns to God and asks, "Why did You send me? Ever since I came to Pharaoh to speak in Your name, he has dealt worse with this people; and still You have not freed Your people at all."

God promises Moses that the people will be liberated.

**THEMES**

*Parashat Shemot* contains three important themes:

1. Pharaoh's war against the Jews.
2. Civil disobedience.
3. Moses' self-doubt and humility.

# PEREK ALEF: *Pharaoh's War against the Jews*

The Book of *Shemot,* or Exodus, continues the history of the Jewish people. Jacob and his family follow Joseph to Egypt, settle in Goshen, and increase in numbers. A new pharaoh comes to power. He has forgotten Joseph's role in saving Egypt and decides to enslave the Israelites.

Why? What brings the Egyptian ruler to such a decision? Does he worry that the loss of slave labor will ruin Egypt's economy and his plans for building great cities and monuments to himself? Does he calculate that if he liberates the Israelites

others will demand their freedom? Or is it possible that the Jews themselves bring on their own persecution and enslavement?

*Sarna*

Biblical scholar Nahum M. Sarna speculates that the new pharaoh feared an invasion of foreigners from the East. Like many Egyptian leaders, he knew of his country's national humiliation and defeat by the invading Hyksos during an earlier period (1700–1680 B.C.E.) and was determined that no such shame would happen during his rule. Sarna explains that the Israelites were living in the Delta region, where an invasion from the East would begin. Pharaoh's "anxiety," he writes, was "quite understandable." He feared that the Jews would join Egypt's enemies. For that reason he decided to enslave the Israelites and to reduce their numbers and power.

Sarna also provides another reason for Pharaoh's decision. He wished to build his capital in the midst of Goshen, or in the Delta region because it was a very fertile land, closer to the critical borders of Syria and Canaan. Enslaving the Jews produced a double benefit. It forced them to give up their lands and provided Pharaoh with an abundance of cheap labor for the construction of his capital cities. (*Exploring Exodus: The Heritage of Biblical Israel*, Schocken Books, New York, 1986, pp. 15–17)

---

**Under the Hyksos**
*Under the Hyksos domination, Egyptian culture had sunk so low that the period has been described as the "Great Humiliation." But the successful war of liberation against the Hyksos led to an Egyptian revival on such a grand scale that the period of the New Kingdom which followed, especially during the eighteenth and nineteenth dynasties (about 1570–1200 B.C.E.), has been called the Golden Age. . . . (Harry M. Orlinsky,* Understanding the Bible through History and Archaeology, *Ktav, New York, 1972, p. 54)*

---

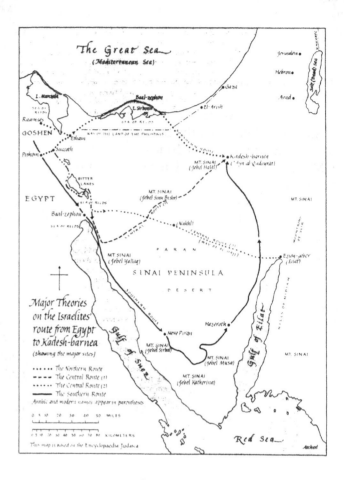

Major Theories on the Israelites' route from Egypt to Kadesh-barnea (showing the major sites)

ting them to work on his projects. He chose Egyptian officers to command them and then allowed the Egyptians to enslave the Jews for their own projects and homes. In this way all of Egypt profited from Jewish slave labor. (On Exodus 1:10)

*Ramban (Nachmanides)*

*Hirsch*

Nachmanides also believes that Pharaoh began his campaign against the Israelites for both strategic and economic reasons. Pharaoh, he says, was afraid that the Israelites would join an invading enemy and escape with a considerable portion of Egypt's wealth. Instead of killing off the Israelites, Nachmanides explains, Pharaoh cleverly developed a plan for taxing their property and for put-

Rabbi Samson Raphael Hirsch believes that Pharaoh's war against the Jews had to do with the weakness of his government. He had just come to power and was seeking a way of rallying the people behind his rule. So he encouraged the masses to oppress the Jews, hoping that his popularity would increase because he had allowed his people to engage in violence and to enrich themselves through theft against strangers living in their midst. (On Exodus 1:8–10)

Hirsch's view is not far from an interpretation offered by a group of ancient rabbinic commentators. Based on the Torah's observation that "a new king arose who did not know Joseph," these commentators taught that the people had come to Pharaoh demanding the right to attack the Israelites. At first he refused, telling them that it would be wrong to harm them since Joseph had saved all the people from ruin. But the people did not listen. They threatened to remove Pharaoh from power. Finally, he was persuaded to go along with their plan to enslave the Jews. The Torah calls him "a new king" because he ceased his protest and accepted the "new" view of those who plotted to destroy the Jewish people. (*Exodus Rabbah* 1:8)

---

**The cause for the oppression**
*The root and beginning of this indescribable maltreatment was the supposed lack of rights of a foreigner, as such. . . . In Egypt, the cleverly calculated lowering of the rights of the Jews on the score of their being aliens (foreigners) came first, the harshness and cruelty followed by itself, as it always does and will, when the basic idea of Right has first been given a wrong conception. (S.R. Hirsch, translator,* The Pentateuch, *L. Honig and Sons Ltd., London, England, 1959, on Exodus 1:14)*

---

In contrast with those who believe that Pharaoh's persecution and enslavement of the Israelites may be blamed on the Egyptian leader's political, economic, or strategic considerations, others argue that Jewish suffering was the fault of the Jews themselves.

For instance, some interpreters believe that after Joseph died the Israelites of Egypt stopped practicing the ritual of circumcision. They said to one another, "Let's be like all the other Egyptians." Other rabbis say that they began to attend sports events at amphitheaters and to visit circuses for entertainment. Their attraction to such events became more important to them than their own traditions and faith. They also moved into homes in Egyptian neighborhoods rather than remaining together in their own "Jewish communities."

Because Jews chose to abandon their traditions and to assimilate, they were oppressed by Pharaoh. He became suspicious of their motives. So did the Egyptian people, who did not want Israelites invading their neighborhoods or competing with them for business opportunities. These commentators maintain that, had the Jews remained loyal to their people and not tried to act like Egyptians, they might not have become targets for Pharaoh's oppression. (*Exodus Rabbah* 1:8–9, *Yalkut Shimoni, Ha-Emek Davar,* as in Nehama Leibowitz, *Studies in Shemot,* World Zionist Organization, Jerusalem, 1980, pp. 2–3)

---

**Causes of anti-Semitism**
*Historian Barbara Tuchman identifies three "principles" regarding anti-Jewish sentiment: (1) "It is vain to expect logic—that is to say, a reasoned appreciation of enlightened self-interest"—when it comes to anti-Semitism. (2) Appeasement is futile. "The rule of human behavior here is that yielding to an enemy's demands does not satisfy them but, by exhibiting a position of weakness, augments them. It does not terminate hostility but excites it." (3) "Anti-Semitism is independent of its object. What Jews do or fail to do is not the determinant. The impetus comes out of the needs of the persecutors and a particular political climate." (Newsweek, February 3, 1975)*

---

*Leibowitz*

Nehama Leibowitz blames the Israelites for not protesting against Pharaoh's decision to enslave them. She says that the Jews were without heros, without those who were brave enough to stand before Pharaoh and say no to his oppression. There was no resistance, no battle for their rights. As a result, Pharaoh easily did away with their freedoms and enslaved them. (*Studies in Shemot* pp. 15–17)

As we can see, a number of theories have been

developed by interpreters to explain the causes for Pharaoh's oppression of the Jewish people. In many ways the ancient story of Israel's enslavement in Egypt is a parallel to the treatment of Jews and other minorities by host nations. Oppression is often the tragic result of suspicions, jealousies, inferiority complexes, together with economic and social rivalries. Only when these are overcome can mutual trust and respect lead to peaceful and productive coexistence.

## PEREK BET: *When Is Civil Disobedience Justified?*

The power of Pharaoh in Egypt was absolute. No one dared defy his rule or his whim. He was honored, not only as the king of Egypt, but as a god. His command was the law of the land. Those who disobeyed him were subject to death.

That is what makes the story of the Hebrew midwives, Shiphrah and Puah, so unusual. Pharaoh commands them to kill every male child born to a Jewish woman. It is an easy order to follow. After all a new mother is weak and defenseless at the birth of her child. Yet, according to the Torah, both Shiphrah and Puah refused to carry out Pharaoh's command.

Why? What moved them to say no to Pharaoh, endangering their own lives by disobedience to his rule?

Many commentators believe that the answer is quite clear. The midwives were Jewish. As Jews they had no choice. No Jewish midwife could kill a Jewish baby. Jewish tradition forbids murder.

*Rashi*  *Ibn Ezra*  *Ramban (Nachmanides)*

This line of reasoning is followed by Rashi, ibn Ezra, and Nachmanides. They base their opinions on the earlier observation of the famous talmudic teachers, Rav and Samuel. Rav taught that Shiphrah was another name for Yocheved, Moses' mother, and that Puah was actually Miriam, the sister of Moses and Aaron. Samuel disagreed, holding that Puah was not Miriam but rather

Elisheva, Aaron's wife. (*Sotah* 11b, *Exodus Rabbah* 1:13)

Other rabbinic interpreters praise Shiphrah and Puah as brave Jewish heroines. These interpreters point out that the two midwives revived babies that were close to death because of difficult deliveries, and, when Pharaoh summoned them to his court and asked, "Why are you not obeying my orders?" they refused to answer. Instead, they defiantly offered him simple excuses: "The Hebrew women are vigorous. They have their babies before we arrive to help them."

Rabbi Isaac argues that Puah, who he believes was Miriam, not only defied Pharaoh, but also bravely criticized her own father, Amram. He maintains that Amram became so depressed about Pharaoh's order to kill all Jewish male babies that he stopped having sexual intercourse with his wife for fear that she would become pregnant. Then he divorced her. When other Hebrew slaves saw what he had done, they also decided to divorce their wives.

According to Rabbi Isaac, Puah confronted Amram and told him that he was acting more cruelly than Pharaoh. "The king ordered the death of all Jewish male children, but you are preventing the conception and birth of all children. Furthermore, because you are a leader, others are following you." Hearing her criticism, Amram immediately remarried his wife, and the other Israelite men followed his example. (*Exodus Rabbah* 1:13)

---

***What the midwives did***
*The rabbis whose comments are included in the Midrash praise the midwives for many acts of kindness during the oppression of Pharaoh: (1) They took food and drink from the rich and brought it to the houses of the poor and hungry. (2) They prayed that each child would be born in good health and not crippled in any way. (3) They prayed that no child or mother would die at childbirth. (4) They made Abraham's hospitality a model for themselves by opening their homes to all who required food and shelter. (Exodus Rabbah 1:15)*

Rabbi Akiba agrees with those who argue that Shiphrah and Puah were brave Jewish women. He even goes so far as to state that "God liberated the Jewish people from Egypt because of the heroic and righteous deeds of the women." Akiba justifies his observation by pointing out that, when they saw their husbands suffering as slaves—overworked, starved, and beaten—they did not think selfishly of themselves, but they went out to comfort them in the fields. They took food. They brought them water and bathed them. They even insisted on having sexual intercourse, telling their husbands that they had to preserve the Jewish people. They did not allow their husbands to become physically weak or to lose faith in the future. For all of their disobedience to Pharaoh's orders, Akiba says, these women are credited with the liberation from Egypt. (*Exodus Rabbah* 1:12)

Not all interpreters, however, agree that Shiphrah and Puah were Jewish. Nor is there any proof within the Torah text that the midwives were Yocheved, Miriam, or Elisheva. The meaning of the Hebrew of the Torah is unclear. While *meyaldot ha-Ivriyot* could mean "Hebrew midwives," it could also mean "midwives of the Hebrews" and be understood as Egyptian midwives of the Hebrews.

Both the commentator-philosopher Philo, who lived in Alexandria, Egypt (20 B.C.E.–40 C.E.), and the historian-general Flavius Josephus (37 B.C.E.–105 C.E.) maintain that Shiphrah and Puah were Egyptian. Others agree.

 *Abravanel*    *Luzzatto*

Both Don Isaac Abravanel and Samuel (Shemuel) David Luzzatto, known also as Shadal, argue that the midwives must have been Egyptian. "How," they ask, "would Pharaoh order Jewish women to put to death children of their own people and not expect that they would make such a plan public?" It is only logical, they conclude, to assume that the Egyptian king gave his orders to Egyptians, whom he thought he could trust to carry them out.

---

> **They were converts**
> *Some interpreters, noting that the Torah says that Shiphrah and Puah "feared God," believe that they were Egyptians converted to Judaism. Out of reverence and loyalty to God, Jews are commanded to die rather than commit idolatry, incest, or murder. Therefore, the Egyptian midwives must have converted to the Jewish faith.*
> (Imrei Noam, *as in N. Leibowitz,* Studies in Shemot, *p. 34*)

If Shiphrah and Puah were Jewish or converts to Judaism, then their defiance of Pharaoh's order was a heroic act against the oppression of their people. By demanding that they murder every Jewish male newborn, Pharaoh had declared war on the Jewish people. Once Pharaoh began to oppress them, their loyalty was to their people and to God, not to the ruler or to the laws of Egypt. As Jews, they were victims. Their disobedience of Pharaoh's orders was justified by their obedience to the law of God and to the survival of their people.

But, if Shiphrah and Puah were Egyptian, what justification might they offer for their "civil disobedience" to Pharaoh?

Modern biblical scholar Nahum M. Sarna observes that the Torah provides us with an explanation of their motivation. We are told that Shiphrah and Puah refused to follow Pharaoh's order out of "fear of God." They believed in the sanctity of human life. For them each human being was sacred and filled with possibilities for creativity and good. They acted out of a conviction that there is a "Higher Power" than Pharaoh "who makes moral demands on human beings" for the preservation of life. Their belief, Sarna explains, led them to reject the Egyptian ruler's command to murder the newborn babies of the Hebrews. "Here we have history's first recorded case of civil disobedience in defence of a moral cause." (*Exploring Exodus*, pp. 24–26)

---

> **Questions for civil disobedience**
> *Civil rights leader Bayard Rustin once suggested these questions as a guide for civil disobedience:*

*"(1) Have I exhausted the available constitutional methods of bringing about the desired change? (2) Do the people I urge to join me sincerely seek to improve the society or do they wish to excite passions that would destroy society itself? (3) What is likely to be the effect of the resistance on me, on others, and on the community? (4) Are my own motives and objectives clear to myself and to others; is my aim genuine social change or mere self-gratification? (5) Given that I oppose specific laws, am I prepared, out of my deep respect for law itself, to suffer the consequences of my disobedience."* (New York Times Magazine, *November 26, 1967*)

*Peli*

### Civil disobedience and liberation
*We may understand how Hebrew women would muster the courage to disobey the king's orders and refuse to kill Hebrew children. But consider the significance of their deed if Shiphrah and Puah were valiant Egyptian women who rebuffed the great pharaoh. They did not say, "My country, right or wrong. . . ." The case of the Hebrew midwives is proof that dissenting individuals can resist evil and thus start a whole process of liberation. (Pinchas Peli,* Torah Today, *B'nai B'rith Books, Washington, D.C., 1987, p. 58)*

The midwives bravely said no to Pharaoh's command that they kill every male Jewish baby. They refused to follow their national leader because they considered his order to be immoral. Instead of making excuses that they were "only following orders" or that "good citizens uphold the law even if they believe it is unjust," Shiphrah and Puah refused to carry out Pharaoh's demand. Forced into making a difficult decision, one that risked their safety, they chose the higher principle of saving life over carrying out Pharaoh's command. Their conviction that each human being is created "in the image of God" led them to disobey Pharaoh's order to murder Jewish babies.

## PEREK GIMEL: *Moses: Fear, Courage, Self-Doubt, or Humility?*

When Moses is called by God to return to Egypt to lead the Jewish people to freedom, his first response is a question: "Who am I that I should go to Pharaoh and free the Israelites from Egypt?" When God tells him, "I will be with you," Moses is unsatisfied and asks for proof. After God tells him what to say to the Israelites, Moses still has his doubts. "What if they do not believe me and do not listen to me?" he asks. Even after God shows him signs and gives him a staff with which to perform magical wonders, Moses continues to hesitate. He offers excuses. "I have never been a man of words," he says, hoping that God will choose someone else to lead the Israelites to freedom.

Why didn't Moses happily and quickly accept God's call to leadership? Why does he offer excuses? Is he afraid? Has he no courage? Is it his way of showing humility?

*Zugot*

### What should a person do?
*Rabbi Hillel taught: "If I am not for myself, who will be for me? But, if I am only for myself, what am I? And, if not now, when?*
(Avot *1:14*)

*Rabbi Judah taught: "Which is the right path to choose? One that is honorable in itself and also wins honor from others."*
(Avot *2:1*)

*Rabbi Hillel said: "In a place where people are without courage, act bravely!"*
(Avot *2:6*)

Interpreters throughout the ages have wondered about Moses' reaction and response to God. For example, the rabbis who wrote the Midrash speculate that it took God an entire week to convince Moses to return to Egypt to work for the liberation of his people. Some of the rabbis explain that he hesitated because he did not want to hurt or anger his older brother, Aaron. Aaron had led the people in Egypt for eighty years. Moses felt that he could not suddenly return and announce that he was replacing him.

Others argue that Moses was truly humble. He feared that he did not possess the political or spiritual skills to liberate his people, especially the talent of public speaking. So he pleaded with God to choose someone else for the task. (*Exodus Rabbah* 3:14,15)

Rabbi Nehori, who lived in Israel during the second century C.E., claimed that Moses weighed the situation and decided that what God was asking him to do was impossible. The rabbi imagines Moses arguing with God: "How do You expect me to take care of this whole community? How shall I shelter them from the heat of the summer sun or the cold of winter? Where shall I find food and drink for them once I have taken them out of Egypt? Who will care for the newborn babies and all the pregnant women?" For Rabbi Nehori, Moses was a realist asking hard questions and concluding that he was being asked to take on an impossible mission. (*Exodus Rabbah* 3:4)

Rashbam, the grandson of Rashi, also believes that Moses hesitated to accept God's call to liberate the Jewish people because he was a realist and saw no chance for success. Seeking to understand Moses' logic, Rashbam explains that Moses must have asked himself: "Is Pharaoh such a fool as to listen to me and send his slaves away to freedom?" Filled with such doubts, Moses, says Rashbam, concluded that his mission to free the Israelites would end in failure. (On Exodus 3:11)

Shadal provides another excuse for Moses' hesitation. He says that by the time God called Moses to return to liberate his people, Moses was an old man. He was weak and felt infirm from many years of shepherding from early in the morning until late at night. Since he had spent most of his time in silence, he could not imagine himself standing before Pharaoh and arguing for the freedom of his people. So, argues Shadal, Moses made excuses to God and asked that someone else be sent to free the Jewish people. (On Exodus 4:10)

Modern writer Elie Wiesel speculates that Moses had another reason for refusing God's request that he return to Egypt. Wiesel writes that "Moses was disappointed in his Jews." When he had defended a Jew being beaten by an Egyptian, no Israelite came forward to help him. Instead, two Jews criticized him the next day for what he had done. Nor had any Israelites offered help to him when Pharaoh put out a warrant for his arrest. "Clearly," Wiesel comments, "Moses had no wish to return to his brothers, no wish to reopen a wound that had still not healed." (*Messengers of God*, Random House, New York, 1976, pp. 188–190)

---

*Jewish tradition and humility*
*No crown carries such royalty as that of humility.*
(*Rabbi Eleazar ben Judah*)

*The summit of intelligence is humility.* (*Ibn Gabirol*)

*The test of humility is your attitude to those who are working for you.* (Orhot Tzadikim *12c, ch. 2*)

*Humility for the sake of approval is the worst arrogance.* (*Nachman of Bratzlav*)

---

In contrast to Wiesel's explanation of Moses' reluctance to return to Egypt, Rabbi Daniel Silver suggests that Moses' response to God was very typical of Middle Eastern behavior at the time. It was a matter of good manners to plead that you were unworthy of taking on major responsibilities. To say "I am not capable" or "I do not possess the right talents" or "let others more able than I do the job" was considered not only correct behavior but also a demonstration of strength of character. Bragging about yourself or singing your own praises was unacceptable. It was a sign of weakness and false pride. So Moses demonstrated his fitness for leadership through his hesitation to accept God's command to free his people. His humility was proof that he was truly the right person for the job.

---

*Prophetic reluctance*

*When Amos was questioned about being a prophet, he told Amaziah, the priest of Bethel: "I am not a prophet, and I am not the son of a prophet. I am a cattle breeder and a tender of sycamore figs. But the Lord took me away from following the flock. . . ." (Amos 7:14–15)*

*It is reported that, when Isaiah was chosen by God to become a prophet, he responded by saying: "Woe is me; I am lost! For I am a man of unclean lips and I live among a people of unclean lips. . . ." His lips were then touched with burning coals, and he was sent on his way to speak to the people of Israel. (Isaiah 6:5–6,9)*

*After Jeremiah was appointed by God to become a prophet he responded: "Ah, Lord God! I don't know how to speak, for I am still a boy." And God answered him: "I will put My words into your mouth." (Jeremiah 1:6,9)*

---

Moses' hesitation to take on the task of leading his people is very similar to the reluctance later expressed by the great prophets Amos, Isaiah, and Jeremiah. They also doubted their abilities and asked God to find other messengers. Like Moses, they feared that they were incapable of doing what God wanted of them. Their hesitation arose out of genuine modesty, a feeling that they were unworthy of the burden of leadership. Judging from their accomplishments, however, their humility was proof of their real strengths and of their loyalty to God.

Moses, too, has serious doubts about his ability to rescue his people. He knows that the challenge is enormous and that the dangers are great. Pharaoh is the most powerful ruler in the world. The Israelites are weakened by years of slavery, beaten into submission. Moses' fears and hesitations are understandable. There is realism and wisdom in his modesty. He knows that the liberation of his people depends upon his ability to inspire their confidence, courage, and hope. He wonders if he will ever be able to convince them that God is calling them to march out of Egypt into freedom.

Great leaders are not blind to the difficulties they face. They realize the difficulties of the challenges before them. At times they feel unworthy and filled with doubts about themselves and those they lead. Sometimes they want to run away and hide rather than face the hard decisions that need to be made.

Perhaps that is how Moses felt when God called him to return to Egypt. He may have hesitated out of fear that he was incapable of doing what God asked or out of a sense that he could do nothing about a hopeless situation. In the end, however, he had the strength and faith to take on the task. He returned to Egypt and worked for liberation of his people.

## QUESTIONS FOR STUDY AND DISCUSSION

1. Author Israel Zangwill has commented: "If there were not Jews, they would have to be invented [as a] guaranteed cause for all evils." Did Pharaoh need a scapegoat, or was it out of fear that he oppressed the Israelites? Would you agree that those who assimilate or abandon Jewish tradition may cause anti-Semitism?
2. Shiphrah and Puah refused to carry out Pharaoh's orders to kill Jewish babies. Under what other conditions is civil disobedience necessary and justified?
3. Moses expresses doubts about his ability to lead his people out of Egyptian oppression. How do you interpret his motives? Was his "humility" a demonstration of weakness or strength, of fear or leadership?

# PARASHAT VA'ERA
## *Exodus 6:2–9:35*

*Parashat Va'era* begins with God saying to Moses: "*Va'era*. . . . 'And I appeared to Abraham, Isaac, and Jacob.' " We are told of the relationship between God and the Jewish people and of the promise to give the Land of Israel to the people. God tells Moses that the time has come to free the Israelites from Egyptian bondage. Moses is told that he should go before Pharaoh to ask that the Egyptian ruler allow the Israelites to depart. Twice Moses responds by saying that Pharaoh will not listen and apologetically explains that, because of a speech impediment, he is not the right person to represent the Jewish people. God answers by declaring that Moses' brother, Aaron, will accompany him as the spokesman.

The two brothers appear before Pharaoh to request the freedom of their people, but Pharaoh refuses to liberate them. As a consequence, terrible plagues are set upon Egypt. The waters of the Nile are bloodied; then the land is filled with frogs and swarms of insects; then there is the death of Egyptian livestock; and later there is destructive hail. These plagues are sent to punish Pharaoh and to force him to free the Israelites.

## OUR TARGUM

· 1 ·

Moses returns to Egypt and speaks to the Israelites. He tells them that God, who was called *El Shaddai*, meaning "God Almighty," by Abraham, Isaac, and Jacob, appeared to him by the name *Yahveh* and instructed him to return to Egypt and say to the Israelites:

"I will free you from the burdens of the Egyptians and deliver you from their bondage. . . . I will take you to be My people, and I will be your God. . . . I will bring you into the land which I swore to give to Abraham, Isaac, and Jacob, and I will give it to you for a possession."

When Moses shares God's promise with the people, they reject it. Their spirits have been crushed by slavery.

God then tells Moses: "Go to Pharaoh and tell him to free the Israelites." Moses refuses, arguing that, if the Israelites would not listen to him, Pharaoh will also reject his request. He also reminds God of his speech impediment. God answers Moses by declaring that his brother, Aaron, would be his spokesman.

### · 2 ·

God also warns Moses that Pharaoh will not easily be convinced that he should free the Israelites. "I will harden Pharaoh's heart," God tells Moses. "I will lay My hand upon Egypt and deliver My ranks, My people, the Israelites, from the land of Egypt with heavy punishments. And the Egyptians shall know that I am the Lord. . . ."

### · 3 ·

The first time Moses and Aaron approach Pharaoh they follow God's direction, and Aaron magically turns his staff into a serpent. Pharaoh's magicians respond by turning their staffs into serpents, but Aaron's serpent swallows theirs. Pharaoh's heart, however, is hard; he will not listen to their plea for the freedom of the Israelites.

So Aaron and Moses appear before Pharaoh a second time as he is finishing his morning swim in the Nile River. Speaking for God, Moses says to him: "Let My people go. Today I will turn the waters of the Nile into blood. All the fish will die. The stink will fill Egypt, and no one will be able to drink the water." Aaron waves his staff over the river, and everything God has predicted comes to pass. But, when Pharaoh's magicians perform the same act, Pharaoh's heart hardens once again.

Seven days later, God tells Moses to return to Pharaoh and threaten him with a plague of frogs unless he frees the Israelites. When Aaron waves his staff and brings the frogs, the Egyptian magicians also perform the same act. This time, however, Pharaoh tells Moses that, if God will remove the frogs, he will allow the Israelites to depart and worship God. But, when Moses removes the frogs, Pharaoh's heart once again hardens, and he refuses to free the Israelites.

God then instructs Moses to have Aaron strike the earth with his rod. When he does, Egypt is suddenly filled with lice. Afterwards, the Egyptian magicians try to produce lice, but they cannot. They say to Pharaoh, "This is the power of God," but Pharaoh's heart remains hard.

During the next days, Moses pleads with Pharaoh on behalf of God, but each time Pharaoh refuses to listen. God sends swarms of insects; then God kills off Egypt's livestock (horses, asses, camels, cattle, sheep). Afterwards, boils appear on the bodies of all Egyptians; then hail storms are sent. After each terrible event, Pharaoh seems to weaken. He promises to free the people, but then, quite suddenly, his heart hardens, and he refuses.

Speaking for God, Moses warns the Egyptian ruler: "Let My people go to worship Me. For this time I will send all My plagues upon your person, and your courtiers, and your people, in order that you may know that there is none like Me in all the world."

**THEMES**

*Parashat Va'era* contains two important themes:

1. Different "names" for God.
2. The "hardening" of Pharaoh's heart.

## PEREK ALEF: *Why So Many Names for One God?*

This Torah portion begins with a surprising statement. Using the name *Yahveh,* God speaks to Moses, telling him that Abraham, Isaac, and Jacob all called God by the name *El Shaddai* ("God Almighty"), but they did not know God by the name *Yahveh.* Why does the Torah use two names for *one* God?

While the question is logical, the fact is that the Torah uses many different names for God. For instance, earlier, as Moses speaks with God at the burning bush (Exodus 3), Moses inquires: "When I come to the Israelites and say to them, 'The God of your fathers [Abraham, Isaac, and Jacob] has sent me to you,' and they ask me, 'What is God's name?' what shall I say to them?" God tells him to say *"Ehyeh-Asher-Ehyeh.* Tell them *'Ehyeh* sent me to you.' "

---

**Ehyeh: another view**
*Philosopher Hugo Bergmann writes that "Ehyeh is an imperfect tense (I will be)," and it teaches us that God is the "yet to be perfected 'I.' "*

---

Commentators and Jewish philosophers have tried to unravel the meaning of the phrase *Ehyeh-Asher-Ehyeh,* just as they have sought to understand the meaning of *Yahveh* and all the other names for God found in the Torah. Since the Hebrew of *Ehyeh* translates into "I will be," many accept the translation "I will be what I will be" as the name for God. By comparison, the most likely Hebrew root for *Yahveh* is *hayah,* meaning "to be." Both *Yahveh* and *Ehyeh-Asher-Ehyeh* suggest that God is not a fixed thing, or person, or object of any kind known to human beings; God is rather an evolving, mysterious, dynamic power that is always in the process of becoming more than what it was or is.

Jews believe that God can never be fully defined. All we can know are traces of God's wonder. We perceive hints of God in the beauty and order of nature, in the triumphs of justice and freedom in history, in the advance of human knowledge, or in the quest for love and peace by human beings. Nonetheless, Jewish tradition counsels great caution when it comes to speaking or writing about God.

For example, through the centuries, Jews were forbidden to say the word *Yahveh.* Instead, it was pronounced *Adonai,* which means "my Lord." Only once a year, on Yom Kippur, was the name used and then only by the High Priest at the Temple in Jerusalem. (*Yoma* 39b) Later, among some Jews, it became the custom to refer to God as *ha-Shem,* "the Name," and to write the word "God" with a hyphen, "G-d." In this way, referring to God was separated from the ordinary use of language and uplifted to the highest realm of honor.

Throughout the ages, many names for God other than *Yahveh, El Shaddai,* and *Ehyeh-Asher-Ehyeh* emerged within Jewish tradition. Within the Torah the oldest is *El,* which some scholars speculate means "the Most Powerful." Other names for God within the Torah include *El Elyon,* "the Highest God"; *El Olam,* "the Everlasting God"; *El Ro'i,* "God who sees me"; and *Eloha,* or its plural, *Elohim,* which are used over two thousand times in the Hebrew Bible and mean "God" or "gods."

The rabbis of the Talmud also developed a number of names for God. Among them were *ha-Kadosh Baruch Hu,* "the Holy One, praised be He"; *Ribono shel Olam,* "Sovereign of the universe"; *ha-Rachaman,* "the Merciful One"; *ha-Makom,* "the Place"; *Shamayim,* "Heaven"; *Shechinah,* "Presence"; and *Avinu sheba-Shamayim,* "our Father in heaven." During the Middle Ages,

Jewish mystics who believed that no person could understand the dimensions of God's power called God the *Ein Sof,* "Without End."

What is clear is that, throughout Jewish history, various designations for God have emerged. Why? Why so many different names for *one* God?

Some modern commentators believe that the names used within the Torah actually identify various traditions within early biblical religion. For instance, all the stories that use the name *Yahveh,* or *Jehovah,* are grouped together and called the J documents; those using *Elohim* are called the E documents. Biblical scholar Richard Elliot Friedman suggests that the J documents were created by people living in the kingdom of ancient Judah while the E documents originated in the kingdom of Israel.

Friedman also points out that "E has much less than J about the world before Moses. E has no creation story, no Flood story, and relatively less on the patriarchs. But E has more than J on Moses." The emphasis in E on Moses, Friedman argues, has to do with those authors who traced their history to the liberation from Egypt. For them, the Exodus was the most important event in the history of the Jewish people. So they worked to combine the past as reported by the J tradition with that event. As a result, says Friedman, they were the first to combine the two names for God, *Yahveh* and *Elohim,* and to link them in the story of Moses asking God, "What is Your name?" (*Who Wrote the Bible?* Summit Books, New York, 1987, p. 83)

For other biblical interpreters the names for God are more than a means of identifying the origins of different Torah stories.

*Sarna*

The modern commentator Nahum Sarna explains that names for God in the Torah reveal the "character and nature"—the "makeup of the whole personality"—of God. As for the variety of names for God found in the Torah, Sarna reports that it was a common custom in the ancient Middle East for gods to have many names. Each name provides another valuable insight into how biblical Jews thought about God. (*Exploring Exodus,* pp. 42–45, 50–52)

Sarna's view is close to the one advanced by Rabbi Abba Hillel Silver. Silver says that "it was a common practice among ancient peoples to change the names of their deity or to add an additional one to indicate that the deity had assumed a new or an additional role." Since God was about to liberate the Israelites from Egyptian bondage, a new name, *Yahveh,* was announced to Moses. The new name, Silver speculates, means "accomplisher," or the "God who performs what is promised." God's new name would not only inspire confidence and hope in the hearts of the enslaved Israelites but would be a reminder to all Jews, after their liberation, that God had freed them from oppression. God's name foreshadowed what God was about to do.

The idea that names for God reveal what God does or will do was also held by Rabbi Abba ben Mammel, who lived in Tiberias during the third century. He claimed that God is called *Elohim* when making judgments about people and nations; *Tzevaot,* "Hosts," when making war against evildoers; *El Shaddai,* "God Almighty," when forgiving human beings for harming themselves and others; and *Adonai* when increasing compassion and love in the world. "God's names reveal God's deeds." In other words, just as the names we sometimes give to people identify their most important traits, so also with the names Jewish tradition has given to God. They identify God as a doer of justice, righteousness, compassion, and love. (*Midrash Rabbah* 3:6)

*Peli*

Modern commentator Pinchas Peli argues that the names for God serve a very valuable function. "Human beings are not capable of grasping the essence of God. All they are able to perceive is God's name, to wit, that side of God's being revealed to them through God's acts." For that reason, Peli says, the rabbis claim there are seventy names for God within the Hebrew Bible. God's powers are so great, awesome, and mysterious that even seventy names are not enough to exhaust the number of ways we encounter God in our lives. Peli, however, concludes with a note of warning: "Even after we call God by all the names—the mystery of God's being is not lifted." ("Torah Today," *Va'era*, in the *Jerusalem Post*, January 18, 1985, p. 16)

Psychologist and philosopher Erich Fromm also believes that the mystery of God is beyond human comprehension, but he offers a very different view of names for God in the Torah. Fromm believes that all names for God are forms of idolatry. God, he writes, "cannot be represented by any kind of image, neither by an image of sound—that is, a name—nor by an image of stone or wood." He suggests that the best translation of the answer God gives to Moses after he has asked "What is Your name?" is "My name is *Nameless.*" In other words, names can be misleading, even dangerous if people assume that they are representations of the whole truth. God cannot be grasped or defined by a name. God is beyond all names, all designations, and definitions. (*You Shall Be as Gods*, Holt, Rinehart and Winston, New York, 1966, pp. 29–32)

As we can see, the issue of giving God names is a controversial one among Jewish commentators. Names help us express our understanding of God, our reverence for God. Yet all are agreed that no "name," however clever or beautiful, lofty or wise, can completely describe God's power or the mystery of God's presence in our lives. Names are merely human language, the tools we use to capture and express concepts, ideas, and meanings. God is beyond our "names," beyond the bounds of our wonder. No human being can depict in words or any other forms of expression the essence of God.

## PEREK BET: The *"Hardening" of Pharaoh's Heart*

Our Torah portion presents us with a difficult question. Moses and Aaron come before Pharaoh. They ask that he allow the Israelites to leave Egypt. Pharaoh listens to their request but refuses to let the people go. Then a terrible plague is sent to punish Egypt and to force Pharaoh into changing

his mind. The same cycle is repeated ten times. Each time the Egyptian ruler seems to indicate that he is ready to say yes to the demand for freedom put forth by Aaron and Moses. Then, mysteriously, his "heart hardens," and he says no.

The difficult question is what the Torah means by "hardening of the heart." What happened to Pharaoh each time he was about to say yes and instead said no? Was God overriding the Egyptian ruler or playing with him like a puppet on strings? Or was Pharaoh freely making his own decisions?

Interpreters point out that the Torah mentions the "hardening" of Pharaoh's heart a total of twenty times. The first ten have to do with the first five plagues, and in each case we are told that "Pharaoh hardened his heart." Clearly, it would seem that whatever is happening is being caused by Pharaoh. Yet the next ten references to the "hardened heart" are different. They occur with the last five plagues, and in each case we are told that "God hardened Pharaoh's heart." Here it would seem that God, not Pharaoh, is in control and is bringing about the change in Pharaoh's heart. (Sarna, *Exploring Exodus*, p. 64)

---

**Ten plagues**
*The ten plagues are (1) blood in the Nile River; (2) frogs; (3) swarms of insects; (4) flies; (5) cattle disease; (6) boils; (7) hail; (8) locusts; (9) darkness; and (10) death of the firstborn.*

---

*Hirsch*

One reading of our Torah text might be that God "hardened" Pharaoh's heart in order to demonstrate divine power over all creatures. Rabbi Samson Raphael Hirsch points out that the Torah uses three different Hebrew words to describe the "hardening" of Pharaoh's heart. The first is *kashah*, meaning "to be hard altogether, to let everything pass over one without making any impression." The second is *kaved*, meaning "heavy." One can receive impressions, but there can be a big gap between the impression and the moment one lets oneself be guided by this impression. Finally, the

Torah uses the word *chazak*, meaning "firm," consciously opposing any pliancy, any submission.

Hirsch argues that "Pharaoh's coldness, his apathetic insensibility" was used by God so that "all subsequent ages could derive a knowledge and conviction of the Almightiness, the Presence, and the Direction of God in human history." Never again, Hirsch says, would there be a "necessity for miracles." In other words, God pulled the strings and directed the choices for the Egyptian ruler. God made his heart *kashah, kaved,* and *chazak* in order to demonstrate where the power and control really is!

*Zugot*

Centuries ago Rabbi Yochanan was troubled by an explanation similar to the one offered by Rabbi Hirsch. In contrast, he reasoned that if God is pulling all the strings, and Pharaoh has no free choice, then the Egyptian ruler could not be held responsible for his choices. That would mean that none of us is really free and that our choices between acts of love or hatred, caring or selfishness, justice or indifference are an illusion. "Is that what the Torah teaches us when it speaks of God hardening Pharaoh's heart?" Rabbi Yochanan asked his brother-in-law who was his close friend and study companion, Rabbi Simeon ben Lakish.

Resh Lakish, as he was known, responded by explaining that God gave Pharaoh several opportunities to change his mind and allow the Israelites to leave Egypt. The plagues were warnings. God hoped that Pharaoh would repent and free the slaves. "Since God warned him five times and Pharaoh refused to pay any attention and continued to stiffen his heart, God told him, 'I will now add more trouble to what you have made for yourself.'" That is what the Torah means when it says that "God hardened Pharaoh's heart." Pharaoh brought on the condition by his own stubbornness. (*Exodus Rabbah* 13:3)

---

**Making choices**
*Resh Lakish taught: "If a person seeks to do evil, that person will find a way. If one seeks to do*

*good, to improve oneself, and to better one's society, God will help."* (Shabbat *104a*)

*God does not predetermine whether a person shall be righteous or wicked; that is left to the free choice of each person.* (Tanchuma, Pikude, *3*)

*Every time we disobey the voice of conscience, it becomes fainter and feebler, and the human heart becomes harder to reach and move. Judaism affirms the principle of free will. We are each the master of our own spirit. "One evil deed leads to another."* (Pirke Avot *4:2*) *And, conversely, "One good deed leads to another," and we are that much more liberated from bondage.* (Rabbi Hillel E. Silverman, *From Week to Week, Hartmore House, New York, 1975, p. 57*)

---

*Rambam (Maimonides)*

Moses Maimonides agrees with Resh Lakish emphasizing "that it was not God who forced Pharaoh to do evil to Israel"; the decision was his alone. Free will "is a fundamental principle of Judaism," says Maimonides. "No one forces, preordains, or impels a person to act. People do as they wish to do. Each is absolutely free to perform any deed, be it bad or good." Pharaoh made his choices, one after the other; as he made them, it became more difficult for him to reverse them. One bad choice led to the next and then to the next until his range of choices narrowed, and he could no longer turn back.

Modern psychologist Erich Fromm amplifies Maimonides' view about the hardening of Pharaoh's heart. Fromm writes that the Torah's description presents "one of the most fundamental laws of human behavior. Every evil act tends to harden man's heart, that is, to deaden it. Every good act tends to soften it, to make it more alive. The more man's heart hardens, the less freedom he has to change; the more is he determined already by previous action. But there comes a point of no return, when man's heart has become so hardened and so deadened that he has lost the possibility of freedom, when he is forced to go on and on until the unavoidable end which is, in the last analysis, his own physical or spiritual destruction." (*You Shall Be as Gods,* p. 101)

So Pharaoh's first choices to continue persecuting and oppressing the Israelites ultimately led him to "a point of no return." He must have thought that "if I give in to their demands and do not stiffen my heart and rule them harshly, then both the Jews and the Egyptians will conclude that I am weak and will rebel." Trapped by fear of failure and unable to develop creative solutions to his problems, Pharaoh fell victim to his own bad decisions. In a tragic way, he chose the steep path and, once he was plunging down it, could not stop or save himself from crashing at the bottom.

One other view about this story of Pharaoh's hardening heart deserves consideration. A comment in the Midrash explains that "Pharaoh used to boast that he was a god." Certainly he had more power at his disposal than any other human being alive in his time. He ruled great armies equipped with weapons to slaughter and trample anyone who might rise against him. Through his taskmasters, he dictated the life or death of thousands of slaves building his cities, Pithom and Raamses. The author of the Midrash imagined that, because Pharaoh possessed the power of life and death over so many, the Egyptian ruler concluded that he was invincible. Nothing could defeat him or ruin his plans. (*Exodus Rabbah 8:2*)

---

**The plagues against Pharaoh**
*Pharaoh was destroyed by ten plagues because he claimed to be a god. What did he say? "My Nile is my own, I made it for myself." (Ezekiel 29:3) As a consequence of Pharaoh's claim, God punished him with plagues.* (Exodus Rabbah 8:2)

Leibowitz

*The purpose of the plagues was educational—to instill acknowledgment of God in those who had refused to recognize God's power. . . .*

---

*The purpose of our Torah portion is to "describe the relentless attempt to break Pharaoh's arrogant heart and teach him to "know the Lord."* (*Nehama Leibowitz,* Studies in Shemot, *pp. 170–177*)

*Finally, it must be remembered that the entire story of the plagues is about a contest between the will of the Pharaoh and the will of the God whom only the Israelites recognized. . . . Consequently, the plagues, the ignoble defeat, and the ignominious end of the god-king constitute a saga that breathes contempt for Egyptian paganism.* (*Nahum M. Sarna,* Exploring Exodus, *p. 80*)

---

Yet Pharaoh was defeated. All his armies and weapons were not enough to snuff out the will of freedom God had placed in the hearts of the Israelites. The more Pharaoh brutalized them, the stronger became their determination to be free. Each time he had a chance to stop the plagues and let them go, he hardened his heart. He thought he was battling with weak, beaten slaves. He could not understand that within them God had planted a yearning for liberation against which he was powerless.

Finally, according to those who related this *midrash,* God decided to teach Pharaoh, and all who would hear of him, a lesson. Now God would harden his heart. The Egyptian ruler, who had claimed to be a god and who had brought suffering to thousands, would be destroyed. God would reveal Pharaoh's weakness to all his people and demonstrate that the God of liberation ultimately wins every battle against oppression.

According to this version, the story of God and Pharaoh is not about whether human beings are free or not free to make good or bad choices. Rather, it is about the confrontation between those who claim to be god and God, between those who claim to rule the world and the liberating God of the world. It is the victory of the spiritual God, who wills freedom, justice, and the sacred equality of each human being, over the godlike Pharaoh, who must enslave and crush others to rule them.

The hardening of Pharaoh's heart and the miraculous plagues that are sent to destroy him are all meant to dramatize the power of the God of freedom. Nothing, the Torah claims, neither hard-hearted Pharaoh nor any other ruler or institution, can stop God's will for human liberation. It is always triumphant. God wants us to be free!

## QUESTIONS FOR STUDY AND DISCUSSION

1. How might the various names for God in Jewish tradition help us to understand what Jews believe and do not believe about God and the origins of Torah? If you were creating new names for God today, what might some of them be? Make a list and explain each name you suggest.

2. Erich Fromm claims that "every evil act tends to harden man's heart, that is, to deaden it." Would you agree? Do we bring on our own stubbornness or do other people and stressful situations cause us to become insensitive and incapable of making balanced and just decisions? How was Pharaoh's heart "hardened" each time he changed his mind and refused to free the Israelites?

# PARASHAT BO
## *Exodus 10:1–13:16*

---

*Parashat Bo* takes its name from the first word of God's command to Moses, "Go (*Bo*) to Pharaoh." Moses and Aaron continue to plead with Pharaoh to let the Israelites go free. Because he refuses, the Egyptians are punished with plagues of locusts, darkness, and, finally, the death of their firstborn. Pharaoh tells Moses, "Be gone from me!" God then tells Moses that, after the last plague, Pharaoh will let the Israelites leave. That midnight Moses leads the Israelites out of Egypt and proclaims that each year on the evening of the fourteenth day of the first month a festival lasting seven days will be celebrated in order to recall their liberation from Egypt. *Matzah*, or "unleavened bread," shall be eaten during the seven days, and on the first night of the festival the children will be told how God freed their people from the house of bondage.

---

## OUR TARGUM

### · 1 ·

After sending seven plagues upon Egypt (blood in the Nile River, frogs, swarms of insects, flies, cattle disease, hail, and boils), God, once again, sends Moses and his brother, Aaron, to Pharaoh. Standing before the Egyptian ruler, they ask him, "How long will you refuse to humble yourself before God?" They warn him that, if he does not free their people, God will bring a plague of locusts upon Egypt.

Pharaoh's advisors counsel him: "Let the men go to worship the Lord their God! Are you not yet aware that Egypt is lost?" So the ruler invites Moses and Aaron back to his palace. "Whom do you wish to take with you?" he asks them. Moses tells him: "We will all go, young and old: we will go with our sons and daughters, our flocks and herds; for we must observe the Lord's festival." Pharaoh denies the request and expels Moses and Aaron from the palace.

God then brings a plague of locusts upon Egypt. The whole land is covered with them. When Pharaoh sees what has happened, he calls for Moses. "Forgive me," he cries. Moses pleads for him, and God ends the plague, but Pharaoh's heart hardens once again.

This time God punishes Egypt with a plague of darkness. For three days there is blackness in the land except in the locations where the Israelites are living. Again, Pharaoh calls Moses. He offers him a deal. "Go, worship the Lord! Only your flocks and your herds shall be left behind; even your children may go with you." Moses refuses, and Pharaoh's heart stiffens again. "Be gone from me!" he tells Moses.

God informs Moses that one more plague will be sent upon Egypt. God also instructs Moses to tell the Israelites to borrow objects of silver and gold from their Egyptian neighbors. The Egyptians willingly give the Israelites the objects they request.

God sends the tenth plague upon Egypt. Every firstborn son and every firstborn of the cattle dies. Having lost his own son, and seeing the disaster that has come upon his people and land, Pharaoh summons Moses and Aaron. Broken by God's power, he tells them, "Go, worship the Lord . . . and may you bring a blessing upon me also!"

The other Egyptians urge the Israelites to leave in haste. So they take their dough before it has leavened and the gold and silver that they had requested from their Egyptian neighbors. At midnight, on the fourteenth day of the first month of the year, after living in Eygpt for 430 years, Moses leads the people out of Egypt.

· 2 ·

On that evening of the Exodus from Egypt, Moses declares that God has commanded the people to recall their liberation each year with a special commemoration ceremony. Every household is to take a lamb on the tenth day of the month and slaughter it at twilight on the fourteenth day of the month. Its blood is to be painted on the doorposts of each family house, and its meat is to be roasted and eaten with unleavened bread (*matzah*) and bitter herbs during the night so that it is consumed by morning. Anything left by morning is to be burned.

As the meal is eaten, Israelite men are to dress

with a belt around their waists and sandals on their feet. Each is to hold a staff in his hand and to eat the lamb quickly. When the children see this strange ritual and ask "What do you mean by this ceremony?" they are to answer: "It is the passover sacrifice to the Lord, because God passed over the houses of the Israelites in Egypt when God killed the Egyptians, but saved our houses."

Moses also informs the Israelites that God has commanded them to recall their liberation from Egypt each year by eating only unleavened bread for seven days. All leaven is to be removed from their homes; none is to be found in all their lands during the seven days of the festival. Furthermore, the first day and the seventh day are to be set aside for a solemn gathering of the community. As with the Sabbath, no work is to be done on them.

## THEMES

*Parashat Bo* contains two important themes:

1. Taking the gold and silver from the Egyptians.
2. The creation of the Pesach celebration.

## PEREK ALEF: *Were the Israelites Justified in Taking Gold and Silver from the Egyptians?*

Just before the tenth and final plague is brought upon Pharaoh and the Egyptians, Moses is commanded by God to tell the Israelites "to borrow, each man from his neighbor and each woman from hers, objects of silver and gold." The Torah informs us that the Egyptians willingly gave the Israelites what they requested and that "thus they stripped the Egyptians."

The description raises many troubling questions. Does the Torah justify robbery from the Egyptians? Why were the Egyptians willing to hand over their wealth to the Israelites? Did the Israelites take advantage of the Egyptians when they "stripped" them of their gold and silver?

The Hebrew word for "borrow" is *sha'al*. It can also mean "ask" or "demand." Which is the most accurate translation for this incident? Did the Israelites "borrow," "ask for," or "demand" riches from the Egyptians? Were the gold and silver gifts, or were they the "spoils" of victory?

Among all Jewish interpreters of this significant Torah story, none suggests that the Israelites deliberately set out to rob the Egyptians of their wealth. Nearly all are agreed that the Egyptians willingly presented their gold and silver to the departing Israelites.

Rabbi Ishmael says that the response on the part of the Egyptians was immediate and without qualification.

*Zugot*

Rabbi Jose agrees, explaining that there was a high level of trust and respect between the Egyptian people and the Israelites. For three days the Egyptians were living in a plague of "black darkness" while the Israelites had light in their dwellings. The Israelites could have taken advantage of them and robbed them, but they did not. For that reason, Rabbi Jose maintains, the Egyptians trusted the Israelites and graciously rewarded them with silver and gold. (*Mechilta* on Exodus 12:36)

*Hirsch*

**Jewish honesty**
*Rabbi Samson Raphael Hirsch comments that the Israelites "proved their sterling moral quality" during the three days of darkness. "For three*

*days long their oppressors . . . were completely helpless in their power; for three days long all their treasures lay open in their houses, and no Jew took the opportunity to take the slightest advantage either against their persons or their possessions." (Comment on Exodus 11:2–3, The Pentateuch, p. 119)*

Josephus agrees. He claims that the Israelites did not steal anything. Instead, the Egyptians offered them gifts, insisting on honoring them out of friendship and neighborliness.

Rashbam also believes that the Egyptians willingly turned over their wealth to the departing Israelites. "They merely asked for it, and the Egyptians responded by giving them gifts." Rashbam implies that there was no force, no persuasion.

*Sarna*

Modern commentator Nahum Sarna disagrees. He explains that the silver and gold were not just neighborly gifts but rather spoils of a justified Jewish victory over the Egyptians. For years the Egyptians had treated the Israelites cruelly, insulting their dignity and intelligence as human beings. Taking "gifts" from the Egyptians was a means of restoring Jewish pride. It proved that Jews were equal in every way to their oppressors. The Israelites, Sarna writes, "escaped from Egypt with their dignity intact."

Sarna's explanation, however, differs from early Egyptian interpretations of the story. During the time that Alexander the Great ruled over Egypt (332–323 B.C.E.), many Egyptians complained to him that the Israelites had stolen riches from their ancestors. As proof they cited the Torah report of Jews taking silver and gold from the Egyptians. Hearing what some Egyptians were claiming, Ga-

viha ben Pasisa, a well-known Jewish leader, asked for a public debate. Alexander agreed.

After listening to the Egyptian argument from the Torah, Gaviha answered: "I will also use a proof from the Torah. We are told that Israel 'lived in Egypt four hundred and thirty-six years.' Do you Egyptians not owe the Israelites payment for all their years of slavery?" After hearing Gaviha's argument, Alexander gave the Egyptians three days to formulate an answer. They considered the matter but could not find one. (*Sanhedrin* 91a)

Gaviha's argument that what the Israelites had taken was neither a gift nor stolen property but rather "reparations" or repayment for years of slave labor is also one that other commentators have raised. For instance, the philosopher Philo Judaeus, who lived in Alexandria during the first century, believed that the silver and gold taken from the Egyptians was a just payment to the Israelites for all their suffering and for the wages they had never been paid. The gifts were owed to the Israelites by the Egyptians.

---

*A just payment*
*The Hebrew slaves had worked for their masters . . . they were entitled to their freedom and, therefore, at the same time, to a just farewell payment. Justice demanded it. (Umberto Cassuto on Deuteronomy 23:8)*

---

In 1951 the government of Israel debated the question of whether or not to seek "reparations" from Germany. Six million Jews had been killed by the Nazis. Jewish-owned businesses and properties worth millions of dollars had been confiscated or destroyed. Careers were ruined; hundreds of thousands were left sick, homeless, and orphaned. David Ben-Gurion, then prime minister of Israel, argued that, while the losses could never be fully calculated, the State of Israel was justified in seeking $1.5 billion from Germany as "material reparations." The money would be used "to secure compensation (indemnification) for the heirs of the victims and rehabilitation of the survivors."

By January 1952, Jews throughout the world, but especially in Israel, were locked in heated debate as to whether such reparations should be either requested or accepted. Ben-Gurion explained that the amount of $1.5 billion had been chosen because it was "the minimal sum required for the absorption and rehabilitation of half a million immigrants from the countries subjected to the Nazi regime." Menachem Begin, then head of the opposition Herut party, objected, claiming that the acceptance of reparations would mean "a surrender of political independence" and would represent "the ultimate abomination" of those who had been murdered by the Nazis. After a month of protests against the government proposal, the Knesset voted (61–50) to accept reparations. The payments were spread over a twelve-year period. (David Ben-Gurion, *Israel, a Personal History,* Funk and Wagnalls, Inc., and Sabra Books, New York, 1971 pp. 399–400)

Were these "reparations" from Germany to the Jewish people after the Holocaust a parallel to the gifts of silver and gold that the Israelites took from the Egyptians? Should victims, or their children, accept "payment" for such cruelty? Can a price be placed on a human life—or on six million human lives?

*Ramban (Nachmanides)*

Nachmanides suggests that the gold and silver that the Egyptians gave to the Israelites represented "atonement," a payment of regret, for the damages they had inflicted upon the Jewish people. The Egyptians sought forgiveness with their gifts. It is as if the Egyptians were saying, "We are the wicked ones. There is violence in our hands, and you merit God's mercy." Their gifts were an admission of guilt, a confession of all the wrongs they had done, and a request for pardon. (Comment on Exodus 11:3)

---

**On forgiving others**
*Each night, before retiring, forgive those who offended you during the day. (Asher ben Yehiel, 14th century)*

*Since I myself stand in need of God's pity, I have granted an amnesty to all my enemies. (Heinrich Heine, 1797–1856)*

---

In requesting and accepting Egyptian "gifts," perhaps the Israelites were also expressing their readiness to forgive their oppressors. They were liberating themselves from all the suffering of the past. Reparations would help build a foundation for a strong future. Forgiving their enemies did not mean forgetting the past; it meant rising above it to create new opportunities. Instead of becoming fixed in anger and resentment against those who had caused them so much pain and had reduced them to poverty and slavery, the Israelites accepted the Egyptian gifts and left Egypt to fashion their future as a proud and independent people.

## PEREK BET: *Origins of the Pesach Celebration*

Pesach is one of the most popular celebrations of the Jewish year. On the evening of the fourteenth day of Nisan, families and friends gather for the *seder.* The table is festively decorated with holiday symbols including the *pesach (zeroah),* a roasted shankbone or chicken neck; the *matzah,* unleavened bread; the *maror,* bitter herb; the *charoset,* a mixture of apples, nuts, honey, cinnamon, and wine; the *chagigah (betzah)* roasted egg; the *kar-*

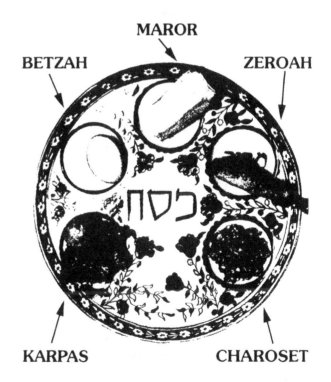

*pas,* parsley; the cups of wine; and one cup of wine set aside for Elijah. At each place is a *haggadah,* a book containing the *seder,* or "order," of the evening's service and the story of the Jewish people's liberation from Egypt.

Those celebrating the *seder* will drink four cups of wine, invite a child to recite four questions, and read about four different children representing four attitudes to the Pesach festival. Near the beginning of the banquet, a *matzah* will be broken, and half of it will be set aside as the *afikoman,* or "dessert." Holding a piece of *matzah,* sometimes at an open door, the leader of the *seder* will say, "Let all who are hungry come and eat. . . ."

The retelling of the Exodus from Egypt will include songs and discussion and a reminder from the rabbis of the *Mishnah* who said, "In every generation a Jew is to see himself or herself as though he or she were escaping from Egypt." The *haggadah* also contains the story of five famous rabbis who extended their celebration from early evening until the break of dawn the next morning. The festive meal concludes with the words, *Le-shanah ha-ba'ah bi-Yerushalayim,* "Next year in Jerusalem!"

What modern Jews celebrate as a *seder* actually evolved over thousands of years. Each generation added important elements to the ceremony while abandoning others. Within our Torah portion we find important descriptions of the first Pesach rituals observed by the people of Israel.

At springtime in ancient times, before the enslavement of Hebrews in Egypt, shepherds set aside a year-old lamb for each household. At twilight on the fourteenth day of the month of Nisan, when the moon was full and bright, the lamb was slaughtered. Its blood was smeared on the doorposts of the houses where it would be eaten, and it was then roasted for the festival feast. When the meat was ready, it was eaten with *matzah* and *maror.*

Early Hebrew farmers also observed a spring festival. Their custom included removing all leavened products from their houses and eating only *matzah* for seven days, from the fourteenth day until the twenty-first day of the month of Nisan.

No one knows when the two traditions of the shepherds and the farmers were combined. That may have occurred at the time Moses liberated the Jewish people from Egyptian bondage—or later. All accounts of the festival within the Torah link it to the historic moment of the Exodus. For instance, we are told that the lamb is to be called "the Pesach sacrifice, because God passed over the houses of the Israelites in Egypt when the Egyptians were killed." (Exodus 12:27) The Torah also contains instructions about eating the lamb. It is to be eaten quickly while each male stands with a staff in his hand, sandals on his feet, and a girdle around his waist. The dress and dramatic posture are of those escaping danger, fleeing for their lives.

All these strange customs were meant to capture the attention of young people. When they saw the lamb killed; its blood painted on the doorposts; their fathers dressed as if they were about to leave on a journey, standing with a staff in their hands and quickly eating the roasted meat, it was hoped that they would ask, "What are you doing? What is the meaning of this strange ceremony?" In answer, fathers were to tell their children how God liberated them from Egyptian slavery.

This early ceremony was known as *Seder Mitzrayim,* or "the *Seder* of Egypt" because it records the early history and rituals of Pesach. The rabbis named the celebration that evolved over the centuries *Seder Dorot,* or "the *Seder* of the Generations." *Seder Dorot* includes many of the old traditions, though they have been changed to meet new circumstances.

For instance, emphasis is still placed upon the festive family meal and upon the importance of eating *matzah* for seven days. *Maror* is still eaten as a reminder of the bitterness of slavery. All that is left of the *pesach* lamb, however, is a roasted shankbone, placed on the *seder* plate and, at the appropriate moment in the ceremony, held up by the leader who explains that it is a reminder of God's saving the Israelite firstborn on the night when all of the Egyptian firstborn were killed.

---

***Each according to his or her ability***
*The rabbis point out that four times the Torah mentions the questions that children will ask on the evening of Pesach. Three of the questions are found in the Torah portion Bo, Exodus 12:26–27; 13:8,14, and one is found in Deuteronomy 2:20–21.*

*One explanation of the four different questions is that they represent four different kinds of human abilities to listen and to learn. "When God spoke to Israel," the rabbis teach, "each person heard according to his or her ability. The elders, the children, the babies, the young, even Moses—each understood what God was saying according to his or her capacity to listen." (Tanchuma on Exodus 19:19)*

### The difference between the "wicked" child and the "wise" child

*The "wise" child asks, "What do the laws and traditions that God has commanded you mean?" The "wicked" child asks, "What does this ritual service mean to you?"*

*What is the difference between them? It has been suggested that the "wise" children ask the reason for the various types of rituals while the "wicked" children do not care about the meanings of the ceremony. For them the festival is merely a burden God has imposed upon the Jewish people year after year.*

*Leibowitz*

*Nehama Leibowitz points out that the real difference between the "wise" and "wicked" children is not in their words but in the introductions to their questions within the* haggadah. *We are told that "the 'wise child' will ask you" and that "the 'wicked child' will say to you." It is the attitude of each that makes the difference. "So long as a child asks, no matter how difficult the questions are, it is a sign that he expects an answer. . . . He is far from being malicious but is a student thirsty for knowledge. The wicked one, however, does not ask and desires no reply. . . . His attitude is fixed and predetermined. He is not interested in your answers but only in*

*what he "will say to you." (Studies in Shemot, pp. 207–208)*

At the *seder*, Jewish fathers no longer dress as if they were about to leave on a long journey, but the *haggadah* created by the rabbis does include four questions to be asked by children at the festive meal. There is also a section about four types of children, each representing different attitudes and learning abilities. The emphasis of the *seder* remains the same as it was in ancient times. It is a unique banquet in which Jews are to relive the historic experience of being liberated from Egyptian oppression and are to pass on that story from generation to generation.

## QUESTIONS FOR STUDY AND DISCUSSION

1. Many commentators argue that the Hebrews were justified in taking gold and silver from the Egyptians when they escaped from bondage because they had been exploited for so many years. Do you agree? Is there a parallel here to the "reparations" paid by Germany to Israel and to Jews who suffered during the Holocaust? What about the payment to Japanese-Americans who were placed in concentration camps in the United States during the Second World War? How should the amounts for such reparations be determined? What about affirmative action that guarantees a percentage of student and job opportunities for those minorities that may have been exploited in the past and whose levels of education and employment may not provide them with openings enjoyed by others within society?

2. Using a *haggadah*, make an outline of the *seder*. Compare it with Exodus 12:1–27, 43–49. What has been added since biblical times by the rabbis who created the *haggadah*? In what dramatic ways is the history of the Exodus from Egypt passed on from generation to generation at the *seder* meal?

# PARASHAT BESHALACH
## Exodus 13:17–17:16

---

*Parashat Beshalach* takes its name from the second word of the Torah portion. *Beshalach* means "when he sent forth" and refers to Pharaoh's decision to free the Israelites. Led by Moses, they depart from Egypt, but Pharaoh changes his mind and decides to pursue them. When the Israelites see Pharaoh and his army approaching, they complain to Moses that he has brought them into the wilderness to die. He assures them that God will save them and leads them through the Sea of Reeds. From the other side they watch as the pursuing Egyptians are drowned. In celebration, Moses and the Israelites sing a song of praise to God. Afterwards they begin their journey through the Sinai desert. Despite their victory over the Egyptians and their liberation, however, the Israelites continue to complain to Moses. They cry out that they have no water to drink, no bread to eat. God grants them water and provides them with "manna," a food substance resembling flour. While the Israelites are camped at Rephidim, they are attacked by the Amalekites. Joshua, who has been appointed by Moses, successfully destroys the Amalekite forces.

---

## OUR TARGUM

### · 1 ·

Upon departing from Egypt, Moses does not lead the people directly to the Land of Israel. Wishing to avoid a war with the Philistines, which might frighten the people and make them want to return to Egypt, Moses takes them south from Goshen towards the Sea of Reeds [Red Sea]. God leads them with a pillar of fire by night and a pillar of cloud by day.

Pharaoh, who has finally agreed to free them, suddenly regrets his decision. He sends his whole army to bring the Israelites back to Egypt. When the Israelites see Pharaoh and all his chariots approaching, they cry out to Moses: "What have you done to us, taking us out of Eygpt? . . . Let us be, and we will serve the Egyptians, for it is better for us to serve the Egyptians than to die in the wilderness." Moses responds by assuring them that God will save them. God then says to Moses, "Tell the Israelites to go forward."

As Moses holds out his hands, the Israelites enter the Sea of Reeds. The waters split and form a corridor through which they pass safely. When the pursuing Egyptian army led by Pharaoh enters the corridor, the waters crash in upon them. The Egyptians panic, their chariot wheels lock, and the whole army is drowned in the sea.

Victoriously, Moses and the Israelites sing a song of praise to God: . . . "Pharaoh's chariots and his army/God has cast into the sea;/And the pick of his officers/Are drowned in the Sea of Reeds./. . . Who is like You, O Lord, among the mighty;/Who is like You, majestic in holiness,/Awesome in splendor, working wonders!/. . . The Lord will reign for ever and ever!" Miriam,

the sister of Moses and Aaron, leads all the women in a festive dance.

· 2 ·

From the Sea of Reeds, the people travel to Marah, or "bitter," so named because of its bitter waters. When the people complain about the taste of the water, God tells Moses to throw a piece of wood into it. He does, and the waters sweeten.

Later, the people journey to the wilderness of Sin. There they turn on Moses again. "If only we had died by the hand of the Lord in the land of Egypt, when we sat by the fleshpots, when we ate our fill of bread! For you have brought us out into this wilderness to starve this whole congregation to death!" Hearing their complaint, Moses and Aaron answer the people: "By evening you shall know it was the Lord who brought you out from the land of Egypt."

That evening, the camp is covered with quail to eat; in the morning, manna, a flaky substance like coriander seed, white in color and tasting like honeyed wafers, rains down upon the people. Moses orders the people to collect an *omer*'s measure, approximately a hand full, for each person and a double amount on the sixth day for the Sabbath.

Nonetheless, some people go out to gather manna on the Sabbath. They find nothing, and God declares to Moses: "How long will this people refuse to obey My commandments and My Teachings? . . . Let the people remain where they are and observe the Sabbath."

· 3 ·

From the wilderness of Sin, Moses leads the Israelites to Rephidim. Finding no water to drink, the people complain once again. "Why did you bring us from Egypt to die of thirst?" Frustrated,

Moses cries out to God, "What shall I do with this people?" God tells Moses: "I will be standing before you on the rock at Horeb. Strike the rock [with your rod] and water will come forth from it." Moses does this, and the people are given enough to drink. The place is named Massah, which means "trial," and Meribah, which means "quarrel."

· 4 ·

While camping at Rephidim, the Israelites are attacked by the forces of Amalek, a group of tribes that live in the Sinai desert. Moses orders Joshua to organize a response to the attack. Joshua successfully overwhelms the enemy, and Moses builds an altar and names it Adonai-nissi, meaning "God is my banner." He declares that "God will be at war with Amalek throughout the generations."

**THEMES**

*Parashat Beshalach* contains three important themes:

1. The "miracle" of the Israelites' escape from Egypt.
2. The Israelites' "complaints" in the desert.
3. Amalek's attack upon the Israelites.

## PEREK ALEF: *Was Israel's Escape from Egypt a "Miracle"?*

The Torah's report of Israel's departure from Egypt makes it clear that the liberation was not only a human effort. We are told that the people were led by an angel of God and by a pillar of fire by night and a pillar of cloud by day. When they arrived at the Sea of Reeds and saw the Egyptian army advancing upon them, God split the waters of the sea so that they could walk safely on dry land to the other side. Then, God rolled back the waters upon the Egyptians, drowning all of them together with their horses and chariots. Upon seeing the "miracle" that God had performed for them, the Israelites sang out: "I will sing to the Lord, for God has triumphed gloriously;/Horse and driver God has hurled into the sea./ . . . You made Your wind blow, the sea covered them;/They sank like lead in the majestic waters." (Exodus 15:1,10)

Is that really what happened? Can we believe that God sent angels to lead the Israelites, split the sea for them, and destroyed the Egyptians by drowning them? Did Moses play any role in the victory? Did the Israelites do anything to save themselves? Is the Torah story an exaggeration beyond belief?

*If I told you what the teacher told us . . .*
*We are told about the ten-year-old whose father was driving him home from religious school. "What did you learn about today?" his father asked. The child responded: "The teacher told us about the Israelites' escape from Egypt. They came to the Sea of Reeds and built pontoons and drove across the water. As soon as the Egyptians and their tanks were on the pontoons, the Israelites sent in their air force and bombed them."*

*The father looked with surprise at his child. "Is that really what the teacher told you?" "Not really," answered the child, "but, if I told you what the teacher told us, you would never believe it!"*

### It was a miracle
*There are always those who will deny the existence of miracles. They claim that the works of ha-Shem (God) are simply natural phenomena. This was the attitude that many nonbelievers assumed in regard to the splitting of the Red Sea. It was caused by an earthquake, they might claim; it was just a freak accident of nature.*

*To forestall any such beliefs, ha-Shem magnified the miracle of the Red Sea. He split not only the Red Sea but also all the waters in the world. Even water that was in a cup gravitated to two separate sides! Because of this no one could deny that the splitting of the Red Sea was a true miracle. . . . (Rabbi Mordechai Katz,* Lilmod Ul'lamade: From the Teachings of Our Sages, *Jewish Education Program Publications, New York, 1978, p. 75)*

According to the author of the *Zohar*, God created one miracle after another to liberate the Israelites. Plagues were sent to convince Pharaoh to free the people. When they reached the Red Sea, God caused the waters to split and harden so that the Israelites could walk safely from one shore to the other on dry land. As soon as Pharaoh and his army entered the sea, God allowed the waters to crash in upon them, destroying the entire army.

Many commentators ask: How can God allow such miracles? Would the world not be destroyed if the laws of nature, like gravity that causes the Red Sea to flow, were suspended even for a second?

The *Zohar* provides an answer. Quoting Rabbi Isaac (perhaps second century C.E.), we are told that, when the Israelites approached the Red Sea, God called upon the great angel who had been appointed to rule over it. "At the time I created the world," God said to the angel, "I appointed you angel over this sea, and I made an agreement with you that, later when the Israelites would need to pass through your waters, you would divide them. Now they have arrived at the sea; open it and allow them to pass through safely." (*Zohar, Beshalach,* 48a–49a)

Clearly, the early rabbis were troubled by the Torah's claim that God had made a miracle at the Red Sea. Rabbi Isaac's explanation seems to overcome the problem by saying that the splitting of the sea had already been fixed or preordained at the time God created the world. In other words, God anticipated the need for dividing the Red Sea and "programmed" the event. Therefore, according to Rabbi Isaac, it was not a matter of a miraculous suspension of the laws of nature. Instead, the splitting of the Red Sea occurred exactly as God had preplanned it!

Other interpreters agree, but their explanations of what happened at the Red Sea are different. Some say that the splitting of the sea occurred in a natural way.

*Hertz*

Rabbi J. H. Hertz speculates that "a strong east wind, blowing all night and acting with the ebbing tide, may have laid bare the neck of the water joining the Bitter Lakes to the Red Sea, allowing the Israelites to cross in safety." Rabbi Hertz also explains that "a sudden cessation of the wind . . . would . . . convert the low flat sandbanks first into a quicksand and then into a mass of waters" which would have drowned the pursuing Egyptians. (*The Pentateuch and Haftorahs,* Soncino Press, London, 1966, pp. 268–269)

*Rambam (Maimonides)*

### Use of miracles
*A miracle cannot prove what is impossible; it is useful only to confirm what is possible. (Moses Maimonides,* Guide for the Perplexed *3:24)*

### Believing in miracles
*In short, I do not believe in miracles. Not if the word be interpreted in its usual sense as exceptions to the laws of nature. I believe in miracles*

*only as occurrences and events that are far too marvelous for me fully to comprehend but that are entirely consistent with nature's accustomed patterns. . . . Do you know any word more descriptive than miracle for the fact that within the tiny, submicroscopic cell each of us was at the moment of conception were already contained the seeds of all the physical traits, all the mental characteristics, all the emotional proclivities, all the creative possibilities of the adults we are today? Compared to that, a sea splitting in two . . . is simple child's play. There are more miracles without magic in this universe than the wisest of us could ever identify. The trouble is that most of the time we're looking for them in the wrong places.* (Roland B. Gittelsohn, Man's Best Hope, *Random House, New York, 1961, pp. 114–118*)

Modern Bible scholar Umberto Cassuto claims that what happened at the Red Sea "is a common occurrence in the region of the Suez." He explains that "at high tide, the waters of the Red Sea penetrate the sand, from under the surface, and suddenly the water begins to ooze up out of the sand, which has been dry. Within a short time the sand turns to mud, but the water continues to rise and ultimately a deep layer of water is formed above the sand, the whole area becoming flooded. . . . Against this natural background the biblical account can easily be understood."

Cassuto, however, does not reject the notion that a "miracle" occurred at the Red Sea. "The miracle," he says, "consisted in the fact that at the very moment when it was necessary, in just the manner conducive to the achievement of the desired goal, and on a scale that was abnormal, there occurred, in accordance with the Lord's will, phenomena that brought about Israel's salvation." (*A Commentary on the Book of Exodus*, Magnes Press, Jerusalem, 1951, pp. 167–168)

Philosopher Martin Buber seems to agree with Cassuto, but from a different point of view. Buber argues that the details of what happened at the Red Sea are not important. "What is decisive . . . ," he writes, "is that the children of Israel understood this as an act of their God, as a 'miracle.'" Buber explains that from a historical point of view a miracle is "an abiding astonish-

ment," a feeling of surprise and awe that people sense in especially significant moments. That is what happened at the Red Sea—and afterwards. The Israelites saw Pharaoh's advancing army drowned and destroyed. They were astonished by the events that saved them. At that moment, as Buber comments, "the people saw in whatever it was they saw 'the great hand of God.'" Afterwards, generations of Jews who retold the story continued to find in it traces of wonder that they identified as the miraculous work of God. (*Moses: The Revelation and the Covenant*, Harper and Row Publishers, Inc., New York, 1958, pp. 75, 77)

Whatever happened at the Red Sea, it is clear that the Egyptians were defeated and the Israelites went forth to freedom. The victory was surprising, a critical turning point in Jewish history. For those who were there, and for those who would tell the tale afterwards, something momentous and "astonishing" happened. God split the sea, saved the Israelites, and assured their liberation. All of this seemed more than the work of ordinary people. Something wonderful occurred, something awesome beyond human comprehension. So they called their victory "a miracle."

## PEREK BET: *Why All the Complaints against Moses and God?*

As astonishing as their victory over Pharaoh's army and their Exodus from Egypt, the Israelites are not portrayed as particularly grateful to God or to Moses. Our Torah portion, in fact, is filled with their complaints, angry questions, and discontent. On four occasions the people turn on Moses and attack him with harsh accusations.

The first time occurs just as they are escaping from Egypt. When the people see Pharaoh's army pursuing them, they ask Moses, "Was it for want of graves in Egypt that you brought us to die in the wilderness? What have you done to us, taking us out of Egypt? Is this not the very thing we told you in Egypt, saying, 'Let us be, and we will serve the Egyptians, for it is better for us to serve the Egyptians than to die in the wilderness'?" (14:10–12)

The second time occurs just after their "miraculous" victory at the Red Sea. They travel for three days and camp at Marah, meaning "bitter," located in the desert region of Shur. Because the water there tastes bitter, the people grumble against Moses and ask him, "What shall we drink?" (15:22–24)

Two and a half months later, they express their displeasure with Moses for a third time. Having just arrived in the wilderness of Sin, they are hungry, hot, and frustrated. So they tell Moses: "If only we had died by the hand of the Lord in the land of Egypt, when we sat by the fleshpots, when we ate our fill of bread! For you have brought us out into this wilderness to starve this whole congregation to death!"(16:1–3)

On the fourth occasion, the people are camped at Rephidim in the wilderness of Sin. Again, they complain about not having sufficient water. Angrily, they ask Moses, "Why did you bring us up from Eygpt, to kill us and our children and livestock with thirst?" (17:1–3)

What accounts for all of these complaints and accusations? Several theories are advanced.

*Rashi*

Rashi explains that the people see "the guardian angel of Egypt marching after them," and they are seized by fear. The guardian angel represents the military power of Egypt. It is advancing quickly upon the Israelites who are unarmed and unable to defend themselves. They are frightened that they will be overtaken and destroyed. Out of fear and disappointment they turn upon Moses, accusing him of leading them to their deaths at the brutal hands of the Egyptians. The terror of death, Rashi believes, generates their complaints.

### Handling our disappointments
*The Israelites were disappointed and angry when they saw the Egyptians pursuing them. They felt tricked and used by Moses when they found themselves in the wilderness without food and water. Given the steps for handling anger suggested below by psychologist Haim G. Ginott, how did the Israelites do when they were "pushed to the brink"?*

*Describe what you see.*
*Describe what you feel.*
*Describe what needs to be done.*
*Do not attack the person.*
(Between Parent and Teenager, *Macmillan, New York, 1969, p. 100*)

*Ibn Ezra*

Ibn Ezra disagrees with Rashi. He points out that there were six hundred thousand Israelites, and they could have easily taken on Pharaoh's army and defeated it. However, they were psychologically incapable. They still saw themselves as slaves, not free people. They thought that they were weak, still subservient and inferior to the Egyptians who had enslaved them. "How would it be possible," they asked themselves, "to go to war and win against those who ruled us?"

According to ibn Ezra it was not fear that brought on the Israelites' complaints. It was their perception of themselves as "weaklings" before their former Egyptian masters. Even though they outnumbered Pharaoh's army, their morale was so low and their self-esteem so shaken that they could not imagine themselves successfully battling the Egyptians. Instead, they turn upon Moses, make him a scapegoat for their frustrations, and blame him for bringing them out to the desert to die. (14:13)

Rabbi Eleazar of Modi'im explains their behavior from a different point of view. As soon as the Israelites left Egypt, he says, they began to experience the difficulties of thirst and hunger in the desert. They were uncomfortable, anxious, and irritable. As a result they began to look back upon their slave experience with nostalgia. They forgot about the beatings and humiliation; they remembered the abundance of food on their tables.

From where did such recollections come? Rabbi Eleazar points out they were based on their experience in Egypt. The people had been slaves to rulers and had been permitted "to go out to the markets and fields to help themselves to grapes, figs, and pomegranates, and no one would stand in their way."

Facing the hardships of the desert, the people began to idealize their situation in Egypt, to look at it through "rose-colored glasses." Rabbi Eleazar says it was out of that twisted point of view about the conditions of their slavery in Egypt that the Israelites complained to Moses. (*Mechilta, Vayasa,* on Exodus 15:27–16:3)

*Zugot*

### They were testing God
*Rabbi Joshua said: The Israelites argued that if God is truly the Power over all things, then we shall serve the Lord. If not, then we shall not serve God. Rabbi Eleazer claimed that they argued that if God fulfills our needs for food, water, and shelter, then we shall serve the Lord. If not, we shall not serve God. This is what the people meant when they said, "Is the Lord among us or not?"* (Mechilta, Vayasa, *on Exodus 17:7*)

*Leibowitz*

Nehama Leibowitz, quoting an observation found in the commentary *Hemdat ha-Yamim*, observes that the Israelites may have lied to one another about their slave existence in Egypt. They recalled all the positive aspects of slavery, not the negative ones. "There was not an ounce of truth in their words" to one another, Leibowitz writes. Like all slaves they were free "from responsibility for their own destiny, their own economic and social ordering. They were in the charge of a taskmaster who forced them to work, beat them, urged them to finish their tasks but also fed them that they might have strength for their labor. Now they were free, no longer dependent upon taskmasters who beat and fed them! The whole burden of taking care of themselves was theirs. This was

the source of their discontent." In other words, the Israelites grumbled at Moses because they now had to make their own decisions, find their own food and shelter. They resented the burdens of freedom. (*Studies in Shemot,* p. 265)

*Ramban (Nachmanides)*

Ramban sees the situation of the Israelites in a different way. They had left Egypt bravely and were now in the desert. They had thought that Moses would lead them to a city or safe place where they would find food, drink, and shelter; they believed it would not be long before they entered the Promised Land of Israel. However, after a month of wandering in the desert, their provisions were nearly gone. They were thirsty and hungry. Their essential needs were not being met, and they feared for the safety of their children. So they said to Moses, "What shall we eat? With what will this great wilderness into which we have come supply us?" Their complaints were not only understandable but both realistic and justified. (Comment on Exodus 16:2)

### They were disloyal to God
*God performed marvels . . . split the sea and took them through it . . . split rocks in the wilderness and gave them drink as if from the great deep. . . .*
*But they went on sinning against God, defying the Most High in the parched land . . . because they did not put their trust in God, did not rely on God's deliverance.* (Psalms 78:12–13, 15, 17, 22)

*Sarna*

Nahum Sarna rejects the notion that the people were justified in their complaints. Instead, he argues that they were like spoiled children. Moses had led them out of slavery. God had freed them from bondage. Even after they had been given sweet water at Marah and manna to eat, they still found reasons to murmur against Moses and God. They remained skeptical, doubtful of God's goodness and of Moses' intentions.

When the Israelites should have been grateful to both God and Moses for their liberation, they appear selfish and unfaithful. "The extreme language of the complaints betrays profound lack of faith in God and base ingratitude," Sarna argues. He points to Psalm 78 as an indication that Jerusalem poets living during the time of the Temple (second century B.C.E.) also saw in all the grumbling of the Israelites an example of their ingratitude, faithlessness, and disloyalty to God.

One other explanation may provide a significant understanding of their behavior. In his *Guide for the Perplexed*, Moses Maimonides makes the observation that God deliberately tested the Israelites with difficulties and challenges. When the time came to leave Egypt, God instructed Moses to take the Israelites the long way through the desert to the Promised Land rather than the direct route across the northern border of the Sinai peninsula, which would have taken only ten days. In the wilderness, God tested the people with thirst and hunger. All these tests, Maimonides explains, were meant to toughen the people and to prepare them for conquering the Land of Israel.

"It is a fact," Maimonides argues, "that the Israelites would not have been able to conquer the land and fight with its inhabitants if they had not previously undergone the trouble and hardship of the wilderness. . . . Ease destroys bravery while trouble and concern about food create strength. This strength that the Israelites gained was the ultimate good that came out of their wanderings in the wilderness." (3:24)

Maimonides viewed the complaints as natural. The people were tried by unpleasant conditions. One would expect them to grumble about their troubles and difficult circumstances. What was important, however, was not their complaints but the lessons they were learning. In coping with all the hardships of the wilderness, they were preparing themselves to conquer the Promised Land.

In the variety of explanations for the people's many complaints against Moses and God, we encounter not only different approaches to our Torah text but also a rich array of opinions about motives for human behavior. The Talmud teaches that "a person is to be judged by his anger." Might it also be correct to say that a person and a community are also judged by their "complaints"?

## PEREK GIMEL: *Amalek's Attack upon the Israelites*

Near the end of our Torah portion and again in Deuteronomy 25, we are told about the Amalekites' attack on the people of Israel. The version in Exodus 17:8–16 informs us that Amalek declares war upon Israel while the newly liberated people are camping at Rephidim. In response, Moses appoints Joshua to take troops and to engage the enemy in battle. While the war wages, Moses climbs to the top of a hill known as Hur and holds up his staff in prayer to God. After Joshua's victory, God instructs Moses to write out the following promise and reminder: "I will utterly blot out the memory of Amalek from under heaven."

The other version of the war with Amalek, as reported in Deuteronomy 25:17–19, adds some interesting details to the story. We are informed that the Amalekites attack the Israelites by surprise when they are "famished and weary," and they deliberately target the weak "stragglers," who are at the end of their lines. As in Exodus, after their victory, the Israelites are commanded: "You shall blot out the memory of Amalek from under heaven. Do not forget!"

Why this unforgiving command concerning the Amalekites?

Within Jewish tradition the Amalekites are identified as a nomadic people, who lived in the Sinai peninsula and were the descendants of Edom. (Genesis 36:12) In two major wars, the Amalekites were defeated by the Israelites, first under the leadership of King Saul and then under the leadership of King David. (I Samuel 15:5 ff. and 27:8 ff.) In the Book of Esther (3:1), Haman, who schemed to destroy the Jewish people, is described as a descendant of Agag, king of Amalek.

According to Jewish tradition, the Sabbath before the festival of Purim, when the Book of Esther is read, is called *Zachor* ("Remember"), and the Torah passage designated for that Sabbath day is from Deuteronomy 25:17–19, containing the commandment not to forget Amalek. In this way, the tradition preserves the connection between the Amalekites and wicked Haman.

---

**Why remember Amalek?**
*Possibly the fact that the Amalekites were the first foes Israel met after its liberation stamped them in the people's mind as the archenemy, the prototype of all whom they would and did meet subsequently. This sentiment is reflected in an old midrash: Moses was to write the judgment on Amalek in a document to let all men know that those who harm Israel will in the end come themselves to harm. (W. Gunther Plaut, editor,* The Torah: A Modern Commentary, *Union of American Hebrew Congregations, New York, 1981, p. 511)*

---

There can be no doubt that the attack of the Amalekites upon the newly liberated Israelites left bitter memories. Yet, there were many other battles and wars in Jewish history; other peoples sought to destroy Israel and to prevent it from occupying its national homeland. Why then does the Torah single out Amalek for special condemnation, calling for the end of its existence upon earth? Why are we commanded to "remember Amalek" rather than to "forgive Amalek"?

These questions obviously bothered those who studied Torah and sought to understand its meanings. As a result, several commentators provide us with their explanations.

Rabbi Joshua and Rabbi Eleazar Hisma both agree that Amalek's attack was brought about by Israel's behavior and lack of faith in God. From their viewpoint, the people of Israel had not "occupied themselves with the study of Torah." Therefore, they deserved the assault upon them. The command to "remember Amalek" was meant to remind Jews of the consequences of disloyalty to God's commandments. If Jews refuse to study Torah and observe its laws, then God will send enemies like Amalek to persecute and even destroy the people of Israel.

This explanation by Rabbi Joshua and Rabbi Eleazar Hisma, however, represents a minority point of view. By contrast, Rabbi Eleazar of Modi'im, who was put to death by his nephew, Bar Kochba, when he refused to cooperate with the plans for rebellion against Rome in 135 C.E., believed that the Amalekites were condemned because of the tactics they used in their war against Israel. "Amalek," Rabbi Eleazar of Modi'im explains, "would sneak under the wings of the cloud at the rear of the Israelite lines, steal people away, and kill them." In other words, the Amalekites are to be remembered for their trickery and treachery. They deliberately ambushed the weak, exhausted, and hungry. They surprised their victims from behind and then brutally murdered them. Because of their shocking and deplorable tactics, the Amalekites are never to be forgotten.

Another teacher, Rabbi Eliezer, presents the very opposite argument. He argues that the Amalekites did not attack the Israelites secretly, but "defiantly." They did not hide in the darkness of night or use the cover of the cloud at the rear of the Israelite lines. Instead, they maimed and murdered the poor, innocent, and weak during the day, publicly so that everyone could see what they were doing. Amalek stands for random killing and torture without cause—or just for the "sport" of it. The Amalekites are remembered for their public brutality in defiance of respect for the sanctity of human life.

Rabbi Jose ben Halafta offers another view. For him, the evil done by the Amalekites was not a matter of their tactics but of their efforts to solicit and organize other nations to aid them in their effort to destroy the people of Israel.

Rabbi Judah agrees with Rabbi Jose and points out that, in order to attack Israel, the Amalekites had to travel through five other nations. From each nation they sought allies for their plans to exterminate the Israelites. Rabbi Judah warns that we dare not forget their deliberate, cool, and calculated design to end Jewish existence. Remembering Amalek, he says, reminds us to be careful and always on guard about the safety and survival of the Jewish people. (*Mechilta, Amalek,* I)

Modern commentator Nehama Leibowitz presents a different observation. She points out that the Torah's report about Amalek makes it clear that the killing of the weak and feeble was because "they did not fear God." Leibowitz says that "we were commanded to blot out the memory of Amalek since they came and fell upon the defenseless and weary without any pretext whatsoever. The children of Israel were not entering their territory, and it was purely a wanton attack." In other words, had the Amalekites honored the worth of each human life as created in the image of God, it would have been impossible for them to kill without any cause. "Where the fear of God is lacking," Leibowitz points out, "the stranger who is homeless in a foreign land is liable to be murdered." We are urged to recall Amalek so that we guard against those who have no fear of God and, consequently, do not believe that each human being is created in God's sacred image. (*Studies in Devarim,* World Zionist Organization, Jerusalem, 1980, p. 253)

*Hirsch*

Rabbi Samson Raphael Hirsch finds another reason for not forgetting the Amalekites' war against the Israelites. Hirsch claims the Amalekites were seeking fame. Because they wanted to demonstrate their bravery and strength, they took up arms against those who had just defeated Pharaoh. "This seeking renown by the force of arms is the first and last enemy of the happiness of mankind," Hirsch writes. Human beings need to be reminded of the danger of seeking fame through the power of arms and military might. For that reason, the memory of Amalek must never be forgotten.

*Peli*

Pinchas Peli believes that Amalek's war against the Jewish people was not only calculated to take their lives but was also intended to rob them of their enthusiasm for freedom. "Amalek rushed to pour cold water on the fire of enthusiasm and faith generated by Israel and its miraculous deliverance from Egypt." Recalling the observation of Jewish mystics that the numerical value of the name "Amalek" in Hebrew adds up to 240, which equals the word *safek* (meaning "doubt"), Peli concludes that the Amalekites represent doubters and cynics, who see their roles as "undermining, defaming, delegitimatizing, cutting off in its bud, any sign of hope wherever it appears." In remembering Amalek, Peli observes, we make certain that the cynics and doubters, those who tear down dreams with their contempt and defeatism, are not allowed to triumph. (*Jerusalem Post,* September 13, 1986, p. 22)

To have forgiven the Amalekites and forgotten their attack might have robbed the Jewish people and the world of valuable lessons. The Amalekites have emerged through the ages as a prototype for aggressive, dangerous human behavior. Understanding the consequences of such evil, and battling against it, may be critical for human survival. Remembering Amalek is a first significant step.

## QUESTIONS FOR STUDY AND DISCUSSION

1. Which explanation for the "miracle" of Israel's Exodus from Egypt makes the most sense?
2. Martin Buber defines a miracle as an "abiding astonishment." Of other human experiences that can be recalled, which are so wonderful that people refer to them as "miracles"? What do they have in common with the Exodus of Israel from Egypt?
3. Why do the Israelites offer so many complaints against God and Moses? Do the reasons given by the various commentators also explain why so many people complain about their lives today? What lessons might we learn from the way the early Israelites handled their gripes and grievances?
4. Why does Jewish tradition insist on encouraging people to "remember Amalek"? Wouldn't it be better for people "to forgive and forget"? Why make a mitzvah out of remembering the past—especially if that past is filled with unhappiness, horror, and fear?

# PARASHAT YITRO
## *Exodus 18:1–20:23*

*Parashat Yitro* continues the journey of the Israelites across the Sinai desert. Before returning to Egypt, Moses had left his wife, Zipporah, and his two sons, Gershom and Eliezer, with his father-in-law, Jethro. Hearing that Moses has freed the Israelites from Egypt, Jethro brings Zipporah and her children to the Israelite camp. Moses tells his father-in-law about the Israelite liberation, and they offer sacrifices of thanksgiving to God. The next day Jethro observes that the people are bringing all their problems to Moses. He suggests that the burden is too great for one person to bear and advises Moses to choose trustworthy people to share leadership with him. Moses takes his advice. Three months after entering the Sinai desert, Moses and the Israelites camp at Mount Sinai. Moses goes up to the top of the mountain, and God speaks to him, giving him the Ten Commandments. Below, the people hear thunder and see lightning. They remain at a distance while Moses communes with God.

## OUR TARGUM

### · 1 ·

Jethro, Moses' father-in-law, hears that the Israelites have escaped from Egypt. He takes Zipporah, Moses' wife, and his grandsons, Gershom and Eliezer, to where Moses and the Israelites are camping in the Sinai desert. Moses tells Jethro about the wondrous liberation from Egypt. Jethro is delighted and says: "Blessed be the Lord who delivered you from the Egyptians and from Pharaoh. . . . Now I know that the Lord is greater than all gods."

During the next day Jethro sees large numbers of people bringing their disputes to Moses. "Why do you act alone?" he asks him. Moses explains that the people need a judge to deal with their disagreements and a teacher to instruct them in God's laws.

"What you are doing is wrong," Jethro tells him. "The task should not be done by one person." Jethro urges Moses to find "trustworthy people who will not take bribes" and appoint them as "chiefs of thousands, hundreds, fifties, and tens. Let them . . . decide every minor dispute themselves. Make it easier for yourself, and let them share the burden with you."

Moses follows Jethro's advice. Later Jethro returns to Midian.

### · 2 ·

Three months after departing from Egypt, Moses leads the people to the wilderness of Sinai. They camp before Mount Sinai, and God tells Moses to say to the people: "You have seen what I did to the Egyptians, how I bore you on eagles' wings and brought you to Me. Now then, if you will obey Me faithfully and keep My covenant, you shall be My treasured possession among all the peoples. . . . You shall be to Me a kingdom of priests and a holy nation."

Hearing God's words, the Israelites respond: "All that God has spoken we will do!"

### · 3 ·

Three days later Moses leads the people to Mount Sinai. The mountain appears to be on fire. Smoke rises from its peaks. The people hear the loud blasts of a horn and are frightened. Moses leaves them and goes to the top of the mountain. There he receives the Ten Commandments.

1. I the Lord am your God who brought you out of the land of Egypt, the house of bondage.

2. You shall have no other gods beside Me. You shall not make for yourself a sculptured image, or any likeness of what is in the heavens above, or on the earth below, or in the waters under the earth. You shall not bow down to them or serve them. . . .

3. You shall not swear falsely by the name of the Lord your God. . . .

4. Remember the Sabbath day and keep it holy.

5. Honor your father and mother. . . .

6. You shall not murder.

7. You shall not commit adultery.

8. You shall not steal.

9. You shall not bear false witness against your neighbor.

10. You shall not covet your neighbor's house; you shall not covet your neighbor's wife, or his male or female slave, or his ox or his ass, or anything that is your neighbor's.

## THEMES

*Parashat Yitro* contains two important themes:

1. Sharing leadership of the community.
2. Appreciating what happened at Mount Sinai.

## PEREK ALEF: *The Burden of Leadership*

During Jethro's visit to the Israelite camp, he notices long lines of people waiting to bring their disputes before Moses. Sitting alone from morning until evening, Moses listens to each argument, hears each problem, and states his judgment on each situation brought before him. Jethro is astounded. "What is this thing that you are doing for the people?" he asks Moses. "Why do you act alone, while all the people stand about you from morning until evening?"

Noting that Jethro was deeply upset with Moses, an ancient sage suggests that what disturbed Jethro was not that Moses appeared overworked but that Moses had become full of self-importance. Moses, he says, was "behaving like a king who sits on his throne while all the people stand."

Rabbi Judah of the village of Akko also detected a dangerous element of conceit in Moses. Why, he asks, did Moses tell Jethro that "the people are coming to *me*" instead of saying that "the people are coming to *God*"? Rabbi Judah's question raises other questions about Moses. Did he believe that he was superior to his people or even to God in helping them solve their problems? Was he beginning to assume that he alone had the wisdom to advise them?

Rabbi Judah's questions seem to imply that Jethro was upset with Moses because he saw him losing his humility, becoming a pompous leader who believed only he could make decisions for his people. For that reason, Rabbi Judah argues, Jethro criticized Moses and told him to find others with whom to share the responsibilities of leadership. (*Mechilta, Amalek,* IV)

While most interpreters do not criticize Moses for holding himself above his people or for playing the role of "king of the Israelites," many cite the dangerous consequences of his decision to judge the people by himself.

*Zugot*

For instance, Rabbi Joshua comments that Jeth-ro's warning to Moses was a practical one. Jethro saw that Moses had taken on too much. The work was overwhelming. Fearful that Moses would collapse from exhaustion, Jethro told him, "They will tire you out and cause you to fail in your leadership of them."

Rabbi Eleazar of Modi'im agrees that the danger to Moses was "exhaustion," but he offers a different perspective. He claims Jethro also believed that Moses was exhausting the people. By insisting that he was the only one who could hear their problems and disputes, he forced them to stand in long lines for many hours in the hot desert sun. As a result they became irritable. They turned to one another with complaints. "Moses is taking too long to hear these cases. By the time he hears us he will be too tired to make a fair decision." Rabbi Eleazar says that Jethro heard their dissatisfaction and warned Moses: "The people will despise and reject you with their criticisms." Jethro saw that Moses' desire to do everything himself was wasteful and inefficient. Instead of helping the people, it was creating frustration and dissatisfaction among them. (*Mechilta, Amalek,* IV)

*Ramban (Nachmanides)*

Nachmanides observes that the trouble with Moses' decision to hear all the disputes and make all the judgments by himself was not simply the frustration of the people but the danger of increasing violence and injustice among them. Jethro, Nachmanides says, told Moses that the people "will tolerate the violence committed against them because they have no opportunity to tell it to you. They do not want to abandon their work and affairs to wait for a free moment when they will be able to approach you." In other words, Jethro saw that, as the people lost faith in Moses' ability to hear their cases, they began to take the law into their own hands. Because they refused to waste their time waiting for him to make judgments, violence and injustice increased among them.

Essentially, in Jethro's critique of Moses, Nachmanides sees a very important criticism of courts not equipped to handle the large number of cases brought to them. The results are long delays, mounting frustration, a loss of faith in the system's capacity to deliver justice, and, often, the decision of some people to take the law into their own hands. Because, at first, Moses insisted on doing everything himself, he increased the dangers of violence and injustice, rather than providing for efficient and fair judgment. (Commentary on Exodus 19:22)

---

**Excellence in management**

*The excellent companies have a deeply ingrained philosophy that says, in effect, "respect the individual," "make people winners," "let them stand out," "treat people as adults." (Thomas J. Peters and Robert H. Waterman, Jr.,* In Search of Excellence, *Harper and Row Publishers, Inc., New York, 1982, p. 277)*

**Participating in management**

*(Decentralization) . . . increases the amount of discretion and autonomy that individuals have at work by decentralizing decision-making and increasing participation in decision-making processes as much as possible. . . .*

*The benefits of decentralization in terms of reduced distress and strain are illustrated in the experience of an officer of a hospital equipment corporation. Over a ten-year period, this officer had worked for two different corporations. One company was very centralized; the other used a very decentralized decision-making approach. During his ten years in the centralized corporation, he had insomnia, depression, and nightmares about going to jail and about running afoul of corporate policies and procedures. . . . After a year of this distress, he left the centralized corporation and subsequently joined the decentralized corporation. Following the move to the new corporation, his insomnia and depression cleared. . . . His family reported that he was much easier to be around, and he was more the man they used to know. (James C. Quick and Jonathan D. Quick,* Organizational Stress and Preventive Management, *McGraw-Hill, New York, 1984, pp. 163–171)*

---

*Sarna*

Modern interpreter Nahum Sarna agrees with Nachmanides' observation. "Jethro," he says, "is appalled at the inefficiency of the system of justice, with its inevitably debilitating effects on Moses himself and the hardships it imposes on the public." It is for that reason that he suggests a new system to Moses. He recommends that he appoint judges for thousands, hundreds, fifties, and tens, allowing them to hear disputes and make judgments. "Make it easier for yourself," he counsels Moses, "and let them share the burden with you." (*Exploring Exodus*, pp. 126–127)

The benefits of sharing the burden of leadership, of "decentralizing" seem clear in this situation. Justice will be dispensed more quickly. The people will be less frustrated and less likely to take the law into their own violent hands. Trust will be established and strengthened by confidence in a system of justice that works. Leadership will be more rested, more alert, and more accessible. Jethro's suggestion to Moses about dividing up the burdens of leadership is both functually wise and socially just.

Jethro, however, not only recommends the sharing of leadership but offers a critique for choosing leaders. He tells Moses: "You shall seek out from among all the people those who are capable and fear God, those who are trustworthy and spurn ill-gotten gain." Not surprisingly, interpreters from all ages have explored the meaning of this remarkable definition of leadership.

*Rashi*

One ancient sage suggests that "capable" means "wealthy, people of means." Rashi agrees, saying that people of "wealth will not need to flatter others or show them favor."

Nachmanides disagrees. "A capable person," he argues, is "wise, alert, and fair" in the administration of justice and is "strong and alert" when it comes to "organizing troops for battle." (*Mechilta, Amalek,* IV; Rashi on Exodus 18:21; Nachmanides on Exodus 18:21)

*Ibn Ezra*

Ibn Ezra offers another point of view. He writes that the phrase "capable people" means "people who have the strength to tolerate without fear the hardship of those who criticize their decisions." For ibn Ezra leadership means independence, confidence in one's opinions, and the strength to stand behind them. (Comment on Exodus 18:21)

Sforno believes that when the Torah uses the words "capable people" it has in mind individuals "who possess the talent to lead Jews out of a fight, and a sufficient enough knowledge of an enemy's strategies and resources to guarantee victory." "Capable people" are those who understand how to compromise and resolve differences between angry parties. But they are not naive. According to Sforno, they also realize that not all disagreements can be settled. Often there are anger, hard feelings, and threats of violence between parties. In such a situation a "capable person" will know how to judge the weaknesses and strengths of the opponent, and how to make efficient and effective use of all resources available for victory. (Comment on Exodus 18:21)

The commentators also ask the question: What can the description "trustworthy people who spurn ill-gotten gain" mean?

Rabbi Joshua suggests that the phrase describes those "who would never accept money while they were sitting in judgment." Clearly, Joshua has in mind people who refuse to accept bribes or judges who, while hearing a case, refuse to accept any money from anyone for fear that it might appear as though they were accepting bribes.

Rabbi Hanina ben Dosa and his friends argue that the phrase "spurn ill-gotten gain" describes "those who do not put great importance on their own money." According to Rabbi Hanina and his friends, such people are to be respected and revered. They are to be trusted because "if they do not put great importance on their own wealth, then they are not likely to place much importance upon taking the money of others to increase what they possess." (*Mechilta, Amalek,* IV)

<blockquote>
*Rules for judges*
*Any judge who takes money from the judgments he makes is no longer qualified to be a judge.* (Baba Batra 58b)

*Any judge who is in the habit of borrowing things from his neighbors is forbidden to act as a judge in a lawsuit involving them.* (Ketubot 105b)
</blockquote>

Nachmanides explains that people who do not place much importance upon their own wealth are likely to be trustworthy because they will not be intimidated by those who offer bribes or threaten their property. Instead, they will say, "Even if this person will burn my property, or destroy it, I will render a just decision." Such people, Nachmanides argues, "love the truth and hate oppression. When they see oppression and violence, they cannot tolerate them. Therefore, they put all their efforts into 'rescuing those who are robbed from those who defraud them.'" (Comment on Exodus 18:21 with quote from Jeremiah 21:12)

Commenting on Jethro's suggestion to Moses that he share the leadership of the community with others, the ancient sage Rabbi Nehemiah taught that "as soon as a person is appointed to leadership, he or she must no longer say: 'I live for my own benefit. I do not care about the community.' For now the whole burden of the community is on his or her shoulders. If a person is seen causing harm to another, or breaking the law, the leader must act to prevent the wrongdoing or be punished." (*Shemot Rabbah* 27:9)

Leadership has always been a serious responsibility. Caring for the safety of a community and preserving its culture and traditions are complex tasks. Jethro appreciated the need to share the burden, and the interpreters of his advice to Moses creatively define for us the qualities of leadership required by Jewish tradition. It is a high ethical standard, which continues to be useful as a measure for excellence in leadership today.

## PEREK BET: *What Happened at Mount Sinai?*

The giving of the Ten Commandments at Mount Sinai is one of the most important events in Jewish history. It is also a moment filled with mystery. The Torah reports that, while the people of Israel stood at the bottom of the mountain, they not only saw flames and smoke rising from it but also heard the blare of horns and felt "the whole mountain tremble violently." According to the report, the people were so frightened that they remained below while Aaron and Moses climbed to the top. Afterwards, Moses descended and presented the Ten Commandments to the Israelites.

From that moment until today, Jews have asked the question: "What happened at Mount Sinai?" Is the Torah report an accurate recording of history or a legend in which some kernels of truth are hidden?

---

**How the Torah was given**

*The Torah was given portion by portion.* (Gittin 60a)

*The Torah was not given to angels.* (Berachot 25a)

*When the Torah was given, God showed Moses all the details of Torah and all the innovations that would later be introduced by the rabbis.* (Megillah 19b)

*Moses received the Torah at Mount Sinai and handed it on to Joshua. Joshua handed it to the elders, and the elders handed it to the prophets. The prophets handed it on to the people of the Great Assembly.* (Avot 1:1)

---

There are many differing views about what happened at Mount Sinai. For instance, Rabbi Yochanan claims that God's voice was divided into seven voices, and the seven voices were further divided into the seventy languages spoken by all the peoples of the world at that time. Other rabbis of Yochanan's time disagree. They claim that God spoke with a single voice.

Rabbi Isaac taught that "the message of all the prophets who were to arise in later generations—people like Isaiah, Jeremiah, Ezekiel, Amos, Micah, and Hosea—was given to Moses with the Torah." Rabbi Simeon ben Lakish agrees. (*Exodus Rabbah, Yitro,* 38:6)

Extending this idea that all the books of the Hebrew Bible were given to Moses at Mount Sinai, some of the ancient rabbis claim that God gave two Torahs to Moses. One they call *Torah Shebichetav,* "Written Torah," comprising the Five Books of Moses: Genesis, Exodus, Leviticus, Numbers, and Deuteronomy. The other they call *Torah Shebealpeh,* "Oral Torah," made up of all the books of the Prophets, the *Midrash Agadah,* the Talmud, and all decisions and explanations of Jewish law by rabbinic scholars through the ages.

Agreeing that two Torahs were given by God to Moses and the Jewish people, other sages explain that God said to Moses: "Write down everything I tell you, for I have made a covenant with Israel." God then dictated the Torah, the Talmud (*Mishnah* and *Gemara*), the Midrash, and even answers to all the questions that leading rabbis in the future would require when they were asked "What did God say to Moses on Mount Sinai?" (*Tanchuma, Ki Tisa,* 58b; *Pesikta Rabbati* 7b)

Clearly, the ancient rabbis have added their own versions of what actually happened between God, Moses, and the people of Israel at Mount Sinai. Their belief that two Torahs were given, including answers to all questions that might arise throughout all time, not only adds to the mystery of whatever occurred at Mount Sinai, but also grants special authority to all subsequent interpreters. This is an important point that should not be overlooked. As a result of their theory of "two Torahs," rabbis now have the right to say that their own interpretations or decisions are "the law according to Moses at Mount Sinai!"

*Rambam (Maimonides)*

### The whole Torah
*I believe with perfect faith that the whole Torah, now in our possession, is the same that was given to Moses our teacher.* (Moses Maimonides, Principles of Faith, #8)

This view of what happened at Sinai became the most dominant interpretation among Jews from early rabbinic times until the beginning of the nineteenth century. Philosopher Yehudah Halevi, for example, writes that "the people believed that Moses held direct communication with God, that his words were not creations of his own mind. . . . They did not believe Moses had seen a vision in sleep, or that someone had spoken with him between sleeping and waking so that he only heard the words in his imagination but not with his ears, that he saw a phantom and afterwards pretended that God had spoken with him." Halevi concludes by citing proof of God's speaking to Moses at Mount Sinai. He says there was no "trickery" there. "For God's speaking was followed by God's writing. For God wrote the Ten Commandments on two tablets of precious stone and handed them to Moses." (*The Kuzari*, New York, Schocken Books, 1964, pp. 60–61)

Orthodox Jews continue to claim that God gave the Torah, both the Written Law and the Oral Law, to Moses on Mount Sinai. It was a onetime gift or revelation. A complete Torah with everything that Jews would ever need to know was presented to Moses and passed on afterwards from generation to generation as *Torah mi-Sinai*, "Torah from Sinai." As proof for this claim today's Orthodox authorities, like Halevi in his time, cite the Torah text itself. It says, they argue, that "God spoke all these words." Therefore, they conclude that is obviously what happened.

A few Orthodox thinkers, however, disagree. Like Rabbi David Hartman of Jerusalem, they do not believe that the Torah given at Mount Sinai

was "a complete, finished system." Hartman explains that "belief in the giving of the Torah at Sinai does not necessarily imply that the full truth has already been given and that our task is only to unfold what was already present in the fullness of the founding moment of revelation." What happened at Mount Sinai, he says, "gave the community a direction, an arrow pointing toward a future filled with many surprises. . . . The Sinai moment of revelation . . . invites one and all to acquire the competence to explore the terrain and extend the road. It does not require passive obedience and submission to the wisdom of the past." (*A Living Covenant*, The Free Press, New York, 1985, p. 8)

### Torah for Reform Jews
*Torah results from the relationship between God and the Jewish people. The records of our earliest confrontations are uniquely important to us. Lawgivers and prophets, historians and poets gave us a heritage whose study is a religious imperative and whose practice is our chief means to holiness. Rabbis and teachers, philosophers and mystics, gifted Jews in every age amplified the Torah tradition. For millennia, the creation of Torah has not ceased and Jewish creativity in our time is adding to the chain of tradition.* (From "A CCAR Centenary Perspective: New Platform for Reform Judaism," Reform Judaism, *November 1976, p. 4*)

### What the Torah reveals
*There is little reason to question that Moses, who led our people in the wilderness and organized them into a nation, also gave them laws. Those laws formed the basis of the various decisions and practices by which the Israelites lived after they entered the Land [of Israel]. In the course of time, those decisions and practices were recorded, compiled, and edited, a process which continued down to the time of Ezra (420 B.C.E.), some centuries after the sojourn in the wilderness. . . . The Torah reveals the working of God in the life of our people in that it articulates the earliest striving of our people to live up to the highest potentialities of human nature.* (Mordecai M.

*Kaplan,* Questions Jews Ask: Reconstructionist Answers, *Reconstructionist Press, New York, 1956, pp. 167–168*)

Hartman's view—what happened at Mount Sinai was an unforgettable "founding moment" in Jewish history but not the conclusion of God's gift of Torah to the people of Israel—is close to the view held by Rabbi Jakob J. Petuchowski, a leading Reform Jewish scholar. In explaining what occurred, Rabbi Petuchowski comments: "The thunders and lightnings at Sinai, as they appear in the biblical narrative, are an echo sounding through the ages of what had happened there. They testify to the fact of Revelation, to the impact it had on the people. But it is only the man of a prosaic mind, the man lacking in imagination, who would read this biblical account as if it were a news bulletin reporting in every detail what has actually happened."

For Petuchowski, the giving of Torah at Sinai was a momentous event in the history of the Jewish people, but it is not to be seen as the moment in which the entire Torah was given to Moses. Quite the contrary. "The laws and commandments of the Torah," Petuchowski writes, "do not all go back to that moment—at any rate, not in the form in which we read them today. They have evolved in the course of the centuries. Different circumstances called forth different responses. Life in the days of the Hebrew monarchy was different from life in the days of the Judges. And the generations engaged in the task of settling in Palestine faced different problems from those that beset the wanderers in the desert. Yet all the different responses to all the different challenges were made from the perspective of the initial commitment at Sinai. . . . The 'giving of the Torah,' therefore, is not confined to the occasion at Sinai. . . . What parts of the Torah really and truly took on their present form already at Sinai we shall probably never know. . . ." (*Ever Since Sinai,* Milwaukee, Wisconsin, Arbit, 1979, pp. 67–80)

Petuchowski's view of an evolving Torah of commandments and their interpretations is shared by Rabbi W. Gunther Plaut who, in considering what happened at Mount Sinai, asks the question: "What precisely was revealed?" Plaut argues that "the traditional answer that the Written and Oral Laws in their entirety were entrusted to Moses at Sinai is unacceptable to me. Only the Written Law then? I rebel equally against this thought." Plaut bases his conviction that the entire Torah tradition evolved over the long course of history on the basis of archeological and historical research.

So what does Plaut believe happened at Mount Sinai? In answering the question, he recalls the explanation of modern philosopher Franz Rosenzweig, who believed that the people did not hear words spoken at Mount Sinai at all. What happened there and what left a lasting impression, Rosenzweig speculates, is that the people encountered God. It was at Sinai that the people began the process of searching out what God wanted of them. From that moment on, the Jewish people has been engaged in a covenant, a partnership with God. "A Jew," Plaut comments, "by the very condition of his Jewishness, pays the continuing price of Sinai. If Jewishness remains his fate, Judaism remains the framework of his native spiritual existence, and God his partner. . . . Each generation should regard itself as standing at Sinai." (*The Case for the Chosen People,* Doubleday, New York, 1965, pp. 90–95)

This conviction that something wonderful and awesome took place between God and the people of Israel at Mount Sinai is also central in the philosophy of Rabbi Abraham Joshua Heschel. He comments that "a cosmic fear enveloped all those who stood at Sinai, a moment more staggering than the heart could feel." Heschel explains: "*What* we see may be an illusion; *that* we see can never be questioned. The thunder and lightning at Sinai may have been merely an impression; but to have suddenly been endowed with the power of seeing the whole world struck with an overwhelming awe of God was a new sort of perception. . . . Only in moments when we are able to share in the spirit of awe that fills the world are we able to understand what happened to Israel at Sinai."

Heschel's conception of the wonder-filled event at Mount Sinai maintains that something extraordinary took place between God, Moses, and the Jewish people. He does not, however, identify what of the Torah might have been revealed at that time. What is significant about the moment at Mount Sinai is that God spoke and the people of Israel responded. "It was both an event in the life of God and an event in the life of humanity. . . . The wonder of Israel's acceptance was as decisive as the wonder of God's expression. . . . Without that power to respond, without the fact that there was a people willing to accept, to hear, the divine command, Sinai would have been impossible." (*God in Search of Man: A Philosophy of Judaism,* Farrar, Straus and Cudahy, New York, 1955, pp. 195–197, 259–260)

So what did happen at Mount Sinai? According to Heschel, God spoke, and the people of Israel listened. They heard the commandments and responded that they would live according to them. The moment was one of the most important in Jewish history because in it God chose and challenged the Jewish people to live according to Torah, and the Jewish people answered, "All that God has spoken we will do!"

We have discovered many theories about what actually happened at Mount Sinai between God, Moses, and the Jewish people. Perhaps two complete Torahs were given by God in that wonder-filled moment. More likely, a God-inspired Moses delivered the Ten Commandments, and later generations, also inspired, wrote down the other commandments that were compiled and edited into what we know today as the Torah. No one can be sure.

All that can be said with certainty is that, whatever happened at Mount Sinai, the people of Israel never forgot the wonder of it. They recalled it as momentous, mysterious, and awesome. They believed that God had spoken and that they had been chosen to become a "treasured people . . .

a holy nation." At Sinai, God and the Jewish people entered into a sacred covenant filled with mitzvot—ethical and ritual responsibilities that not only continue to evolve but give meaning to Jewish lives and justification for the existence of the Jewish people.

## QUESTIONS FOR STUDY AND DISCUSSION

1. What problems do the commentators believe Moses created for the Israelites by setting himself up as their only judge? Do these same problems exist today? How might Jethro's advice to Moses help solve contemporary problems?

2. Is "decentralization" really necessary for good management and effective institutions? What are some of the negative aspects of "sharing leadership" rather than relying upon one strong personality? How might some of these problems be overcome? How did Jethro anticipate such problems?

3. Orthodox Rabbi J. David Bleich writes: "The text of the Bible as we have it today—that of the Torah scroll read in the synagogue—is identical in every significant detail with the original scroll of the Torah written by Moses in the wilderness." How do the interpreters in our chapter agree or disagree with Bleich?

4. How has the Oral Torah tradition of evolving new interpretations of Jewish law and practice actually guaranteed the survival of the Written Torah? Is there a parallel between the Constitution of the United States and its interpretation by the courts and the Torah with its long history of rabbinic interpretations?

# PARASHAT MISHPATIM
## *Exodus 21:1–24:18*

*Parashat Mishpatim* presents the *mishpatim,* "rules" or "laws," that govern the ancient Jewish community. The code of law deals with the treatment of slaves; crimes of murder and kidnapping; personal injuries; damages through neglect or theft; offenses against others through lying, witchcraft, idolatry, oppression, unfair business practices; and unjust treatment by judges. This Torah portion also includes a warning against following others to do evil, along with directives to care for the distressed animals of your enemy and to show impartiality in making judgments. Israelites are reminded to demonstrate sensitivity to the stranger because they were strangers in the land of Egypt. Finally, the portion presents rules for the Sabbath, sabbatical year, Pesach, Shavuot, and Sukot. Upon hearing all these laws, Moses gathers the people at Mount Sinai to offer sacrifices and declares, "All the things that God has commanded we will do!"

## OUR TARGUM

### · 1 ·

While still at Mount Sinai, Moses presents the people with the laws that will govern their community.

About slavery, which was common among all peoples at that time, Moses declares that a slave will be free after seven years and clarifies the rights of slaves and their children in cases of marriage.

Those who deliberately murder are to be put to death. Those who accidentally kill another person are provided a safe place where they can seek

judgment. Kidnappers or those who curse their parents are to be put to death.

If a person injures another in a quarrel, payment is to be made for both the cure and loss of work time. If the injured party is a pregnant woman who happens to miscarry, then the one responsible will pay damages agreed to by her husband. If, however, the injury is to the body, the penalty will be "life for life, eye for eye, tooth for tooth, hand for hand, foot for foot, burn for burn, wound for wound, bruise for bruise."

If an ox gores a man or woman, the ox will be stoned or put to death; but, if the ox is known

to be dangerous and its owner has not taken steps to guard it, both the ox and the owner shall be put to death. When a person's ox kills another ox, the owners are to sell the live ox and split the money received for both the live and dead animals. However, if it was known as a dangerous ox and the owner did not guard it, he must restore it with a live ox and keep the dead animal.

If a person digs a pit and neglects to cover it, he is responsible to pay for whatever falls into it and is harmed.

Fines shall be paid for stealing, for allowing one's animals to graze on another's property, for damages related to starting a fire, for misappropriation of property, for animals that are borrowed and die of injuries, and for seducing a virgin.

Witchcraft is forbidden; also forbidden is having sex with an animal or offering sacrifices to other gods.

Jews are forbidden to wrong or oppress the stranger. They are to remember that they were strangers in Egypt.

Widows and orphans must be treated with care. The poor are to be given interest-free loans. If a person gives a garment as guarantee for a loan, that garment must be returned by sunset so the person will be safe from the chill of night.

Spreading rumors, cursing leaders, joining with others to give false testimony, siding with others to do wrong, showing favoritism to rich or poor in courts of law, making false charges, or taking bribes are all forbidden.

Returning an enemy's lost animal or caring for it if it is in distress is considered the right thing to do.

· 2 ·

Serving God includes not only the ethical conduct commanded above but also the celebration of special rituals. The firstborn of the flocks are to be sacrificed to God as thanksgiving offerings. Eating the flesh of beasts killed by other animals is forbidden. The Sabbath is to be observed each week, and a sabbatical year in which the fields are allowed to rest from planting is to be practiced every seventh year. A kid is not to be boiled in its mother's milk.

Three times a year, on Pesach, Shavuot, and Sukot, the people are to celebrate before God.

· 3 ·

God promises the Israelites that, if they will be faithful to these laws and not follow the idolatrous practices of other peoples, God's angel will lead them victoriously into their land.

Moses is instructed to climb Mount Sinai along with Aaron, Nadab and Abihu, and seventy of the elders of Israel. On Sinai, Moses repeats all the laws, and the people answer, "All the things that God has commanded we will do!" Moses offers a sacrifice to mark their commitment to God's laws. Afterwards, he ascends Mount Sinai to receive the stone tablets of the law. He disappears from sight inside a cloud at the top of the mountain, where he remains for forty days and nights.

## THEMES

*Parashat Mishpatim* contains two important themes:

1. The importance of the *mitzvot,* or "commandments."
2. Care for the *ger,* or "stranger."

## PEREK ALEF: *Ethical and Ritual Mitzvot*

*Parashat Mishpatim* begins with the words of God to Moses, "These are the rules that you shall set before them." It then continues with a detailed list of the mitzvot or commandments that the people are to follow. It is a long list containing a wide variety of rules. There are commandments having to do with the treatment of slaves; the consequences of murder, kidnapping, or cursing one's parents; the responsibilities of one person to another in cases of damage or neglect; concern for the stranger and the poor; warnings to judges and witnesses about honesty and fairness in court. There are also mitzvot dealing with the observance of the Sabbath, the sabbatical year, the festivals of Pesach, Shavuot, and Sukot, along with those prohibiting the boiling of a kid in its mother's milk, of worshiping idols, or even mentioning the names of other gods.

While this Torah portion is called *mishpatim,* or "laws," it is not the only portion containing such a list of commandments. Throughout the five books of the Torah we find hundreds of commandments or mitzvot that begin with the words

"You shall . . ." or "You shall not. . . ." Many of these are repetitious. The Ten Commandments, for example, mentioned in Exodus 20:2–14 are repeated in Deuteronomy 5:6–18, and many of the rules recorded in *Mishpatim* are also found scattered throughout Leviticus and Deuteronomy.

Perhaps the first commentator to ask the question "How many mitzvot did God give to the Jewish people at Sinai?" was Rabbi Simlai. Simlai, who taught in both the Land of Israel and Babylonia during the fourth century C.E., declared that Moses received 613 commandments at Sinai. Simlai divided these into two categories: 248 were *mitzvat aseh,* "positive commandments," which begin with the words "You shall . . ." and correspond to the 248 parts of the human body; 365 were *mitzvat lo ta'aseh,* or "negative commandments," which begin with the words "You shall not . . ." and correspond to the number of days in the solar year. The commandments, Simlai emphasized, were meant to guide human beings in the use of all their physical powers during each day of the year. (*Makot* 23b)

Other commentators divide the mitzvot of the Torah into two different categories. Those commandments dealing with the observance of the Sabbath, holidays, diet, and other religious practices are called *mitzvot bein adam le-Makom*, "commandments between the human being and God." Those commandments dealing with the ethical and moral relationships between human beings are labeled *mitzvot bein adam le-chavero*, "commandments between the individual and other human beings. (*Yoma* 85b)

This division of the mitzvot into ritual and ethical categories, however, does not mean that the interpreters of Jewish tradition considered one set of commandments more important than the other. Both were of equal significance, and often commentators point out that the ritual mitzvot lead a person to ethical action. For instance, a part of fulfilling the mitzvah of making a Pesach seder is to invite "all who are hungry to eat."

Despite the fact that early commentators had created two categories of mitzvot and that Rabbi Simlai uses the figure of 613 mitzvot, it is not until the eighth century that the Babylonian teacher Simeon Kairo actually tried to identify which of the hundreds of commandments mentioned in the Torah were to be counted among them. Kairo offers an explanation for each mitzvah, but he also differs with Rabbi Simlai in his count of the positive and negative commandments. Kairo lists 265 positive mitzvot and 348 negative mitzvot. Following Kairo, many other scholars offer their own explanations and lists of what has become known as the *Taryag Mitzvot* (made up of the letters *tav*, representing the numerical value of 400, *resh*, representing the value of 200, *yod*, representing the Ten Commandments, and *gimel*, representing the value of 3).

While most commentators agree with Rabbi Simlai and Kairo that *Taryag Mitzvot*, 613 commandments, were given by God to Moses, there is no agreement about which of the commandments were to be included on the list. Great scholars like Sa'adia Gaon, poets like Solomon ibn Gabirol and Elijah the Elder, as well as philosophers like Hafetz ben Yatzliah—all differ with one another. Each offers a different point of view, underscoring the fact that Jewish tradition was never static and unchanging but always made room for the evolution of new insights and interpretations of how Jews should practice their faith.

### Rambam (*Maimonides*)

It was the great teacher Moses Maimonides, however, who formulated the most authoritative list of the *Taryag Mitzvot*. Writing in Egypt, in 1168 C.E., at the age of thirty-five, Maimonides created his *Sefer ha-Mitzvot*. Using as his basis both Rabbi Simlai's division of the 613 commandments and the two categories of *mitzvot bein adam le-Makom* and *mitzvot bein adam le-chavero*, Maimonides offers an explanation for each mitzvah and arguments for living one's life according to the discipline of each one. He argues that the commandments are "meant to suppress the human being's natural tendency . . . to correct our moral qualities and to keep straight all our doings." (*Mishneh Torah*, bk. 9, chap. 4)

But Maimonides also realizes that there are many commandments that do not seem to improve human behavior. Such commandments as not eating pork or crab meat or those having to do with sacrifices during Temple times do not seem to have any meaning at all. How shall we explain them? How can we even justify continuing their observance? In response, Maimonides writes: "It is fitting for a person to meditate upon the laws of the holy Torah and to comprehend their full meaning to the extent of his ability. However, a law for which a person finds no reason and understands no cause should not be considered trivial. . . . One should be on guard not to rebel against a commandment decreed for us by God only because the reason for it is not understood. . . ." (Ibid., chap. 8)

Like Maimonides, many other commentators have tried to understand the reasons for the mitzvot of Jewish tradition. While some agree with Maimonides that it is difficult and often impossible to find meanings for all the commandments, most believe that the mitzvot have special purpose and significance.

**Reasons for doing mitzvot**

*Ibn Ezra*

*The essential reason for the commandments is to make the human heart upright.* (Abraham ibn Ezra, Commentary on Deuteronomy 5:18)

*Each commandment adds holiness to the people of Israel.* (Issi ben Akabia, Mechilta, *Exodus 22:30*)

*The purpose of the mitzvot is . . . to promote compassion, loving-kindness, and peace in the world.*
(*Maimonides*, Yad, Shabbat, *1180, 2, 3*)

The talmudic teacher Rab holds that the commandments were given by God to the Jewish people in order to discipline them. Through their observance they will be refined and strengthened in character and behavior. Another ancient interpreter claimed that it made no difference to God how animals were slaughtered. All the mitzvot having to do with ritual slaughter, and others as well, were meant "to purify the people of Israel." In other words, the commandments were considered exercises, a means of training people to be more sensitive to one another and to the world in which they live.

Another teacher suggests that the commandments are meant to make us more righteous. Each of us has the potential of adding kindness and justice to the world, or of adding to the pain and suffering of others. We should see ourselves as half-good and half-evil. By observing mitzvot we become more just and loving and add to the good in our lives and in the world. (*Genesis Rabbah* 44:1; *Tanchuma, Shemini*, 5; *Pesachim* 50b)

For Rabbi Abahu the commandments were not necessarily just a way of improving human behavior but also a means of preserving the survival of the world! He argues that God created the world as a gardener creates a beautiful orchard. The commandments given to Israel are like instructions given to those chosen to tend the garden. If they are followed, the orchard would survive, flower, and feed all who require its food. (*Exodus Rabbah* 30:9)

Other interpreters believe that the purpose of the mitzvot is only partially connected to improving human behavior or to promoting the survival of the world. The commandments, they maintain, are meant to guarantee entrance into the *olam ha-ba*, "the world to come," or "heaven." "All the mitzvot that the people of Israel do in this world will come and testify in their favor in heaven," says one teacher. Another poetically declares that "each commandment a person does in this world forms a thread of light in heaven, and all of the threads are spun together to form a garment for that person to wear when he dies and goes to heaven." For these commentators, the mitzvot are the means through which one insures a place and "a garment" in the world to come. (*Avodah Zarah* 2a; *Zohar* III:113a)

*Sarna*

In his study of Exodus, contemporary interpreter Nahum Sarna makes an observation about the unique nature of the ethical and ritual laws found within the Torah and, especially, within *Parashat Mishpatim*. While the laws of other ancient people are divided between secular and religious matters, the Torah presents an "indiscriminate commingling and interweaving . . . of cultic topics and moral imperatives" for which there is "absolutely no analogy." Within the Torah there is no attempt to separate ethical and ritual concerns. They are combined. Ritual commandments and celebrations often lead to ethical action. "The Torah," Sarna writes, "treats life holistically"; everything a person does, secular or religious, is seen as a potential mitzvah meant to serve God and uplift life with meaning. (*Exploring Exodus*, p. 174)

Sarna's view is shared by Rabbi Abraham Joshua Heschel. For Heschel, Judaism is "a science of deeds" or mitzvot that are meant to add the "taste or flavor" of holiness to human life. Being a Jew, Heschel explains, is not just a matter of performing rituals and moral deeds. It is realizing that in the doing of the mitzvah one is seeking to do what God wants of us. It is lighting a lamp before God. It is changing or transforming ourselves by that light so that we "absorb the holiness of deeds." The purpose of the mitzvot, Heschel says, "is to refine man. They were given for the benefit of man: to protect and to ennoble him, to discipline and to inspire him." (*God in Search of Man,* chap. 34)

While for Heschel the doing of mitzvot is meant to elevate us to new levels of holiness, to deepen our sensitivities and our awareness of what God requires of us, for Rabbi Herman E. Schaalman, we are to do the mitzvot "because we are the descendants of those ancestors, the children of those parents who said at Sinai: *Na'aseh ve-nishma,* 'We shall do and we shall hear.' " The commandments, in other words, are our historical inheritance. They are the way in which God continues to speak to us.

Rabbi David Polish agrees. "Mitzvot," he says, "are 'signs' of the covenant, affirmed and reaffirmed through the ages at various turning points in which Jewish existence stood in the balance. . . . Thus the mitzvot around birth, *milah* (circumcision), naming, education, marriage, and death take on added meaning because in each case the individual is made conscious of his own role in Jewish history." For these thinkers, the doing of each commandment is a way of identifying as a Jew. It is a means of linking oneself to the historical covenant of the people of Israel with God. (Simeon J. Maslin, editor, *Gates of Mitzvah,* Central Conference of American Rabbis, New York, 1979, pp. 100–107)

The 613 commandments form the essential core of Jewish practice and tradition. Their blend of both the ethical and ritual is unique. Perhaps that explains why Jews in every age sought to understand the purpose and meaning of the mitzvot and felt compelled to shape their lives and the quality of their community by practicing them.

In ancient times Rabbi Ishmael taught that the commandments were given to the people of Israel so they might *"live"* by them." In other words, the

mitzvot are for enhancing life, for celebrating it with special meanings, for filling it with deeds of justice, kindness, and peace. Today the challenge of living a mitzvah-filled life continues as the central goal of Jewish tradition.

## PEREK BET: *Caring for the Stranger*

Twice in the midst of *Parashat Mishpatim* we find a commandment dealing with care for the *ger,* or "stranger." (Exodus 22:20; 23:9) This emphasis upon the treatment of aliens or foreigners—those who are new to a community or society—is not unusual within the Torah. Early Jewish tradition emphasizes the pain of the outsider and seeks solutions to it. Commandments calling for sensitivity and justice for the *ger* are found in thirty-six different places within the Torah, more than the mention of any other mitzvah.

Even the language of the commandments dealing with the *ger* is special. At times we are given a positive formulation such as "you shall love the stranger . . ."; in other places, a negative formulation such as "you shall not oppress the stranger. . . ." Treatment of the stranger is one of those rare rules that is listed not only among the 248 *mitzvat aseh* but also among the 365 *mitzvat lo ta'aseh.* Frequently, the mitzvah also includes the reminder that "you were strangers in the land of Egypt."

Many commentators note this unique emphasis of the Torah upon justice for the stranger and ask: "Why all these warnings? Why all this attention to the *ger?*"

Early rabbinic interpreters offer a variety of opinions. Many understand that the word *ger* does not mean only "stranger." They point out that it also translates as "convert." For instance, we are told that "God so loves *gerim,* or 'converts,' that God postponed Abraham's circumcision until he was ninety so future converts would know one can become a Jew at any age." Another sage suggests that Jews are commanded to love converts because the Torah uses similar descriptions for both Jews and *gerim.* Both are called "servants," "ministers at the altar," "friends of God." Even the notion of a covenant with God is mentioned in connection with both.

The treatment of converts is a sensitive matter. Entering a new group, whether religious or secular, is always frightening. One is not sure of what to expect and, therefore, is uncertain and uncomfortable. The welcome given by a family or group to a newcomer can make the difference between feeling accepted or rejected. Perhaps that is why Jewish tradition emphasizes reaching out with friendship to the *ger* to make certain that he or she is "at home" within the Jewish community.

For many early rabbinic interpreters, all this concern for the feelings of the *ger* meant that Jews had a special obligation to treat converts fairly, never to take advantage of them, insult them about their past, or find fault with them. "Converts," the rabbis declare, "are beloved by God." (*Mechilta, Nezikin,* 18, on Exodus 22:20)

Later commentators not only note that Jews must welcome and appreciate converts but also treat any *ger* justly. They point out that the Torah cautions us not to oppress the *ger* because "you know the feelings of the stranger, having yourselves been strangers in the land of Egypt." This warning, say these teachers, raises significant questions: Do memories of the past, especially a painful past, teach us to be more sensitive to the feelings of others? Can those who recall being abused or oppressed prevent themselves from abusing or oppressing others?

*Rashi*

In answer to these questions, there is a serious division of opinion among interpreters. For example, Rashi's view is that for many people memories of cruel treatment do not teach sensitivity and that what the Torah really meant by its warning was that, if you oppressed the *ger*, he or she might answer by reminding you of your own lowly origins. You might be told, "Don't try to elevate yourself by demeaning me. After all, you also come from strangers. Your people were *gerim* in Egypt!"

On the other hand, Rashi does allow for those who might be more enlightened and made aware of the suffering of the stranger through their study of Jewish history and their understanding of how their people were persecuted in Egypt. Commenting on the Torah's observation, "you know the feelings of the stranger," Rashi suggests that because you have been in pain "you know how painful it is for him when you oppress him." (Comment on Exodus 22:20; 23:9)

Sixteenth-century commentator Moshe ben Alshekh, who spent most of his life in Safed, amplifies Rashi's view with his own. He maintains that the Torah's linkage of the warning about "knowing the feelings of the stranger" with the reminder that "you were strangers in Egypt" is deliberate. The Torah, Alshekh claims, teaches us not to oppress the stranger by noting our own treatment by God. "When you lived in Egypt," Alshekh explains, "you worshiped idols. Afterwards you accepted the Torah. Just as God did not look down on you for having worshiped idols and [thus] decide not to give you the Torah, so you must not look down upon the stranger." Clearly, it is Alshekh's conviction that Jews who recall their origins before being given the Torah will be more sensitive to the feelings of strangers and will treat them with more understanding and fairness. (Comment on Exodus 22:20)

*Ramban (Nachmanides)*

Nachmanides presents a differing point of view. For him the linkage between the commandment not to oppress the stranger and the observation "for you know the feelings of the stranger, having yourselves been strangers in the land of Egypt" is not simply a reminder about "common origins."

It is a warning about how God works in history on behalf of the oppressed.

Nachmanides argues that God speaks through the words of Torah, saying to the people: "You should not think that the stranger has no one to save him from the violence or oppression of your hands. On the contrary, you should know that, when you were strangers in Egypt, I saw the oppression with which the Egyptians were persecuting you and I brought punishment upon them. For I see the sufferings that are inflicted by evildoers on people and the tears of the oppressed who have none to comfort them. And I free every person from hands of violence. Therefore, do not afflict the stranger, thinking there is no one to save him. For he will be helped more than any other person!" (Comment on Exodus 22:20 and 23:9)

Nachmanides' view is that the Torah's reminder to the Jewish people that "you were strangers in the land of Egypt" is not just for the purpose of recollecting their painful status as persecuted people. It is also a lesson about whose side God takes in situations of oppression. God, Nachmanides teaches, stands by the persecuted. God comforts and heals the wounds of the abused, and God refuses to rest until, like the enslaved Israelites, they are free. The recollection of what God did for the Israelites in Egypt is meant to encourage Jews, who are God's partners, to help the oppressed.

*Leibowitz*

Differing with Nachmanides, modern commentator Nehama Leibowitz looks carefully at the Torah text and questions whether the memory of persecution really prevents one from becoming a persecutor. For the enlightened, she argues, such a recollection of history may be sufficient. It may lead to sensitivity and to a genuine concern for the strangers. For others, however, this is not the case. "The hate, persecution, and shame the individual or community experiences in the past do not act as a deterrent, preventing them from adopting the same attitude to those entrusted to their power, later on."

> **On abuse and oppression**
> Enlarging upon her observation, Leibowitz writes, "The fact that 'you were strangers in the land of Egypt' is certainly no adequate motivation for not oppressing or troubling the stranger. On the contrary, how often do we find that the slave or exile who gains power and freedom, or anyone who harbors the memory of suffering to himself or his family, finds compensation for his former sufferings by giving free rein to his tyrannical instincts when he has the opportunity to seize power over others?" (Studies in Shemot, p. 384)

Contemporary studies of abuse in marriage, or by parents or teachers, demonstrate the correctness of Leibowitz's observation. Tragically, patterns of battering and harassment often repeat from generation to generation. Those who are victimized and oppressed often turn their frustration and anger upon others and become brutal oppressors themselves.

What is true about physical abuse is also the case with "substance" abuse. Alcoholics, smokers, and drug addicts have often inherited their "habit" from parents or other adults in their environment. Having suffered from the results of neglect and even violence by substance abusers or having seen the illness and destructive results of narcotics, drinking, and smoking does not necessarily lead to a rejection of them. More often than not the cycle of violence to oneself and others continues. Victims take up the "habit," and the tragedy becomes a bitter cycle.

The answer to these cycles of abuse, whether of "substances" or of strangers, requires two different kinds of education, according to Leibowitz. The first is to appeal to the intellect and to teach people sensitivity by allowing them to learn the harmful effects of violence through a study of history. However, many people, Leibowitz maintains, are incapable of learning such a lesson. They require a second form of education. Memories of their own suffering do not act as a deterrent to their oppression of others. The only way to break the cycle of violence, argues Leibowitz, is by shocking such people with the realization that they will pay a high price for taking advantage of the stranger or for abusing substances. Only then will they change their patterns of behavior.

As we have seen, many interpreters understand that the Torah identifies the *ger,* or "stranger," as a *convert* to Judaism. Yet not all commentators adopt this rather narrow reading of the Torah text. For many Jewish teachers through the ages, the word *ger* meant any stranger, anyone new to the community, whether Jew or non-Jew.

---

### Protecting the *ger*

Ger *was the term applied to the resident non-Israelite who could no longer count on the protection of his erstwhile tribe or society. . . . The ger was to be given every consideration, and care must be taken that not only his rights but his feelings as well were safeguarded. He must never be shamed. . . . (Plaut, editor,* The Torah: A Modern Commentary, *p. 582)*

*It is forbidden to wrong or oppress the stranger . . . the reason given is purely ethical: you yourselves suffered as sojourners in a strange land, and you know the soul of the sojourner; therefore, take heed not to embitter the life of the sojourner living in your midst just as you did not wish the Egyptians to embitter your lives when you dwelt among them. (Umberto Cassuto, comment on* Exodus 22:20 and 23:9)

---

*Hirsch*

Protecting the stranger, as Leibowitz notes, is a matter of high ethical priority within Jewish tradition. More is at stake, however, than the feelings or rights of the alien. Rabbi Samson Raphael Hirsch makes this clear in his comment that "the treatment given to strangers is always the surest standard by which to measure the respect for human rights and the humanitarianism that prevails in any state." For that reason, Hirsch argues, the Torah places great emphasis upon assuring justice and charity for the alien and protection from oppression and harassment. "The granting of un-restricted rights of living, working, and earning a livelihood to aliens is demanded from the community or nation."

For Hirsch, however, the treatment of the stranger is also a special test of living ethically as a Jew. Because of their history of persecution, Jews should be more sensitive to the suffering of foreigners or strangers. "Though others may discriminate against the Jew," Hirsch says, "you must not fail to recognize every stranger as a human being! . . . show that you are a Jew—hold the stranger sacred." (Comment on Exodus 23:9; also in *Horeb: A Philosophy of Jewish Laws and Observances,* translated by I. Grunfeld, Soncino Press, New York, Fourth edition, 1981, pp. 254–256)

Rabbi Leo Baeck agrees with Hirsch. For him, as well, treatment of the stranger is a test of the creative power of Jewish teachings in the lives of Jews. Baeck points out that within the Torah the word *ger* takes on a special meaning because all human beings are called "strangers," "pilgrims," or "aliens." We are told that God says, ". . . the land is Mine; for you are strangers and settlers with Me." (Leviticus 25:23) That statement, Baeck argues, reminds us that no people is superior to any other, no person is more sacred than any other. We are all strangers and must care for one another. (*The Essence of Judaism,* Schocken Books, New York, 1948, pp. 197–198)

As we have noted, Jewish tradition emphasizes just treatment for the *ger,* or "stranger." For some commentators that meant special concern and sensitivity for converts to Judaism. Many others understood that the term *"ger"* meant any stranger. Jews were commanded by God to protect the rights and feelings of the alien, not only because such treatment was just, but also because they themselves had been persecuted strangers in Egypt and throughout their history. The Torah's attitude toward the *ger* is perhaps best summed up in the commandment "You shall love the stranger as yourself." (Leviticus 19:34)

## QUESTIONS FOR STUDY AND DISCUSSION

1. How do the commentators see the relationship between ethical and ritual mitzvot? How

would you describe the purpose of mitzvot in Jewish life?

2. In the *Centenary Perspective* of Reform Judaism, adopted in 1976 by the Central Conference of American Rabbis, it is stated that "the past century has taught us that the claims made upon us may begin with our ethical obligations but they extend to many other aspects of Jewish living, including: creating a Jewish home centered on family devotion; lifelong study; private prayer and public worship; daily religious observance; keeping the Sabbath and the holy days; celebrating the major events of life; involvement with the synagogue and community; and other activities that promote the survival of the Jewish people and enhance its existence." Is it true that the doing of mitzvot guarantees the survival of Jews and Judaism?

3. What have "strangers" and "converts" in common, justifying that, in Hebrew, both are called *gerim*?

4. Do you agree or disagree that the repetition of the reminder that Jews were strangers in Egypt has tended to teach greater sensitivity for the plight of the stranger and the alienated? How do you create conditions of just treatment for strangers?

# PARASHAT TERUMAH
## *Exodus 25:1–27:19*

*Parashat Terumah* is about building the first sanctuary, or the Tabernacle. The Israelites are still wandering through the Sinai desert. Moses instructs each person to bring a *terumah,* or "donation," "gift," for the building of the sanctuary. The contributions may be of gold, silver, and copper; of blue, purple, and crimson yarns, fine linen, goats' hair; tanned ram skins, dolphin skins, and acacia wood; oil for lighting, spices for the anointing oil and for the aromatic incense; lapis lazuli and other precious stones for the *ephod* and breastplate. Concerning the Tabernacle, God says to Moses, "And let them make Me a sanctuary that I may dwell among them." Instructions for the architecture of the sanctuary are detailed. The ark and poles for carrying it shall be made of acacia wood overlaid with gold. Two gold cherubim with large wings are to be placed above the ark, facing each other. A table of acacia wood overlaid with gold is to be made, along with special bowls and jars for offering sacrifices. Moses is also instructed to build a *menorah,* or "lampstand," of pure hammered gold to hold seven lamps. As for the sanctuary itself, Moses is given details of its size, the material to be used in its construction, and instructions on how to assemble it.

## OUR TARGUM

### · 1 ·

While still on Mount Sinai after receiving the Ten Commandments, Moses is also given instructions for building the sanctuary in which the people will worship God during their wanderings through the desert. God tells him to ask each Israelite to bring a *terumah,* or "gift," "contribution," for the construction. God says to Moses, "And let them make Me a *mikdash* ["sanctuary"] that I may dwell among them."

### · 2 ·

Details for the creation of each aspect of the sanctuary are given to Moses.

The ark and two poles for carrying it are to be of acacia wood overlaid with gold. A cover of gold is also to be made for it, along with two winged gold cherubim who are to be placed facing each other above the ark. "There I will meet with you, and I will speak to you . . . and I will command you concerning the Israelite people," God tells Moses.

### · 3 ·

Moses also receives instructions about making a table and poles to carry it. They are to be made of acacia wood overlaid with gold. Special bowls, ladles, jars, and jugs are to be fashioned to hold the liquids for offerings to God.

Along with the table and its poles, other furnishings for inside the sanctuary include a seven-branched lampstand, or *menorah*. There are to be three branches on each side of its center. Each branch will contain three cups shaped like almond-blossoms with calyx and petals. The center lamp-stand is to contain four cups shaped like almond-blossoms. Moses is told, "Note well, and follow the patterns. . . ."

### · 4 ·

Moses is also given an architectural plan and instructions for the materials to be used in creating the Tabernacle. Included are the sizes for the acacia wood planks for the walls, the number of cloths of goats' hair for coverings, and the number of sockets for attaching the planks and cloths. A curtain of blue, purple, and crimson yarns and fine twisted linen with the design of cherubim worked into it is to cover the ark.

### · 5 ·

The plan of the altar, which will be made of acacia wood, calls for a horn overlaid with copper on each of its four corners. Pails, scrapers, basins, flesh hooks, and fire pans—all for use when sacrifices are offered—are also to be made of copper. Poles of acacia wood overlaid with copper are to be used in carrying the altar when it is moved.

A description of the Tabernacle's inside furnishings includes hangings of fine twisted linen, silver-banded posts, copper pegs, and sockets.

## THEMES

*Parashat Terumah* contains two important themes:

1. The function of the *mikdash*, or "sanctuary," in Jewish tradition.
2. The Torah's emphasis upon the "details" of the sanctuary.

## PEREK ALEF: *The Sanctuary in Jewish Tradition*

Before the creation of the first *mikdash*, or "sanctuary," the Hebrews worshiped God on hilltops, beside streams, or wherever they felt moved to pray. Abraham and Isaac traveled to Mount Moriah; Jacob encountered God in a lonely place on the desert and near the river Jabbok; Moses met God through an ordinary bush and at the top of Mount Sinai. Now, after their liberation from Egypt and the acceptance of the laws given to them at Mount Sinai, the people are commanded to build a sanctuary.

The sanctuary is to contain the Ark of the Covenant with its sacred stones on which the Ten Commandments are inscribed. It is to be placed in the Holy of Holies chamber inside the inner tabernacle. The opening of the Holy of Holies chamber is to be covered by a curtain. Outside the curtain is a special altar for incense, a table for the shew bread, and a golden *menorah*, or "lampstand." In front of the inner tabernacle is another curtain, outside of which are the laver and an altar for burnt offerings. Clearly, the sanctuary is designed for offering sacrifices and prayers to God.

Some scholars believe that the description of the *mikdash* did not belong to the original Torah but was added to the story of the Exodus by later priests who wanted to justify the existence of the

*Tabernacle*

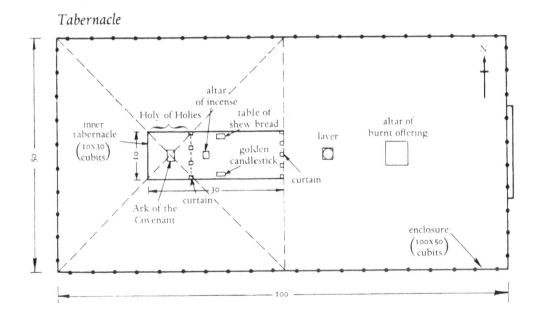

Temple and priesthood in Jerusalem. To prove their point, these critics argue that many of the materials mentioned in the Torah's description of the *mikdash* were not available to the ancient Israelites in the Sinai desert.

Other scholars disagree, maintaining that the *mikdash* was one of the earliest of all Jewish institutions, though later authors of the Torah may have exaggerated about how it was built or about the materials used in its construction. H. M. Orlinsky explains: "Acacia wood—cedar, cyprus, or olive was later used in Canaan—ramskins, lambskins, cloths of goats' hair, and the like are all manifestations of nomadic existence." (Plaut, *The Torah: A Modern Commentary,* p. 599)

While we may never be able to prove when the *mikdash,* or the first Jewish sanctuary, came into existence, the Torah does seek to clarify its purpose. Moses is instructed by God to tell the people, "And let them make Me a sanctuary that I may dwell among them."

What do these words really mean? Is it possible God was telling the people that, without a sanctuary, a building, a place for the Ark of the Covenant, or altars for sacrifice, they would not sense the presence of God in their lives? Are sanctuaries necessary for worship, for finding God? Does God require a building in order to "dwell" among human beings?

---

*Where does God dwell?*
*O God, where shall I find You?*
*All hidden and exalted is Your place;*
*And where shall I not find You?*
*Full of Your glory is the infinite space. (Yehudah Halevi)*

*There is no place without God. (Sa'adia ben Joseph Ha-Gaon)*

*Wherever you find a human footprint, there God is before you.* (Mechilta *to Exodus 17:6)*

*The Kobriner Rabbi turned to his Chasidim and said: "Do you know where God is?" Then he took a piece of bread, showed it to them, and continued: "God is in this piece of bread. With-*

*out God's nurturing power in all nature, this piece of bread would have no existence."*

*"Where is the dwelling of God?" This was the question with which Rabbi Mendel of Kotzk surprised a number of learned people who happened to be visiting him. They laughed at him: "What a thing to ask! Is not the whole world full of God's glory!" Then he answered his own question: "God dwells wherever we let God in."* (Martin Buber, Tales of the Hasidim: The Later Masters, *Schocken Books, New York, 1961, p. 277)*

---

Jewish tradition teaches that we experience God in many ways. God is to be found in the beauty and mystery of nature, in the love and friendship we share with others, in the spiritual impact of a ritual or celebration, and in the work done to promote justice, generosity, and peace. There is no exclusive "place" for God. There are many places where God dwells. King Solomon, who built the first Temple in Jerusalem, admitted that God, who could not be contained by all the heavens, could certainly not be limited to "this house that I have built!" (I Kings 8:27)

If that is so, if no *mikdash,* or "sanctuary," can be the exclusive place of God, then what can the Torah mean when it reports that God said to Moses, "Make Me a sanctuary that I may dwell among them"? What is the purpose or the function of the sanctuary in Jewish tradition?

The early rabbis offer an answer through an imaginary conversation between God and the people of Israel. They picture the people explaining to God that all human rulers have beautiful palaces, rooms where offerings are brought to them and where the people can demonstrate their loyalty and love. The people say to God, "Shouldn't You, our Ruler, have such a palace?" And, according to the rabbis, God responds, "My children, I have no need for such a place. After all, I do not eat or drink. Obviously, however, you have a need for such a place. It will help you experience Me. For that reason, build a sanctuary and I will dwell in your midst."

What the early rabbis sensed was our human need for a place of worship, a special space set aside for meditation and prayer. It is the nature of human beings to uplift the importance of ordinary buildings by assigning them unique functions and names. Out of bricks and mortar, steel and poured concrete, we create and decorate structures we call "capitals," "museums," "concert halls," theaters," and "courts." Sometimes we add to their importance by linking to them the names of popular personalities or donors.

Like capitals, museums, or concert halls, religious sanctuaries serve a significant function. They are the unique spaces we set aside for our "meetings" with God through prayer, study, and sharing with others. Does that mean that they are the only places where "God dwells"? Of course not. Just as we enjoy music and art in a variety of places outside of concert halls and museums, we can pray and encounter God in many different places as well.

We create religious sanctuaries, however, out of our need for beautiful and inspiring environments where we can find moments for reflection, comfort, and hope in difficult times, direction and wisdom when we face moral choices, and beautiful rituals with which to celebrate the most important moments of our lives. Our sanctuaries provide us with spaces where we can share with others and sense the support and enthusiasm of a community. As the early rabbis taught, our sanctuaries answer our human and spiritual needs.

Commentator Umberto Cassuto sees another purpose in the creation of the sanctuary. He points out that the people of Israel experienced God in a powerful way at Mount Sinai. They heard the Ten Commandments and felt themselves connected to God in a unique covenant. "But once they set out on their journey [away from Mount Sinai]," says Cassuto, "it seemed to them as though the link had been broken, unless there was in their midst a tangible symbol of God's presence among them."

In other words, the *mishkan* was a tangible, visible assurance of the bond that God had forged with the people of Israel at Mount Sinai. While they would journey to distant places from that wonderful mountain where God addressed them, their sanctuaries with their arks and eternal lights would be a constant reminder that "God dwelled

among them." Every synagogue sanctuary is an extension of Mount Sinai. (*A Commentary on the Book of Exodus*, p. 319)

---

### Why a "sanctuary"?

*Peli*

*The* mikdash *was not a dwelling place for God but a place set aside for people to come and experience more intensely the in-dwelling presence of God in the world at large. It represented a way of re-creating the universe in the center of which is God. (Pinchas H. Peli, "Torah Today,"* in the Jerusalem Post, *February 20, 1988)*

*Our sages believed that the building of holy palaces, the exercise of piety, prepares the heart for godliness. People who build sanctuaries are more likely to feel the spirit of holiness, the mood of sanctity. (Jacob J. Weinstein,* The Place of Understanding, *Bloch Publishing Company, New York, 1959, p. 58)*

*If you would know the mystic source from where
Your persecuted people facing slaughter drew
In evil days the strength and fortitude
To meet grim death with joy, and bare the neck
To every sharpened blade and lifted ax . . .
If you would know the bosom where streamed
Your people's tears, its heart and soul and gall . . .
If you would know the fortress where
Your ancestors carried to a safe haven
Their Torah scrolls,
The sacred treasure of their yearning souls . . .
If you would know the shelter which preserved
Immaculate, your people's spirit . . .
Then go to the house of prayer. . . . (Chaim Nachman Bialik)*

*Hirsch*

Rabbi Samson Raphael Hirsch offers another view of the Torah's command "And let them make Me a sanctuary that I may dwell among them." For Hirsch, the *mikdash* symbolizes the unique relationship between the Jewish people and God. The people create the sanctuary when they seek to shape their lives with the commandments of Torah. And the direct result of fulfilling all the commandments is that God's "protecting and blessing-giving presence" is experienced in their "private and national lives." The sanctuary is much more than a building. It is a symbol reminding Jews of their covenant relationship to God. If they observe the mitzvot of their contract with God, then their "reward" will be the joy of knowing that God dwells among them. (Commentary to Exodus 25:8)

Rabbi Morris Adler differs from Samson Raphael Hirsch in his discussion of the sanctuary. Rather than seeing it as a symbol, Adler emphasizes its important functions. He identifies four "tasks" for the ancient *mikdash* and for the modern synagogue.

The first is "to conserve, to guard against oblivion the great insights and concepts that have been developed" by human beings through the ages. Adler points out that new generations often destroy their past, and it is the role of religion to preserve "the accumulation of insights" of human wisdom. Our religious sanctuaries proclaim, "Do not destroy the ancient landmarks."

The second task of the sanctuary "is to scrutinize, to criticize, to evaluate." Religious sanctuaries, Adler argues, must constantly present "an ethical code that does not surrender to expediency, that does not give way to hysteria, that sees the problems of our time from the perspective of a great background of experience and faith."

The third function of the sanctuary is "to enlarge the lives of people." Religion seeks to tell people, "Do not starve yourself by limiting yourself only to the struggle for a livelihood. Do not become the prisoner of your own ego."

Finally, Adler says that "the Jewish sanctuary seeks to remind the Jewish community that what keeps Jews together is not a common sorrow . . . is not charity, not defense, but common history, common culture, and common hope." (*The Voice Still Speaks*, Bloch Publishing Company, New York, 1969, pp. 175–178)

Throughout the ages, the *mikdash*, or "temple," "synagogue," has functioned as a *bet tefilah*, "a house of prayer," a *bet midrash*, "a house of study," and a *bet knesset*, a "house of meeting." It has been the sacred space where Jews have worshiped and celebrated together, educated themselves and new generations, and met to face new challenges. It is the meeting place between God and the Jewish people. Today, the synagogue, like the ancient *mikdash*, remains the most significant institution of Jewish life; it is the guarantor of Jewish tradition and survival.

## PEREK BET: *"Exactly as I Show You . . . So Shall You Make It"*

Following the commandment to construct the *mikdash*, the Torah presents several chapters containing hundreds of detailed descriptions of every object and material to be used in the building of the ancient sanctuary. The text reads like a combination architect's blue print and decorator's design.

For example, we read that the sanctuary planks should be made of acacia wood, each plank ten cubits in length and a cubit and a half in width. We are informed that there should be twenty planks on both the north and south sides and six on the front and rear sides. Each plank is to have two silver sockets and two tenons overlaid with gold.

The same attention to details is given to the creation of the curtain, the ark, the altar, and all other aspects of the sanctuary. With each description we are given specific measurements, colors, instructions about the various materials to be used, and how the ancient tent is to be fastened together.

Why? Why all this attention to details? Why does the Torah present God as concerned about every single item used in the creation of the sanctuary?

*Sarna*

Bible scholar Nahum Sarna explains that the Torah's detailed description of the sanctuary "belongs to a common Near Eastern genre of temple building reports." In other words, such descriptions were common among ancient peoples, who believed that God ordered every feature and design of their sacred shrines. So what we have here is not surprising or even special. It is similar to other temple plans passed on within the religions and cultures of the Middle East.

*Abravanel*

Many other commentators disagree. Through the ages, various rabbinic scholars saw in the details of the sanctuary many different meanings. Don Isaac Abravanel, for example, maintains that the entire sanctuary and each of its parts have "allegorical meaning." When the Torah speaks about the *mikdash*, it is not only describing a sacred building in which worship takes place but it also has in mind the body of each human being. That is to say, each human being is a sacred sanctuary. Each detail, Abravanel explains, teaches an ethical lesson meant to guide people in their relationships with one another and with God.

As an example of his allegorical explanation, Abravanel points out that the *menorah* is made of "pure gold," teaching the truth that one must be careful of impure ideas. He also suggests that the *menorah* is to be placed so that it faces the Holy of Holies. The placement reminds us that true wisdom is always in harmony with the teachings of Torah.

Agreeing with Abravanel's allegorical approach, other commentators provide a number of fascinating insights about the meanings of the various sanctuary details.

Moshe ben Adrianopolis Alshekh compares the *menorah* to the "human soul," which also provides light. Just as the *menorah* is made of "beaten gold,"

so human beings "can only become a lamp of pure gold through the cleansing and refining effect of suffering." When one learns humility—not to answer back with anger and insults but rather with kind, pure, caring words—then one becomes like the *menorah,* full of light for others.

Describing the ark, the Torah informs us that it was to be overlaid with gold on the outside and inside. Why, some teachers ask, should gold, which would not be seen, be used inside? Is that not a waste of precious metal?

In answer, early Jewish teachers suggest the principle *tocho kevaro,* "the outside must match the inside." As Rabbi Hillel Silverman comments: "This is the true meaning of integrity. A person's exterior—words and deeds—must reflect his inner being and character. We must mean what we say, and say what we mean." (*From Week to Week,* p. 74)

Basing his own comments on those of both Rashi and Nachmanides, Joseph of Piavinitz seeks to explain why the description for the cherubim, the two angel-like creatures placed above the ark, includes the command "They shall face each other. . . ." Again, his interpretation is allegorical. The cherubim are symbols for how God wants human beings to care about one another. They are to make an effort to see one another, to understand what brings pain or joy into one another's lives. It is forbidden to turn away, to avoid others, to practice indifference. Like the cherubim, human beings are meant to serve God by keeping their eyes upon the needs of others.

Samson Raphael Hirsch offers another view. He observes that the description of the ark includes details about the poles used to carry it from one place to another. The Torah says, "The poles shall not be removed." "Why not?" asks Hirsch. After all, nothing is said about removing the carrying poles for the table and lampstand of the sanctuary. Why are the poles of the ark singled out for such prohibition?

"The poles of the ark symbolize . . . the mission of the ark and what it housed," says Hirsch. The message is that "the Torah is not parochial, not restricted to the particular country where the Temple is situated." It is always ready to move with the people, to be their guide, their source of wisdom and faith. Since no one knows when it will be necessary to move, or where the Torah's teachings will be required, the poles of the ark must always be in place so that it can be carried to where it is needed. (Commentary on Exodus 27:7)

Clearly, Jewish commentators found many significant lessons in the Torah's detailed descriptions of the *mikdash*. For many of them, the Torah offered more than quaint architectural plans or decorative descriptions. Each detail had hidden meaning, and like creative detectives they sought to uncover and reveal them. Sometimes they focused attention on the entire sanctuary, at other times on a small feature.

More often, however, they combined approaches, pointing out that the sanctuary symbolizes all our human achievements. In its details are all the small, seemingly unimportant, efforts we make on the road to our successes. No real achievement is possible without attention to detail. The musician must practice note after note, day after day, to play with excellence. The athlete must stretch, run, and lift weights to compete successfully. Students must gather facts one by one, detail after detail, to master a subject. Genuine accomplishments, like magnificent sanctuaries, are the products of hard work, deed after deed, and careful attention to every detail.

So why does the Torah spend so many chapters describing the building of the *mikdash*? Modern biblical scholars see nothing special about the details of these chapters in Exodus. They say they are very much like other descriptions of temples found in ancient Middle Eastern literature. Rabbinic commentators, however, look upon the Torah's portrait of the *mikdash* as a sacred work of art. Multiple meanings and messages are present in each detail. The challenge to the student of Torah, like to the student of great art, is to appreciate the beauty and mystery of the object.

## QUESTIONS FOR STUDY AND DISCUSSION

1. Some historians believe that the synagogue was the most important institution in the survival of the Jewish people. What other institutions helped to preserve Jewish life? What important place does today's synagogue play in guaranteeing the survival of Jewish tradition and culture?

2. Given our discussion of the sanctuary, what can we mean when we say that "God dwells in this place"?

3. As we have seen, many commentators interpret the description of the sanctuary and its details in a symbolic way. Review "Our Targum." What "symbolic" interpretations and lessons come to mind?

# PARASHAT TETZAVEH
## *Exodus 27:20–30:10*

*Parashat Tetzaveh* continues the description of the *mikdash*, begun in the previous Torah portion. It includes commandments to create a *ner tamid*, "a constantly burning light," above the sanctuary ark and to appoint Aaron and his sons as priests to manage the sacrifices offered in the sanctuary. Also included are detailed instructions about clothing for Aaron. He is to wear an *ephod*, a breastpiece, a robe, a fringed tunic, a headdress, and a sash. Aaron's ceremony of ordination as priest is described, along with instructions for the slaughtering of the offerings. The portion concludes with directions for building an altar for burning incense before the ark.

## OUR TARGUM

### · 1 ·

The Israelites are commanded by God to bring clear oil of beaten olives to the sanctuary and to use it for the *ner tamid*, or "continually burning light." Aaron and his sons are to keep the light over the ark burning continually from evening to morning.

### · 2 ·

Aaron and his sons, Nadab and Abihu, Eleazar and Ithamar, are appointed priests with the responsibility for managing all the sacrifices and offerings of the community at the *mikdash*. Aaron is to wear eight specially decorated garments crafted by skilled artists: (1) the *ephod*, an apron of gold, of blue, purple, and scarlet yarns, and fine linen, with a belt around the middle and two shoulder straps, each containing a lazuli stone inscribed with six names of the twelve sons of Jacob; (2) the breastplate of judgment, a square-shaped container decorated on the front with four rows of precious stones, each framed and mounted in gold, and each bearing a name of the twelve sons of Jacob. The breastplate is attached by gold chains to the shoulder straps of the *ephod*; (3) the Urim and Thummim, a small box through which it was believed God spoke; it was worn by the priest inside the breastplate of judgment; (4) the blue robe embroidered with a hem of pomegranates of blue, purple, and crimson yarns with bells of

gold; (5) the gold plate engraved with the words "Holy to the Lord" and attached to Aaron's headdress so that it hung on his forehead; (6) a fringed linen tunic; (7) a linen headdress; and (8) an embroidered sash.

Aaron's sons are to wear tunics, pants, sashes, and turbans for dignity and beauty.

### · 3 ·

The ceremony of consecrating Aaron as priest includes leading him to the *mikdash*, bathing him and dressing him in his special garments, and pouring anointing oil over his head. His sons are also brought forward and dressed in their priestly garments.

A bull is brought forward for slaughtering. Aaron and his sons lay their hands upon its head. After it is slaughtered, some of its blood is painted on the horns of the altar; the rest is poured at the base. The fat of its entrails, the lobe above the

liver, and the two kidneys are burnt on the altar; the rest of its flesh is put into a fire outside the borders of the camp. Following the sacrifice of the bull, rams are slaughtered; Aaron and his sons are sprinkled with anointing oil and the blood of a ram. At one point in the ceremony, Aaron and his sons hold pieces of the sacrificed ram in one hand, and flat loaves of bread, cakes of oil bread, and wafers in the other hand. They wave them before God as an offering. The ram's flesh is then boiled and eaten by Aaron and his sons.

The ceremony of ordination lasts seven days. On each day the sacrifices are repeated in order to purify the priests and the altar. At the end of Aaron's life, his priestly garments and duties are to pass on to his sons.

The priests and sacrifices in the *mikdash* remind the people that God is in their midst and that God brought them out of the land of Egypt to abide among them as their God.

·4·

An acacia altar, overlaid with gold, decorated with horns, and carried by acacia wood poles also overlaid with gold, is to be placed in front of the curtain before the ark. Aaron is commanded to burn incense on this altar every morning and evening at the time he extinguishes and kindles the lights. Once a year, he is to consecrate the altar by painting the horns with the blood of a sin offering.

## THEMES

*Parashat Tetzaveh* contains two important themes:

1. The meaning of the *ner tamid*, or "continually burning light."
2. The significance of the priestly dress of Aaron and his sons.

## PEREK ALEF: *What Is the Ner Tamid?*

For centuries, the light hanging just above the ark where the Torahs are kept on the eastern wall of a synagogue has been called the *ner tamid*, or "eternal light." It is part of the architecture and religious symbolism of every Jewish sanctuary. Sometimes it is an electric light; at other times it may be a flame fueled with oil. Often it is artfully crafted out of precious metal or glass.

Many commentators believe that the origin of the *ner tamid* is found in the opening lines of our Torah portion, Exodus 27:20–21. There is disagreement, however, over how the original Hebrew of those lines is to be translated and understood. Compare the following versions.

● *From* The Torah, *Jewish Publication Society of America:*
*You shall further instruct the Israelites to bring you clear oil of beaten olives for lighting, for kindling* lamps regularly.

● *From* The Jerusalem Bible, *Doubleday and Company:*
*You are to order the sons of Israel to bring you pure olive oil for the light and to keep a* flame *burning there perpetually.*

● *From* The Living Torah, *Aryeh Kaplan, translator:*
*You [Moses] must command the Israelites to bring you clear illuminating oil, made from hand-crushed olives, to keep the* lamp *constantly burning.*

It is clear from these three different translations that there is disagreement as to whether one light or many lights are to be kept burning. In one version, the words *ner tamid* are translated "lamps regularly." In the other two versions, the translation refers to one "flame," or one "lamp." So which is the correct translation of *ner tamid?* Is it one light or many lights? Did it always burn or was there a specially designated time when it was kindled?

If one reads the original Hebrew sentence in context with the sentence that follows it, the meaning of the *ner tamid* becomes clear. We are told: "You shall command the Israelites to bring you clear oil of beaten olives for lighting, for kindling the *ner tamid* [continually burning lamp]. Aaron and his sons shall set *them* up in the Tent of Meeting, outside the curtain which is over the Pact [ark], [to burn] from evening to morning before the Lord."

In context, it becomes clear that the *ner tamid* of the *mikdash* was a lamp with several flames. How else can we explain the word *"them"* appearing in the sentence after the command? The lamp with its multiple flames stood in front of the ark curtain and was lit every evening at sundown and kept burning through the night until dawn. In the only other reference within the Torah to the *ner tamid*, we are informed that this lamp with many flames had its own seven-branched lampstand (*menorah*). (Leviticus 24:2–4)

Later, during the time of the Jerusalem Temple, the *ner tamid* was also called *ner ma'aravi*, or "western light," because it lit up the Holy of Holies (containing the Ark of the Covenant), which was on the western end of the Temple. It became the custom to light six wicks of the *menorah* from sunset to sunrise and to keep one of its wicks burning *tamid*, "continually," twenty-four hours a day. When the Temple was destroyed by the Romans, they carried the *menorah* off as booty to Rome. Perhaps as a reminder of the Temple's *ner tamid*, a light was kept burning in each synagogue. At times it was placed near the western wall facing the ark, which was on the eastern wall; sometimes it was placed in a container on the eastern wall near the ark. Eventually it became the custom to hang it just above the ark.

For the early rabbinic commentators, the *ner tamid* and its fuel, "the clear oil of beaten olives," were powerful symbols representing the Jewish people. For example, they point out that the prophet Jeremiah (11:16) says that God calls the Jewish people a "verdant olive tree, fair, with choice fruit." What, the rabbis ask, does Israel have in common with an olive tree, or with the clear oil of beaten olives?

The answer is not a happy comparison. The life of the olive, the rabbis explain, is a hard one. It dries and shrivels while still on the tree. Then it is cut down, crushed, ground, and pressed until it yields oil.

So it is, the rabbis claim, with the history of the people of Israel. They have been beaten, chained, imprisoned, and surrounded by those threatening to crush them. Enemies constantly endanger them. Yet they have survived because they were loyal to God, asked God's forgiveness for their errors, and repented their wrongdoings. In this interpretation, the *ner tamid* with its beaten olive oil symbolizes the cruel oppression Jews have endured and their constant faith in God. Like the *ner tamid* that burns forever, the Jewish people will survive forever despite their persecutors.

---

### Does suffering make Jews better?
*The people of Israel is likened to an olive, which yields up its oil only when it is crushed, for the people of Israel reveals its true virtues only when it is made to suffer. (Ya'akov Shmuel Khaquiz, 1672–1761)*

---

### Israel's suffering—a barometer
*And just because it was always a minority, Judaism has become a standard of measurement of the level of morality. How the Jewish community was treated by the nations among which it lived has always been a measure of the extent to which right and justice prevailed; for the measure of justice is always its application to the few. (Leo Baeck,* The Essence of Judaism, *pp. 273–274)*

### Pride in Jewish suffering?
*The story of the Jews since the Dispersion is one of the epics of European history. Driven from their natural home . . . scattered by flight . . . persecuted and decimated . . . shut up within congested ghettos . . . mobbed by the people and robbed by the kings . . . outcast and excommunicated, insulted and injured . . . this wonderful people has maintained itself in body and soul, has preserved its racial and cultural integrity, has guarded with jealous love its oldest rituals and traditions . . . has emerged . . . renown in every field for the contributions of its geniuses, and triumphantly restored, after two thousand years of wandering, to its ancient and unforgotten home. What drama could rival the grandeur of these sufferings, the variety of these scenes, and the glory and justice of this fulfillment? (Will Durant,* The Story of Philosophy, *Simon and Schuster, New York, revised edition, 1961)*

---

In another interpretation, some early rabbis suggest that the people of Israel and the olive oil of the *ner tamid* react in similar ways when mixed with foreign matter. When other liquids are mixed together, they form one substance. Not so with olive oil. When mixed with another liquid, it remains separate; it always floats to the top, above all the other substances.

So it is, say these rabbis, with the people of Israel. Their survival depends on their remaining separate, on Jews marrying Jews and creating Jewish homes in which children experience the celebration of Shabbat and Jewish holidays. Jewish survival also requires that Jews know their language, Hebrew; appreciate their history; visit or live in the Land of Israel; and support the educational, religious, charitable, and social institutions of the Jewish community. Those maintaining this point of view argue that, when Jews demonstrate such loyalty, they are like pure olive oil, which separates above all other liquids. In other words, they rise above all other peoples of the world. Their talents grow into greatness, and they guarantee their own survival. (*Genesis Rabbah* 36:1)

---

### "Light to the nations"

*The Jews regarded themselves as the chosen people, not because of their racial qualities, but because of having been selected to be the servants of God to carry His moral law to the world. They looked upon themselves as a covenanted people, a kingdom, not of supermen but of priests. . . . Admission into this covenant was open to all people of all races at all times, also as a matter of choice. . . . The mission was not conquest or racial mastery or territorial* Lebensraum, *but to be a "light unto the nations." . . . Israel's sole prerogative lay in carrying on an arduous and self-sacrificing moral and religious leadership.* (Abba Hillel Silver, The World Crisis and Jewish Survival, *Richard R. Smith, Inc., New York, 1931*)

---

Other rabbis see the comparison of the olive oil and *ner tamid* to the people of Israel differently. God, they argue, needs Israel as a source of light in the world. It is like two people walking together at night along a rocky path. One is blind; the other can see. Without a light they will stumble and injure themselves. So the one who can see says to the one who is blind, "Hold this light that I may see the path."

So it is with God, explain some of the rabbis. God commands the people of Israel to keep the *ner tamid* burning. Its brightness and pure olive oil are to remind the people that they are responsible for God's light in the world. Just as they need God to show them the way, God needs them to bring the light of justice and the hope for peace into the world. That is the unique purpose of the

Jewish people. God has chosen Israel, as the prophet Isaiah said, to be "a light to all the nations." (*Genesis Rabbah* 36:2)

Still other early rabbis argue that the *ner tamid* is not a symbol for the people of Israel but for the Torah, which provides the light of wisdom and faith to all who study it. These teachers make the comparison to those who foolishly try to walk in a dark place without the help of light. Such people take the chance of falling against stones or injuring their heads against the ground. So it is with those who try to live without the knowledge of Torah.

On the other hand, those who study Torah accumulate wisdom and learn to discipline their desires by its ethical teachings. They are constantly enriched by the cultural and spiritual views accumulated through thousands of years of human experience. Such individuals provide light for themselves and for others. The *ner tamid* in the sanctuary reminds the Jew of that important lesson.

Not so, say other interpreters. The *ner tamid* is really a symbol meant to remind the Jew of all the mitzvot, all the ethical and ritual commandments one should observe in order to brighten the world. Basing their argument on Proverbs 6:23, which says that "the mitzvah is a lamp; the teaching is a light," they point out that every good deed "brightens" the world. Each mitzvah is an opportunity to serve God, to make the world a more just and kind place for all human beings. When, for example, a person gives to charity, supports a friend in time of trouble, visits the sick, cares for the homeless, or feeds the hungry, the world is brightened with God's light. The *ner tamid* symbolizes all the love, kindness, and generosity brought into the world by those who carry out the commandments and teachings of Torah. (*Genesis Rabbah* 36:3)

From the time the ancient Israelites installed the "continually burning lights" in their sanctuary to the creation of the *ner tamid*, or "eternal light," of the synagogue, interpreters have found in the flickering flames a variety of messages. Symbols often evoke different meanings. They reflect the sad and joyous moments of human life, and they function like signals calling people to take on new challenges. Throughout Jewish history, the *ner tamid* has represented a variety of meanings for the people of Israel. Today those meanings continue to challenge the faith and ethical commitment of Jews everywhere.

## PEREK BET: *Priestly Clothing: Fashionable Style or Significant Symbol?*

According to the Torah, Aaron and his sons were not only appointed as priests to carry out all of the special animal sacrifices and rituals inside the *mikdash*, but he as the High Priest and his sons as assistants were to dress in uniquely designed and decorated clothing—or costumes. Aaron is commanded to wear eight different garments: the *ephod*, breastplate of judgment, Urim and Thummim, blue robe, fringed tunic, embroidered sash, linen headdress, and gold plate worn over the headdress. Each garment is to be made by artists out of the finest materials.

Many commentators questioned all this attention to the dress of the priests. Why is the Torah so concerned with costume and style?

*Sarna*

One answer may have to do with the role of priests in early Jewish society. Nahum Sarna suggests that "the priests are set apart from the rest of the people by dedication to the service of God, by their consecration to a distinctive way of life that gives expression to this intimate involvement with the Divine through special duties and restrictions, and by the obligation to serve the people." (*Exploring Exodus*, p. 131)

Because they are set apart from the rest of the people by special duties, it seems logical that their priestly clothing should also call attention to their unique work and role in their society. Throughout human history, uniforms have been used to signify status, membership in a group, special skills, or privileges. Uniforms are symbols of identity. Whether they are the colorful jerseys of a football team, the blue shirts of the police, or the black robes of a judge, special attire signals not only what those who wear it do but also whom they represent. Costumes are often badges of identity.

The garments worn by Aaron, however, appear to have a function beyond identifying him as the High Priest. Modern commentator Umberto Cassuto suggests that Aaron's special costume was "a symbol of his consecration" to God. It was a reminder to him that he played a unique role as God's servant. Wearing the *ephod*, the Urim and Thummim, his blue robe, and the gold plate over his linen headdress made him conscious of his sacred responsibilities. (*A Commentary on the Book of Exodus*, p. 371)

*Hertz*

Rabbi J.H. Hertz agrees with Cassuto. He comments that "these garments distinguished the priest from the lay Israelite and reminded him that even more than the layman he must make the ideal of holiness the constant guide of his life." In other words, the heavy weight of all his priestly garments were a constant signal to Aaron that his duties, and how he carried them out, were a matter of great importance to God and to the people. (*The Pentateuch and Haftorahs*, p. 339)

Most interpreters agree that Aaron's priestly garb distinguishes him from others and reminds him of his sacred duties. However, some suggest that each of the garments may have had special symbolic meaning. These meanings, they maintain, are rich with significant lessons.

*Peli*

Writing about the *ephod* and breastplate of judgment, Pinchas Peli points out that the Torah not only describes the *ephod* with its two precious stones on which are written the names of the twelve tribes of Israel, but it also tells us that Aaron is to wear them over his heart when entering the sanctuary for prayer. (See Exodus 28:29.)

Peli argues that much more than style and decoration are intended in the Torah's description. "It seems that the design of the *ephod* and the breastplate is meant to teach us an important lesson about responsible leadership. There are many leaders who, after they are elected or chosen for high office, swiftly forget the people whom they are supposed to represent. The names of the twelve tribes of Israel were to be carried on the 'shoulders' of Aaron, so that he should never forget the burden of their needs." Furthermore, Peli explains that the symbols were to be "carried on *his* shoulders," so that he would remember "to be a loyal spokesman for them . . ." filling "his heart with love and compassion for each and every one of his people." (*Torah Today,* p. 88)

*Leibowitz*

Nehama Leibowitz sees the symbolism of the breastplate with its twelve gemstones, each engraved with the name of a tribe of Israel, not as a reminder to Aaron of his responsibilities, but as a sign of the people's holiness. Aaron, wearing his linen headdress and gold plate with "Holy to the Lord" inscribed upon it, represented the entire people when he stood before God in prayer. He and his garments, writes Leibowitz, "were not an end in themselves, but both he and the task undertaken by him in the sacred vestments constituted a means of stimulating the awareness and consciousness that Israel is holy to the Lord."

For Leibowitz, the priestly costume is meant to encourage the people to be holy—distinct in their moral standards and performance, as well as loyal to their ritual traditions. The challenge to Aaron was to fulfill all the responsibilities of the High Priest, and the challenge to the people was to be known as "priests of God." Aaron's colorful garments symbolized their mutual mission. (Comment on *Tetzaveh;* also Isaiah 60:6)

Several commentators notice that the Torah calls for Aaron to wear a blue robe underneath the *ephod.* It is to be embroidered with a decorative hem of alternating golden bells and pomegranates. As U. Cassuto points out, the pomegranate was a "common ornamental device" among ancient Middle Eastern peoples. The bells, however, are given a special significance within the Torah's description of them. We are told that "Aaron shall wear it while officiating, so that the sound of it is heard when he comes into the sanctuary before the Lord and when he goes out—that he may not die." (Exodus 28:35)

Were the bells really meant to save Aaron's life? What was the danger of entering the sanctuary that made it necessary for a "noise maker" to protect Aaron?

Cassuto suggests that the ancients saw the sanctuary as the royal palace of God. Just as one would never enter the king's place without a proper announcement, so one is not allowed to enter God's "palace-sanctuary" without ringing the bell. Cassuto puts it this way: "It is unseemly to enter the royal palace suddenly; propriety demands that the entry should be preceded by an announcement, and the priest should be careful not to go into the sanctuary irreverently." Among Hindus and Buddhists, bells are often used to announce the presence of worshipers in the sanctuary and the beginning of sections of prayer. The bells on the Torah crowns are also meant to signal honor for the Torah and the joy of its study. Chimes in a church often announce the beginning or conclusion of prayer. The use of sound in religious ritual is universal.

*Meklenburg*

Jacob Zvi Meklenburg believes that the bells on Aaron's robe represented more than an announcement of his coming and going into the sanctuary. He writes that, unlike the rest of the Israelites, the High Priest had many additional responsibilities relating to the rituals and sacrifices of the people. The bells, Meklenburg explains, functioned as symbols, warning Aaron with each step that he must discharge his sacred duties with care and diligence. They were auditory reminders. With each ring, the High Priest knew that he was an instrument of God, serving not himself but his people. (Comment on Exodus 28:35)

Was all of this attention to the beauty of the priestly garments or the expenditure of community resources for the creation of a magnificent sanctuary necessary? It is clear that the builders of the first *mikdash,* and of the Jerusalem Temples after it, used the finest materials and employed the most skilled artisans. Their standard was one of excellence. They demanded of themselves that their sanctuaries and services be beautiful.

Their motive, however, seems to have been more than the outward appearance of beauty. Perhaps they demanded that their *mikdash* symbolize the kind of world they believed they were commanded to create—one of beauty, harmony, and riches shared by all. They may have insisted also on what later Jewish tradition called *hiddur mitzvah,* a standard that calls upon every Jew to enhance each mitzvah with special enthusiasm, additional effort, and, where appropriate, the highest quality of product affordable. For example, one performs *hiddur mitzvah* when one gives charity, not only generously but in a way that protects the feelings of the recipient. The use of a beautiful silver cup rather than an ordinary goblet for Shabbat *Kiddush* is another example of *hiddur mitzvah.* For the ancients, beautifying the sanctuary was a means of uplifting it to a place of honor.

Additionally, all the attention given to the quality of the material from which the priestly garments were made, including every detail of their decoration, carries the message that valuable creations—whether a sanctuary, a worship service, a sacred garment, or a holy object—are all the result of careful, patient, disciplined hours of artistic skill and work. They do not arise magically; they do not result from indifference, laziness, or neglect. Achieving excellence and beauty requires discipline, time, devotion, and much effort.

## QUESTIONS FOR STUDY AND DISCUSSION

1. Which of the various interpretations of the *ner tamid* is most appealing to you? How would you apply the interpretation today?
2. Would you agree that suffering improves human beings or has made Jews more sensitive to the pain of others?
3. Do you believe that "mixing" with other peoples has weakened or strengthened Jewish survival? Why?
4. The priestly garments with their colors and sounds added beauty to the sanctuary. What can we do today to add "beauty" to the ethical and ritual mitzvot we perform?
5. Which interpretation of the dress and symbols worn by Aaron and his sons has the greatest appeal to you?

# PARASHAT KI TISA
## *Exodus 30:11–34:35*

God instructs Moses to collect a half-shekel from every person over the age of twenty when he takes a census of the community. He is told to make a copper container, fill it with water, and place it in the sanctuary that the priests might wash themselves before approaching the altar; he is also to create a special anointing oil for consecrating the furniture of the *mikdash*. Moses is told that the sanctuary furnishings, including the priestly garments, are to be made under the supervision of Bezalel, a skilled artisan. Moses is commanded to remind the people that in observing the Sabbath they celebrate the covenant between themselves and God. The Torah text now shifts back to the time of Moses standing on Mount Sinai. He is given the two tablets containing God's commandments. Forty days have passed, and below the people of Israel approach Aaron, requesting that he create a golden calf for them to worship. Aaron agrees. God tells Moses what has happened, threatening to destroy the Israelites, but Moses pleads for the people and saves them from God's anger. When Moses sees the idol they have built, however, he shatters the tablets God has given him. Entering the camp, Moses also destroys the golden idol and punishes those who have not shown loyalty to God. Fearful that God will abandon the people, Moses asks for proof that God will continue to lead them. God's Presence is shown to Moses as assurance that neither he nor the Israelites will be abandoned. Afterwards, God directs Moses to carve two new tablets and return to Mount Sinai. God commands the Israelites to observe Pesach, Shavuot, and the Sabbath. When, after the second forty days and nights, Moses returns to the people, his face is bright red, radiant from speaking with God; so he covers it with a veil.

## OUR TARGUM

### ·1·

God explains to Moses that, when a census is taken, each person over the age of twenty shall pay a half-shekel. The donation will assure the forgiveness of all sins for the person enrolled in the census.

### ·2·

God commands Moses to make a copper water container that the priests can wash themselves when they enter the sanctuary to perform their rituals. Moses is also told to create anointing oil out of choice spices and to consecrate the sanctuary furnishings and priestly garments with the oil.

### ·3·

Bezalel, son of Uri son of Hur, of the tribe of Judah, is appointed as the artisan in charge of making all the furniture and priestly garments to be used in the sanctuary. Oholiab, son of Ahisamach, of the tribe of Dan, is designated as his assistant.

### ·4·

God commands the people of Israel to observe the Sabbath, calling it "a sign for all time" of the covenant between the people and their God.

### ·5·

While Moses remains on Mount Sinai, the Israelites protest to Aaron, telling him to make them a golden calf, an idol, to worship, for they did not know what had happened to Moses. Aaron tells them to bring their gold to him. He creates a golden calf, and the people shout, "This is your god, O Israel, who brought you out of the land of Egypt!" The next day they offer sacrifices before the golden calf and sit down to eat, drink, and make merry.

God tells Moses what the people have done and threatens to destroy them. Instead of accepting God's judgment, Moses argues with God on behalf of his people. He tells God, "Let not Your anger . . . blaze forth against Your people . . ." so the Egyptians will not be able to say that "the God of Israel liberated this people,

only to . . . annihilate them from the face of the earth." Moses pleads with God to recall the promises made to Abraham, Isaac, and Jacob that the Israelites would one day be as numerous as the stars of heaven, secure in their own land. His argument convinces God not to punish the people.

Holding the tablets, Moses comes down the mountain. From a distance Moses, accompanied by Joshua, sees the Israelites dancing before the golden calf. In a rage, he shatters the tablets on the ground and burns the calf. He grinds the calf into powder, sprinkles it into water, and forces the people to drink it.

"What did this people do to you that you have brought such great sin upon them?" Moses asks Aaron.

Aaron immediately blames the people, explaining that they requested an idol and that they are "bent on evil." Aaron explains to Moses that he told them to give him their gold, which he threw "into the fire and out came this calf!"

Judging that the people are out of control, Moses calls upon all who are loyal to God to join him. All the Levites come forward and, following his direction, they kill those who have demonstrated disloyalty to God. In addition, a plague is sent among the people as punishment for the sin of creating the golden calf.

God promises to give the Land of Israel to the people—after driving out the Canaanites, Amorites, Hittites, Perizzites, Hivites, and Jebusites—but not to dwell in their midst because they are "stiff-necked." The people react with fear, take off their fine clothing and jewels, and begin to mourn. God instructs them to leave off their fine clothing and jewels, pledging to decide their destiny.

·6·

Moses appeals to God, "Unless You go in the lead, do not make us leave this place." God responds by assuring Moses that he has gained God's favor and that the people will be led by God's Presence. "Let me see Your Presence," Moses challenges. God answers, "You cannot see My face, for no person may see Me and live." Moses is told to hide in the cleft of a rock to await God's Presence.

Afterwards, as instructed by God, Moses carves two new stone tablets and carries them to the top of Mount Sinai. There God's Presence passes before him, declaring: "The Lord! the Lord! a God compassionate and gracious, slow to anger, rich in kindness and faithfulness, extending kindness to the thousandth generation, forgiving iniquity, transgression, and sin."

Moses asks God to forgive the people, and God makes a covenant with them. God will drive out the inhabitants of the land against which the Israelites are advancing. The Israelites are commanded by God to tear down all altars of idol worship, not to marry from among the inhabitants of the land, and to observe Pesach, Shavuot, and Shabbat. In addition, God orders them to bring choice first fruits to the sanctuary for an offering and to refrain from ever boiling a kid in its mother's milk.

Moses writes down all these commandements. After forty days and nights of fasting, Moses returns to the people. The skin of his face is bright red, radiant from speaking with God. When he finishes teaching the people all that God had said, he covers his face with a veil. From that time on, whenever he concludes speaking to the people, he replaces the veil over his face.

## THEMES

*Parashat Ki Tisa* contains two important themes:

1. The sin of the golden calf.
2. Protesting on behalf of others.

## PEREK ALEF: *Why Did They Build the Golden Calf?*

Consider the following facts: Moses returns to Egypt in order to free the Israelites fron bondage.

He and his brother, Aaron, risk their lives in persuading Pharaoh to liberate the Israelites. The people achieve freedom and are saved from pursuing Egyptian troops. They arrive safely at Sinai, hear the words of God spoken to them through

Moses, and are commanded to build a sanctuary for the worship of God. Finally, Moses climbs to the top of Mount Sinai where he stays for forty days and nights in order to bring back the sacred tablets of the Ten Commandments.

Everything seems to point to success for the people of Israel. They have known the bitterness of slavery, the pain of oppression, but now they are tasting the pleasures of victory and liberation. Each day they are fed with manna and, through Moses, are receiving instruction and commandments from God.

With all of these benefits, why do they suddenly lose faith in Moses? Why do they gather before Aaron demanding that he build them a golden calf? Why are they willing to donate their gold for such an idol? Why, after hearing the first of the Ten Commandments, "I am the Lord your God who brought you out of the land of Egypt," and the second, "You shall not make for yourself a sculptured image. . . ," does Aaron deliberately mold a golden calf, saying nothing when the people proclaim, "This is your god, O Israel, who brought you out of the land of Egypt"? What prompts the people to abandon the teachings of both Moses and God?

The answer given by many interpreters is "fear." Forty days and nights have passed since Moses left them and climbed to Mount Sinai. Perhaps he is dead; perhaps he has abandoned them. Their anxiety mounts. What are they to do? Where are they to turn? Who will lead them now? Terrified, filled with uncertainty, they say to Aaron, "Come, make us a god who shall go before us, for that man Moses, who brought us from the land of Egypt—we do not know what has happened to him."

*Peli*

**The masses must have a leader**
*Moses is but a few hours late, and they, without much hesitation, with little reservation, un-*

*ashamedly rewrite history; this calf is your god that brought you out of the land of Egypt. . . . Moses, the teacher and lawgiver, is all but forgotten. . . . How swift and how shocking! And how typical of mass psychology! They, the masses, must have a leader. What a gap between Moses and a handmade calf! But to them this gap does not matter. "Make us a god who shall go before us!" They are ready to follow blindly any leader, be he a Moses or a golden calf.* (Pinchas Peli, Torah Today, *pp. 91–92*)

**What the people might have said**
*Philosopher Martin Buber suggests that the people were in a state of panic and said to one another: Moses "has vanished completely. He said that he is going aloft to the God up there, when we need the God down here just where we are; but he has not come back, and it must be supposed that that God of his has made away with him, since something or other between them was clearly not as it should have been. What are we to do now? We have to take matters into our own hands. An image has to be made, and then the power of God will enter the image and there will be proper guidance."* (Moses: The Revelation and the Covenant, *Harper and Row Publishers, Inc., New York, 1958, p. 151*)

Philosopher Yehudah Halevi agrees with this assessment of their situation and claims that only 3,000 of the 600,000 people liberated actually requested that Aaron build the golden calf. These people were not really idolaters, Halevi explains. In the absence of Moses, they were simply desperate to have "a tangible object of worship like the other nations without repudiating God who had brought them out of Egypt." Having waited so long for Moses to return, they were overcome with frustration, confusion, and dissension. As a result, they divided into angry parties, differing with one another over what they should do. No longer able to control their fears, a vocal minority pressured Aaron into taking their gold and casting it into a golden calf.

Furthermore, argues Halevi, the creation of the golden calf was not such a serious sin. After all, he explains, making images or using them for worship was accepted religious practice during ancient times. God had commanded the people to create the cherubim and place them above the ark. If the people made a mistake, Halevi says, it was not in refusing to worship God, but in their impatience. Instead of waiting for the return of Moses or for a message from God, they took matters into their own hands and acted as if they had been commanded to replace their leader with a golden idol. It was for their impatience, not for creating an idol, that they were punished. (*The Kuzari* 1:97)

Yehudah Halevi's carefully reasoned excuse for the behavior of the Israelites is very different in tone from the criticism of them offered by the author of Psalm 106. Speaking of their liberation, the Psalmist writes, "God delivered them from the foe, redeemed them from the enemy. . . . But they soon forgot God's deeds. . . . There was envy of Moses in the camp, and of Aaron. . . . They made a calf at Horeb and bowed down to a molten image. They exchanged their glory for the image of a bull that feeds on grass. They forgot God who saved them, who performed great deeds in Egypt. . . ." In other words, the creation and worship of the golden calf by the Israelites was a brazen act of disloyalty to the God who had freed them from Egyptian bondage.

Many of the early rabbinic interpreters of Torah agree with the author of Psalm 106. Building the golden calf was an act of idolatry, and the people's worship of it was nothing less than a signal that they accepted idolatry and were defying the second of the Ten Commandments: "You shall have no other gods beside Me. You shall not make for yourself a sculptured image. . . . You shall not bow down to them or serve them. . . ." (Exodus 20:3–5; *Avodah Zarah* 53b)

As to why the Israelites chose idolatry, some of the early rabbis suggest that they found the worship of a God without form, shape, and color very difficult. They wanted a god like the Egyptians— one that was carried from place to place; one of glistening gold; a bull symbolizing power that would march before them and, they believed, protect them. So they came to Aaron and said, "Come, make us a god. . . ." Because the Israelites sought to imitate the Egyptians and practice idolatry, say the rabbis, they were punished for their sin. (*Pirke de-Rabbi Eliezer* 45)

Some interpreters put forward the observation that it was the men, not the women, who were guilty of creating the idol and worshiping it. They point out that Aaron cleverly looked for a way to divert the men from their desire for an idol. Because Aaron knew that the women would refuse to donate their gold rings to such a project, he deliberately told the men: "Take off the gold rings that are on the ears of your wives. . . ." As Aaron had hoped, the women were unwilling to donate their rings. "We will not give our rings to create an idol!" they told the men. So the men removed the rings from their own ears and built the golden calf. (*Pirke de-Rabbi Eliezer* 45)

Other interpreters blame Aaron, not the Israelites, for the sin of creating the golden calf. They maintain that, when the people began to speak critically of Moses and his failure to return after forty days, Aaron failed to provide an explanation to calm their fears.

These same interpreters also embellish the Torah's report. They say that, when Hur, one of Moses' loyal assistants, accused those who were speaking against Moses of being "brainless fools," Aaron said nothing. As a result, the mob murdered Hur. Then they approached Aaron, warning that they would do the same to him. Fearing for his life, Aaron gave into their demands, took their gold, and created the calf. Instead of taking the risk, speaking out, and providing strong guidance in the absence of his brother, Aaron capitulated to the demands of the mob. His lack of courage and leadership, these interpreters believe, brought about his people's shocking sin of idolatry. (*Exodus Rabbah* 41:7)

---

**Aaron refuses to take responsibility**
*When Moses asks Aaron why he allowed the people to create an idol, he protests "that he never intended to fashion a golden calf. It was all a tragic accident. He simply threw the gold into the fire to be melted down, and 'there came out this calf.' He could not foresee the consequences of his acquiescence to the demands of a rebellious people."* (Silverman, From Week to Week, p. 79)

*Steinsaltz*

Modern commentator Adin Steinsaltz agrees with this assessment of Aaron. He labels the episode of the golden calf "the worst failure of his career." Yet, just as Yehudah Halevi sought to excuse the behavior of the Israelites, Steinsaltz offers an apology for Aaron. "When he agreed to cooperate in the casting of the golden calf, he was undoubtedly proceeding along his own mode of leadership—given to compromise and acquiescence—with the accompanying perils of 'distorting the truth for the sake of peace.'" Aaron is willing to indulge in idolatry in order to pacify the people. (*Biblical Images,* Basic Books, New York, 1984, pp. 75–79)

As Steinsaltz portrays him, Aaron leads by testing the wind, by sensing where the pressure is likely to be, and then rushing to carry out the expectations of others. His guiding principle is peace at any price, compromise to avoid confrontation. For that reason, he offers no argument when the people tell him to create an idol. He desperately wants to be loved and to be popular. If the price others demand is a golden calf, that's what he will give them.

*Leibowitz*

Nehama Leibowitz sees in the story of the golden calf not just Aaron's failure, or the sin of the Israelites, but a deliberate warning that human beings are capable of acting nobly at one moment and ugly at the next. Leibowitz observes that "we should not be astonished at the fact that the generation that had heard the voice of the living God and had received the commandment 'You shall not make other gods besides Me' descended to the making of the golden calf forty days later. One single religious experience, however profound, was not capable of changing the people from idol worshipers into monotheists. Only a prolonged disciplining in the laws of Torah directing every moment of their existence could accomplish that." (*Studies in Shemot,* pp. 554–556)

From Nehama Leibowitz's point of view, the story of the golden calf is not just about what happened on the Sinai desert centuries ago. It is about human beings in every age. The Torah relates the tale of the Israelites' sin to teach that yesterday's charity may be followed tomorrow by selfishness and insensitivity. Each day is filled with new choices. The role of constant Torah study is to keep an individual asking, "What is the next mitzvah I must do?"

Why does the Torah include this incident about the golden calf? No one can be sure. It may have been placed in this section of Torah because those who experienced it could not forget it. The shock of the incident remained, and they related it from generation to generation as a story they could neither understand nor give up. Perhaps it is included in the Torah because, as some interpreters suggest, it captures the fear and confusion of the people and Aaron when Moses failed to return from Mount Sinai. Still other commentators may be correct in viewing this incident as an indication of Aaron's lack of leadership or as a significant insight into the way people fall from their good intentions when they are confronted with the glitter of gold.

What can be said is that the story of the golden calf has stimulated the genius of Jewish interpreters throughout the ages. They have found within it a wide variety of meanings and lessons. Today, however, the riddle remains. What is the meaning of this curious tale? Why was it included in the Torah text?

## PEREK BET: *Moses Protests on Behalf of His People*

Imagine Moses carefully making his way down Mount Sinai, holding the heavy carved tablets of the Ten Commandments. Among the words inscribed on them are "You shall have no other gods beside Me. You shall not make for yourself a sculptured image. . . ." For forty days and nights he has been alone at the top of the mountain. Now, as he is descending, God informs him that the Israelites have not only made a golden calf but are worshiping it as their god.

Before Moses has a chance to answer, God tells him that, because the Israelites are a stubborn people, God will destroy them and create another people for Moses to lead.

Moses, of course, could have accepted the offer. He had already experienced many unpleasant moments with the Israelites. They had complained about his leadership and about the lack of food and water on the desert. They had even accused him of liberating them from Egypt in order to let them die in the wilderness. Why not exchange the Israelites for another people?

Despite the arguments in favor of abandoning them, Moses surprisingly seeks to protect the Israelites from God's decision to destroy them. For centuries, Jewish interpreters of this Torah portion have been questioning the reason. Why does Moses choose to intervene and plead for the survival of those who are worshiping a golden calf?

Among the early rabbis, there were those who believed that Moses defended his people because he was convinced that God's judgment was unfair. It was God, they explained, who had brought the Israelites to Egypt where they had learned about idolatry. "How," they imagined Moses asking, "could God now blame them for worshiping a golden calf?"

Rabbi Huna compared the situation to a father who opened a business for his son on a street filled with evildoers. When his son began acting unethically, the father became angry and threatened to punish him. A friend intervened and told the father: "You are as guilty as your son. Did you not place him on a street of evildoers, in a place where he could pick up bad habits? Did you not expect that the environment would have an influence upon him?" (*Exodus Rabbah* 42:10)

*Abravanel*

### The blame for bad habits

*Don Isaac Abravanel believes that Moses said to God: "You know very well that You brought them forth out of the land of Egypt, a land filled with idolatry. . . . Why do You become angry when they fall back on their old practices? For habit has become second nature to them, and that was what led them to build and worship the golden calf."*

In other words, Rabbi Huna believes that Moses intervened on Israel's behalf because he was convinced that their worshiping the golden calf was actually God's fault. The people had not chosen to live among idolaters in Egypt. God had placed them in an evil environment where they had learned bad habits. They were incapable of overcoming the conditions in which they had been reared as children and had survived as adults. Moses understood their burden and, according to Rabbi Huna, intervened to save the Israelites to prevent God from doing a great injustice.

Modern author Elie Wiesel agrees with Rabbi Huna. He sees Moses as a brave defender of his people who argued: "Whose fault is it, God, theirs or Yours? You let them live in exile, among idol worshipers, so long that they have been poisoned; is it their fault that they are still addicted?"

Wiesel also observes: "In spite of his disappointments, in spite of his ordeals and the lack of gratitude he encountered, Moses never lost his faith in his people. Somehow he found both the strength and the courage to remain on Israel's side and proclaim its honor and its right to live." (*Messengers of God,* pp. 200–201)

Excusing the idolatry of the people of Israel because of their exposure to an evil environment, however, is not the only reason given for Moses' intervention on their behalf. The early rabbinic interpreters also point out that Moses was upset by the language God used when talking about the people of Israel. At other times, God had always referred to Israel as "*My* people." Now, in announcing their punishment to Moses for making the golden calf, God called them "*your* people," as if to imply that their evildoing was Moses' fault—when they were "good," they belonged to God, but, when they were "bad," they were Moses' responsibility.

Rabbi Berechiah, quoting Rabbi Levi, compared the situation to a king who had a vineyard that he rented out to a grower. When the wine produced by the grapes of the vineyard was excellent, the king would proudly proclaim, "What fine wine *my* vineyard produces!" When the wine was inferior, the king would blame the grower. "What terrible wine *you* produce!" Upon hearing the criticism, the grower confronted the king and told him, "The vineyard is yours whether it produces superior or inferior wine!"

Moses spoke out, explains Berechiah, because he felt that he was being blamed unfairly for the evil behavior of the people. Berechiah imagines Moses complaining to God: "Ruler of the universe, You can't have it both ways. It cannot be that, when they are good and follow all Your commandments, they are *Your* people, and, when they are unfaithful and do not carry out Your commandments, they are *my* people. They belong to both of us, and neither of us can abandon them." (*Pesikta de-Rav Kahana* 16)

As Rabbi Berechiah sees it, Moses is upset, not only with God's failure to take responsibility for Israel's building and worshiping an idol, but also for blaming him for their evildoing. Such blame is unjust. It is even a sign of disloyalty. How can you abandon that which you love? So Moses intervenes, protesting to God.

---

### Reasons for protest

*U. Cassuto imagines that Moses told God: "Don't let other people conclude that all Your work in liberating this people was done in vain!" And Moses also argued: "These Israelites are Your people. Don't allow the Egyptians to come along and say that You intended to destroy them from the very beginning of their liberation." Furthermore, Cassuto says that Moses reminded God that, if the Israelites were annihilated, God would be known as a liar. Had not God promised Abraham, Isaac, and Jacob, the patriarchs of the people, that their descendants would live forever? It was these arguments, Cassuto explains, that convinced God to forgive the people. (A Commentary on the Book of Exodus, pp. 415–416)*

---

Nehama Leibowitz points to another reason Moses chose to plead for the survival of the people

of Israel rather than allow God to destroy them. It was a matter of God's reputation!

Leibowitz reminds us that Moses challenged God with a warning. "Let not the Egyptians say, 'It was with evil intent that God delivered them, only to kill them off in the mountains and annihilate them from the face of the earth.' " (Exodus 32:12)

According to Leibowitz, Moses feared that God's punishment of Israel, no matter how just, would be misinterpreted by the Egyptians and other peoples. They would conclude that their idols were more loyal and generous than the unseen power of God and that it was dangerous to follow the God of Israel. "Far from educating and promoting the cause of justice," Leibowitz comments, God's destruction of Israel "would bring the divine reputation into disgrace . . . the cause of falsehood would be promoted and that of truth set back." For these reasons, Leibowitz explains, Moses decided to plead with God to forgive Israel rather than to punish the people for making and worshiping the golden calf. (*Studies in Shemot*, pp. 575–576)

Why does Moses intervene to save the people from God's intention to destroy them for creating the golden calf? Interpreters provide a variety of reasons that may have moved the great liberator and leader of the Israelites. He was motivated by sensitivity to their past and to the habits and customs they had learned through long years of living in a corrupt environment of slavery and idolatry. Perhaps he felt pity for them, sensing that the Israelites were frightened and uncertain of where he and God were leading them. It is also possible Moses concluded that destroying the Israelites was a bad strategy for God. It would ruin God's reputation. No one would have faith in a God who liberated in order to destroy and whose promises were lies!

Did Moses really think all these thoughts? No one really knows. Yet the biblical story of his protest to God on behalf of the Israelites captures our attention, just as it appealed to the imagination of commentators. For them, Moses became a model from whom to learn. Just as he intervened to save his people from what he believed was God's unjust punishment, so too were human beings to intervene and save the innocent whenever they were threatened.

Protecting others from harsh judgments by pleading their case, by urging an understanding of those pressures and conditions over which they may have little or no control, is judged within Judaism as a high moral obligation.

*Zugot*

Rabbi Hillel taught: "Judge not another until you are standing in his place." (*Avot* 2:5) Philosopher Hasdai Crescas observed that "true justice is tempered with mercy." (*Or Adonai*)

Moses' intervention on behalf of his people is an ethical model worthy of imitation. Undoubtedly, that is why the *Zohar* praises him above all the heroes of the Torah as the "faithful shepherd" of Israel. (Commentary on Exodus 32:32)

## QUESTIONS FOR STUDY AND DISCUSSION

1. How do fear and frustration cause a people to abandon democracy or freedom? Can you give other examples when, out of confusion or fear, people have given up their liberties and accepted the tyranny of dictatorships?

2. What role did Aaron play in the building of the golden calf? Could he have intervened and stopped the people from creating the idol, from breaking the law? Did he demonstrate weak or clever leadership? Was he a failure or success? Why?

3. Does society today worship idols? What are our "golden calfs"?

4. What do the commentators identify as the reasons for Moses' protest to God on behalf of the Israelites? How would you compare Aaron's agreement to build the golden calf with Moses' defense of the people when God announces that they are about to be destroyed? What arguments does he use to convince God not to punish the people for building the golden calf?

# PARASHAT VAYAKHEL-PEKUDE
## *Exodus 35:1–40:38*

*Vayakhel-Pekude* is one of seven designated Torah portions that, depending upon the number of Sabbaths in a year, is either read as two separate portions or combined to assure the reading of the entire Torah. While this volume will combine them, it will present an interpretation on each of their most important themes.

*Parashat Vayakhel* repeats the commandment to observe the Sabbath, emphasizing that no work is to be done on that day. It continues with Moses asking the Israelites to donate gifts of gold, silver, copper, precious stones, fine linen, wood, oil, or spices to be used for building the *mishkan,* or "sanctuary." Moses appoints Bezalel and Oholiab, skilled craftsmen, to oversee the construction of the sanctuary, and they report to Moses that the people are giving more gifts than are needed. So Moses tells the people to stop bringing their donations. Under the direction of Bezalel and Oholiab, skilled craftsmen work on the cloths, planks, bars, curtains, screens, lampstands, altars, and priestly garments of the sanctuary.

*Parashat Pekude* describes the records kept of all the work and materials used in the construction of the *mishkan,* as well as of all the donations given by the Israelites. When the *mishkan* is completed, Moses and the Israelites celebrate by anointing it. God's Presence fills the sanctuary and leads the people throughout their journeys.

## OUR TARGUM

### · 1 ·

**M**oses gathers the community together, reminding them that, on the Sabbath, they are to do no work or light any fires. It is to be a day of complete rest.

### · 2 ·

He also asks them to bring donations of gold, silver, copper, fine yarns, linen, goats' hair, skins, acacia wood, oil, spices, and precious stones for the construction of the *mishkan,* or "sanctuary." "Let the Israelites contribute whatever their hearts move them to give," Moses tells the people.

He invites all skilled artisans to donate their efforts in building and decorating the sanctuary. Both men and women come forward to help. Bezalel and Oholiab are appointed to receive all gifts from the Israelites and to organize the construction. Shortly afterwards, they inform Moses that the people are bringing more than is required. In response, Moses issues a proclamation: "Let no man or woman make further effort toward gifts for the sanctuary!"

· 3 ·

The Israelites construct the *mishkan*, working on curtains and decorations, planks, sockets, bars and rings, the screens, ark, table, utensils, lampstand (seven-branched *menorah*), and altars.

Records of each object are kept, noting how much gold, silver, copper, and half-shekels are offered. Details of the materials and how they are used in making the priestly clothing, including the breastplate of the High Priest, his robe, and *ephod*, are all described.

After the building of the sanctuary is complete, Moses is told to arrange for its dedication on the first day of the first month of the year, Nisan. The ark, table, and *menorah*, along with all the other furniture and special utensils for the sacrifices, are placed within the *mishkan*. Aaron and his sons are anointed as priests. Moses lights the *menorah* and offers special sacrifices to God.

A cloud hovers over the sanctuary, indicating that God now dwells inside. When the cloud lifts, the Israelites follow it as a sign that God is with them throughout their journeys in the wilderness.

So ends the second book of the Torah, Exodus.

**THEMES**

*Parashat Vayakhel-Pekude* contains three important themes:

1. The Sabbath as a day of *no work*.
2. The obligation of giving charity, *tzedakah*.
3. Accountability of public officials.

## PEREK ALEF: *The Sabbath Is for Celebration, for Rest, Not Work!*

The commandment to celebrate the Sabbath is mentioned several times in the Torah. We are told that, after laboring for six days to create the heavens and earth, God rests on the seventh day and calls it *Shabbat*, "day of rest." (Genesis 2:1–3) The Ten Commandments include the directive "Remember the Sabbath day and keep it holy," along with the statement "Six days you shall labor and do all your work, but the seventh day is the Sabbath of the Lord your God: you shall not do any work. . . ." (Exodus 20:8–9) Once again, the commandment is repeated at the beginning of the Torah portion *Vayakhel*. (See Exodus 35:1–3.)

Moses calls the people together in order to speak with them about building the sanctuary. He is about to ask them for donations of gold, silver, and copper and for their time and talents in the construction of their holy place. First, however, he reminds them that they are to work for six days and then observe a day "of complete rest." Nothing is to supersede celebrating the Sabbath, neither their work nor even the construction of the sanctuary. Working on the Sabbath carries a harsh penalty. Moses warns them that "whoever does any work on it shall be put to death." (Exodus 35:1–2)

Several centuries after Moses, the prophet Isaiah calls the Sabbath "a delight," and Rabbi Hiyya ben Abba, who taught in the third century, tells his followers that the Sabbath is a day "given only for pleasure." Most students of Jewish tradition agree with the evaluation of Rabbi Leo Baeck that "there is no Judaism without the Sabbath." (Isaiah 58:13; *Pesikta Rabbati* 23)

Yet, if the Sabbath is meant to be such a "delight" and "pleasure" and of such importance to the Jewish people, why does the Torah specifically forbid "work"? Furthermore, how does Jewish tradition define "work"? Might there not be certain activities that one person calls "work" and another calls "pleasure"?

The Torah repeats the commandment not to work on the Sabbath twelve times and, specifically, forbids making a fire, baking and cooking, gathering wood, moving from one boundary to another, plowing and harvesting, carrying objects, engaging in business, and buying and selling. (Exodus 35:3; 16:23,29; 34:29; Numbers 15:32–36)

Despite the mention of such activities forbidden on the Sabbath, the Torah contains no definition of "work." It is the early rabbis who created such a definition. They identify thirty-nine different categories of work from their study of our Torah portion and its description of the construction of the sanctuary. Since the people were forbidden to work on the Sabbath, it was assumed by the rabbis that every kind of labor associated with building the sanctuary, or supporting the builders, was prohibited.

Rabbi Judah Ha-Nasi, editor of the *Mishnah*, provides us with the thirty-nine categories. They include: sowing, plowing, reaping, sheaving, threshing, winnowing, cleansing crops, grinding, sifting, kneading, baking, shearing, blanching, carding, dyeing, spinning, weaving, making a minimum of two loops, weaving two threads, separating two threads, tying, untying, sewing a minimum of two stitches, ripping out stiches in order to replace them, hunting a gazelle, slaughtering it, flaying it, salting it, curing, scraping its hide, slicing its hide, writing a minimum of two characters, erasing in order to write them, building, wrecking, extinguishing, kindling, hammering, transporting. (*Shabbat* 7:2)

As one can see, Jewish tradition took seriously the prohibition of any labor on the Sabbath. Why? Why set aside the Sabbath as a day of *no work*? Several answers are suggested.

One suggestion is found within an imaginative dialogue, invented by the rabbis, between God and the Torah. The rabbis say that, after God created the heavens and earth and placed the people of Israel in their land, the Torah came to God with a complaint. "O God," said the Torah, "what will become of me when the Israelites are busy every day of the week with their occupations?" God answered, "I am giving them the Sabbath, and they will devote themselves on that day of rest to studying Torah." (*Exodus Rabbah*)

In other words, for the ancient rabbis, the Sabbath is meant as a time for reviewing and examining important lessons of Torah. Studying each week's Torah portion exposes a person to questions of history, ethical challenges, and to the varying perspectives of great thinkers on some of the most perplexing issues facing human beings. Sabbath Torah study provides food for thought, time-tested insights, and experiences meant to enrich our understanding of ourselves, others, and the world in which we live. One refrains from work on the Sabbath to benefit from the wisdom of Torah tradition.

Rabbi Mordecai M. Kaplan, however, suggests that the Sabbath is more than a time for Torah study. He calls it "a pause in our brush-work" of life and compares its importance to the critical rest moments of an artist. "An artist," he observes, "cannot be continually wielding his brush. He must stop at times in his painting to freshen his vision of the object, the meaning of which he wishes to express on his canvas."

For Kaplan, the Sabbath is a time for pausing, for taking a fresh look at what we are trying to do with our lives. It is a weekly opportunity to scrutinize our goals, hopes, successes, and failures. Getting away from "work" allows us a chance to assess its worth and the value of what we are doing with our energies and talents. After celebrating the Sabbath, we are ready, Kaplan says, "to take ourselves to our painting with clarified vision and renewed energy." (*The Meaning of God in Modern Jewish Religion*, Reconstructionist Press, New York, 1962)

### We are not machines

*The Sabbath . . . prevents us from reducing our life to the level of a machine. The gathered experience of humanity that the break in the routine of work one day in seven will heighten the value of the very work itself is not lightly to be put aside. The Sabbath is one of the glories of our humanity. (Claude G. Montefiore, 1858–1938)*

Not working on the Sabbath, however, is not only connected with gaining a fresh perspective on life. Jewish tradition also celebrates the Sabbath as a "day of liberation." Each Sabbath is welcomed with the singing of the *Kiddush*, the blessing over the wine, which makes reference to the Sabbath as a "remembrance of the Exodus from Egypt."

This connection of the Sabbath with the theme of freedom is also captured in the comments of modern psychologist and biblical commentator Erich Fromm. Fromm claims that "it is no exaggeration to say that the spiritual and moral survival of the Jews during two thousand years of persecution and humiliation would hardly have been possible without the one day in the week when even the poorest and most wretched Jew was transformed into a man of dignity and pride. . . ."

The power of the Sabbath, Fromm argues, "is the expression of the central idea of Judaism: the idea of freedom; the idea of complete harmony between humanity and nature. . . . By not working—that is to say, by not participating in the process of natural and social change—man is free from the chains of time, although only for one day a week." (*You Shall Be as Gods*, pp. 193–197)

For Fromm, the Sabbath celebrates the liberation of human beings from "the chains of time." It frees us from the obligations of meeting a schedule, of producing by a certain hour in the day, of dealing with all the stress and pressures that derive from imposed, and necessary, timetables, agendas, and calendars. The Sabbath liberates us from "slavery" to the clock.

Rabbi Abraham Joshua Heschel agrees with Fromm. "We have fallen victims," he comments, "to the work of our hands; it is as if the forces we had conquered have conquered us. . . . The Sabbath is the day on which we learn the act of surpassing civilization. . . . On the Sabbath we live, as it were independent of technical civilization."

Not working on the Sabbath allows a person

to enter what Heschel defines as a "realm of time where the goal is not to have but to be, not to own but to give, not to control but to share, not to subdue but to be in accord." Resting on the Sabbath, using it as a day for prayer and study and for sharing friendships and the love of family, is a way of ruling time rather than allowing time to rule us. By setting aside the Sabbath, argues Heschel, we seize control of the time of our lives. It becomes ours, and we become liberated. Celebrating the Sabbath is a declaration of our freedom. (*The Sabbath: Its Meaning for Modern Man*, Farrar, Straus and Giroux, New York, 1951, pp. 1–10)

*Peli*

Pinchas Peli extends Heschel's views by pointing out that the purpose of the Sabbath is to remind us of what is really important in human life. For six days we work. We compete. We struggle to shape the world to fit our needs, desires, and expectations. Celebrating the Sabbath as a day of no work reminds us that "the real purpose of life is not to conquer nature but to conquer the self; not to fashion a city out of a forest but to fashion a soul out of a human being; not to build bridges but to build human kindness; not to learn to fly like a bird or swim like a fish but to walk on the earth like a human being; not to erect skyscrapers but to establish mercy and justice; not to manufacture an ingenious technical civilization but . . . to bend our will to God's will."

Yet, not working on the Sabbath, Peli points out, is a discipline. Celebrating the Sabbath is not a matter of occasionally rescuing oneself from exhaustion or of taking "time off" when it is convenient. In order for the Sabbath to make a difference, it must be set aside and welcomed each week. Rest must also be "scheduled" or "created." (*Shabbat Shalom*, B'nai B'rith Books, Washington, D.C., 1988, pp. 59–67)

By uplifting the Sabbath as a special day of no work, Jews reserve time for achieving a fresh perspective on life, for studying the wisdom of Torah, and for celebrating their freedom. Observing the Sabbath each week heightens sensitivity to the essential questions and meanings of human existence.

## PEREK BET: *The Obligation of Giving Charity, Tzedakah*

This Torah portion contains a remarkable story about giving charity, or *tzedakah.*

Moses gathers the people of Israel together and invites them to contribute to the building of their sanctuary. "Let all of those whose hearts move them bring forward their gifts of gold, silver and copper, precious linens, yarns, and goats' hair, along with spices, valuable skins, and precious stones." Apparently Moses was a persuasive fundraiser because, not long after he had invited the people to give, Bezalel and Oholiab, whom he had appointed to oversee the building of the sanctuary, came to him and told him: "The people are bringing more than is needed."

So Moses stops the building campaign! He tells the people, "You are giving more charity than can be used!" It's an amazing and surprising report.

In the process of interpreting its meaning, many commentators draw a very subtle distinction between support for public institutions and *tzedakah* for the needy. While the first biblical sanctuary seems to have been constructed from the generosity of those whose "hearts moved them," we are also informed that the sanctuary and later the Jerusalem Temple were maintained by a system of tithes, or obligatory taxes of 10 percent of one's property. These tithes were not a matter of freewill giving. Like our contemporary taxes, they were collected by community or government representatives and were distributed by the king or those in authority.

During the medieval period such communal taxes were allocated, not only to support local synagogues, but to maintain all other Jewish communal institutions, including schools, libraries, courts, jails, health facilities, ritual baths or *mikvaot*, shelters for the poor and hungry, cemeteries, and the supervision of *kashrut*, or "standards of food preparation for the community."

Giving charity beyond the "taxes" collected by the community to support the needy and maintain institutions, including synagogues, was always considered a mitzvah, an obligation and responsibility of every Jew. The Torah instructs Jews to leave the corners of their fields for the strangers, the poor, the widows, and the orphans. Later the rabbis emphasize that providing for the poor brings one into the Presence of God and those who use their energies for helping others less fortunate than themselves shall be rewarded with "long life, prosperity, and honor." Indeed, giving aid to the poor was considered so important a commandment that Zutra, a leader of the Babylonian Jewish community at the beginning of the fifth century, teaches that "even a poor person must give to charity!" (*Baba Batra* 10a; Proverbs 21:21; *Gittin* 7b)

---

### How much should one give?

*How much should one give to the poor? Whatever it is that the person might need. How is this to be understood? If he is hungry, he should be fed. If he needs clothes, he should be provided with clothes. If he has no household furniture or utensils, furniture and utensils should be provided. . . . If he needs to be spoon fed, then we must spoon feed him.* (Shulchan Aruch, Yoreh Deah *250:1*)

---

With the rise of contemporary Jewish communities, where Jews pay taxes to their governments and support such Jewish communal agencies as synagogues, schools, special family and childrens' services, and various Jewish civil rights organizations, all charitable giving by Jews has become voluntary. As with the first sanctuary, Jews give as their "hearts move them." No longer are they "taxed" by a Jewish authority unless they are living in Israel and paying taxes to the government.

Given this new circumstance, what are the obligations of *tzedakah* in Jewish tradition? Is giving charity simply a matter of making a donation when you are "moved by the cause," or does Jewish tradition "demand" *tzedakah* from each Jew?

The consensus of Jewish teachings through the ages makes giving charity to the needy and maintaining all the institutions of Jewish life a mitzvah, a required duty. Rabbi Assi of the third century teaches: *"Tzedakah* is equal to all the mitzvot, all the commandments!"

Joseph Karo, author of the *Shulchan Aruch*, one of the most important collections of Jewish law in the Middle Ages, writes: "Each person must contribute to charity according to his or her means." Regarding those who might themselves be considered needy, Karo comments: "Even if one can give only very little, yet he or she should not abstain from giving, for the little is equally worthy to the large contribution of the rich." (*Baba Batra* 8–9; *Kitzur Shulchan Aruch* 34:2)

But how much is considered "a little," and what is a "large contribution"? How much is one obligated to give to charity? Does Jewish tradition suggest standards for giving?

The rabbis warn that, while a person should be generous in giving, one "should not give away all that he or she possesses." Others say that "one should not go beyond a fifth of one's property."

Joseph Karo draws a distinction between "the acceptable and meritorious" ways of fulfilling the mitzvah of charity. It is acceptable to give a tithe, or 10 percent of annual profits over and above household expenses. It is meritorious to give a fifth, or 20 percent of one's annual profits over and above household expenses. He also adds to this standard that at the time of death it is appropriate to give as much as a third of one's estate to charity. (*Arachin* 28a; *Ketubot* 50a; *Kitzur Shulchan Aruch* 34:4)

---

### Considering tzedakah

*To the person who has the means and refuses the needy, God says, "Bear in mind that fortune is a wheel."* (*Nachman,* Tanchuma, Mishpatim, *8*)

*Zugot*

*The more charity, the more peace.* (*Hillel,* Avot *2:7*)

*Boasting about the charity you give another cancels the goodness of your deed.* (*Samuel Ha-Nagid,* Ben Mishle *11c,8*)

What about deciding which cause is more important? Does Jewish tradition suggest any priorities for the obligation of *tzedakah*?

Feeding the hungry, sheltering the homeless, clothing the naked are all considered priorities of Jewish charity. So, too, are providing a funeral and burial for the poor, clothing for a needy bride, care for those who are sick, scholarships for poor students, and ransoming those who are held captive.

There is some disagreement about whether funds used to feed the poor may be diminished to pay ransom for a captive or marriage expenses for poor brides. All Jewish authorities are agreed, however, that, when it comes to providing relief for needy men and women, needy women take precedence over men. They also teach that no distinction is to be made between Jews and non-Jews.

Joseph Karo argues that, when it comes to aiding the poor, one must give preference to immediate family members, then to other relatives. After one's relatives, one is obligated to care for the poor servants of one's home, then the poor of one's town, then the needy of another town, then the needy of one's own land, and then beyond. In other words, the needs of the hungry, homeless, and poor who live closest to us have first claim on our charitable giving. (*Sotah* 14a; *Eruvin* 18a; *Shabbat* 127a–b; *Peah* 4:16; *Baba Batra* 8–9; *Tosefta Ketubot* 6,8; *Shulchan Aruch* 34:3,6)

Supporting the needy and maintaining the institutions of the Jewish community have always been considered a mitzvah, a religious responsibility for every Jew. The Torah's report about the Israelites' generous response to Moses' request concerning the building of the sanctuary is pointed to with pride. Their standard of giving immediately and unselfishly became a measure for all *tzedakah*. No excuses for *not* giving charity were acceptable. The rabbis taught that "whether we are rich or poor, we must take from what God has given us and share it with others." (*Tze'enah u-Re'enah, Vayakhel*)

## PEREK GIMEL: *Accountability of Public Officials*

The Torah portions *Vayakhel-Pekude* repeat descriptions of the sanctuary construction, including long, detailed lists of items donated by the Israelites.

*Abravanel*

Biblical interpreter Don Isaac Abravanel counts five repetitions of building plans and donation lists within the Torah. The matter is "puzzling," says Abravanel. "Why keep on recapitulating such details?"

*Ramban (Nachmanides)*

Commentator Ramban answers Abravanel by claiming that all the repetition "reflects the love with which the sanctuary was viewed by God. Such repetition is designed to underscore its importance in the hearts of the Israelites." On the other hand, modern commentator Umberto Cassuto suggests that all the duplication is merely a matter of "style." Ancient Middle Eastern documents, he claims, all contain repetitions of details, especially plans describing sacred places of worship.

Early rabbinic commentators disagree with Cassuto. They believe that the details and lists serve a very important function. Moses, they say, carefully records each charitable gift. Afterwards he reviews the contribution and checks his list against others made by Bezalel and Oholiab. Then he rechecks each entry, making sure that none has been overlooked or misplaced. All this repetition, attention to detail and recapitulation of what was given and how it was used, is a matter of "accountability." For Moses, the rabbis observe, accountability by public officials of what they collect and how they use it is a moral responsibility. Public officials must be beyond reproach.

Furthermore, rabbinic commentators teach that

at least two people are to be appointed to look after the finances of a community. They point out that, in the case of Moses, he was acting alone, and for this reason he insisted on having all the accounts he supervised publicly audited by the people. The repetition of the long lists of donations and how they were used, the rabbis maintain, was the actual public examination of Moses' records. (*Exodus Rabbah, Pekude,* 1–3)

Why did Moses insist on such accountability? Was he not the trusted leader of his people? Could anyone have thought that he was misusing public charity?

Apparently that is the impression the rabbis believe Moses wanted to avoid. There are gossips in every community, those who spread false rumors or question the integrity of public servants. Moses realized, say the rabbis, that there were those who pointed at him and said, "Look how well he is eating and drinking. He is living off our money. He is getting rich from our donations." In order to answer such false rumors and gossip, Moses insisted that his accounting books be public and open to all the Israelites. (*Tanchuma, Pekude,* 7)

The rabbis also claim that, when Moses realized the people were giving more than Bezalel and Oholiab required for the building of the sanctuary, he asked God, "What shall be done with the surplus gifts?" God instructed him to build a special chapel inside the sanctuary. When it was complete, Moses reported to the people: "We spent this amount on the sanctuary, and with the additional funds we built the chapel." Because he accounted for *all* the gifts, even the additional ones, Moses placed himself above suspicion. (*Exodus Rabbah, Pekude,* 1–3)

---

### Stealing

*It is better to eat a poor person's meal and be respected as honest than to eat the richest meal and be hated for swindling and cheating others. Stealing is the worst of all sins.* (Tze'enah u-Re'enah, Pekude)

### Collecting and distributing charity

*Collecting charity for the poor must be done by at least two people jointly. It is to be distributed by a committee of three to assure just criteria and fairness.* (Peah 8:7)

*If collectors of charity must make change or invest surplus funds, they must do so with others present so that no one may suspect them of deriving personal benefit from their transactions.* (Baba Batra 8b)

---

Using Moses as an example, the teachers of the Talmud held that public officials should always be above suspicion. Their actions, and those of their families, should prove their honesty and integrity. The rabbis point out that, as models of behavior, those who prepared the special fine bread offering for the Temple never allowed their children to enjoy any of it. In this way no one could accuse them of profiting from their office. The same rule applied to members of the house of Avtinas, who were experts in preparing spices for the Temple incense. They never allowed their daughters to wear perfume, even as brides, because they did not want anyone to suspect that they prospered or took advantage of their service to the Temple. (*Yoma* 38)

For the teachers of Jewish tradition, the appearance of honesty was a critical factor in assuring public trust. They ruled, for instance, that officials of the Temple treasury, when taking an offering, were not permitted to wear clothing with pockets. Also they were not permitted to wear shoes or sandals. Why? "Because, if such officials become rich, others will assume that they have taken money from the Temple treasury for themselves." (*Shekalim* 3:2)

Jewish tradition maintains that public officials must be above suspicion. The community must have full confidence in the integrity and honesty of those chosen to serve. Handling the funds of others demands open and careful scrutiny. Just as Moses makes a detailed public accounting of his collection and expenditure of funds, so all public officials are to be held to such high ethical standards.

## QUESTIONS FOR STUDY AND DISCUSSION

1. Review Rabbi Judah Ha-Nasi's categories of work. How, in our present society, would you define "work" that should not be done on the Sabbath? What are the benefits of *no work* on the Sabbath? Why, in Jewish tradition, can Sunday not serve as a substitute for the Sabbath?

2. How does Sabbath observance continue to benefit Jews?

3. The Talmud suggests that we give a minimum of 10 percent of our earnings above household expenses to charity and up to 20 percent if we are able. What would you suggest as appropriate standards for *tzedakah* today? Are some charities more deserving of our support than others?

4. Would you agree that standards of accountability for public officials ought to be higher than the standards of those they serve? Why?

# THE
# TORAH
# PORTIONS
# OF
# LEVITICUS

# PARASHAT VAYIKRA
## *Leviticus 1:1–5:26*

*Parashat Vayikra* describes five different kinds of sacrifices to be offered in the sanctuary. They are the *olah,* or "burnt offering"; the *minchah,* or "meal offering"; the *zevach shelamim,* or "sacrifice of well-being"; the *chatat,* or "sin offering"; and the *asham,* or "guilt offering." The manner in which each offering is made is described in detail.

## OUR TARGUM

### · 1 ·

God speaks to Moses concerning the way in which the *olah,* or "burnt offering," should be made by the people of Israel. It is to be a sheep, goat, or bull without a blemish, or a turtledove or pigeon. The person offering the sacrifice is to place a hand upon its head. The animal is then to be slaughtered, and the priests are to pour its blood against the sides of the altar. In the case of a sheep, goat, or bull, the animal is then to be cut up into sections and burned on the altar. If the sacrifice is a turtledove or pigeon, its head is to be removed and the blood is to be poured against the sides of the altar; it is to be torn open by its wings and placed upon the altar to be consumed by the fire.

### · 2 ·

Concerning the *minchah,* or "meal offering," Moses is told it shall consist of choice flour, and oil should be poured upon it, along with frankincense. When it is presented to Aaron and his sons, they are to scoop out a handful of it and place it upon the altar for burning. Afterwards they are to eat the remainder of the offering.

All of the *minchah* offerings are to be of unleavened flour or grain of the finest quality. If the offering is brought on a griddle or pan, it is to be mixed with oil and seasoned with salt. Then a piece of it is to be burned on the altar.

### · 3 ·

The *zevach shelamim,* or "sacrifice of well-being," is to be taken from the herd or flock. The animal offering should be without blemish, and the

priests are to cut it up and offer the entrails and all the fat upon the altar.

### · 4 ·

When a person accidentally fails to fulfill God's commandments, a *chatat,* or "sin offering," is to be made. If the person is a priest, the offering is to be an unblemished bull of the herd. It is to be brought to the entrance of the Tabernacle, where the priest is to lay his hands upon its head. Afterwards it is to be slaughtered, and the priest is to sprinkle its blood seven times inside the Tabernacle before the Ark of the Covenant. All the fat and entrails are to be offered on the altar; the rest of the sacrifice is to be taken outside the camp and burned.

If the community accidentally fails to fulfill God's commandments, the elders of the community are to lay their hands upon the head of a bull. After the bull is slaughtered, the priest is to sprinkle some of its blood seven times in front of the curtain. Some of the blood is to be put on the horns of the altar in the Tabernacle, and some is to be poured at the altar base. The fat is to be burned on the altar, and the rest of the bull is to be burned outside the camp.

If the head of a tribe accidentally sins, that person is to offer a male goat without blemish. If an ordinary person sins, that person must bring a female goat without blemish. After the person's hands have been laid upon the head of the animal being sacrificed, it is to be slaughtered by the priests, and its fat is to be burned on the altar. In this way sins are forgiven.

·5·

If a person is guilty of a wrongdoing, an *asham,* or "guilt offering," shall be made. For example, if a person withholds reporting on a matter seen or heard, touches an unclean carcass or an unclean person, or makes an oath and does not fulfill it, that person offers a "guilt offering." If the person cannot afford a sheep for the offering, a turtledove or two pigeons may be offered. If the person cannot afford the turtledove or two pigeons, a tenth of an *ephah* of choice flour will do for the "guilt offering."

Furthermore, if one deals dishonestly with another in the matter of a loan or a pledge, through robbery or fraud, by finding something lost and lying about it, or by swearing falsely, one must first restore or repay that which has been wrongly taken, along with a fifth of its value. Afterwards one may offer a ram without blemish as a "guilt offering." The priest is to sacrifice it, and the person's wrongdoing shall be forgiven.

**THEMES**

*Parashat Vayikra* contains two important themes:

1. Sacrifice and prayer.
2. Sin and guilt.

# PEREK ALEF: *The Meanings of Sacrifice and Prayer*

The third book of the Torah is named in Hebrew by its first word, *Vayikra,* "And [God] called." In Latin the book is called Leviticus because the priests whose duties it describes were of the tribe of Levi. By the first century C.E., it was known among the early rabbis as *Torat Kohanim,* "Instruction of the Priests."

Most of the book describes in detail how the *korbanot,* or "sacrifices," of the people of Israel were to be offered in the ancient sanctuary. While the descriptions seem to be applicable to the time when Moses and the people were still wandering through the desert, many modern scholars believe this book was written by priests for the priests who presided over the sacrifices offered at the Jerusalem Temple.

In our modern society, the idea of sacrificing animals—of extracting their blood and spilling it on the side of an altar, of cutting out various organs and arranging them for burning—is both foreign and unpleasant. Some would describe it as disgusting and repugnant; others would call it "cruelty to animals," protesting it as morally offensive.

> *Beauty of the sacrifice*
> *The author of* Sirach, *a book of the* Apocrypha, *provides the following description of the sacrifice service in the Jerusalem Temple:*
>
> *How glorious he (Simon the High Priest) was when the people gathered round him as he came out of the inner sanctuary!*
> *. . . When he put on his glorious robe and clothed himself with superb perfection and went up to the holy altar . . . when he received the portions from the hands of the priests, as he stood by the hearth of the altar with a garland of brethren around him . . . with the Lord's offering in their hands, before the whole congregation of Israel. Finishing the service at the altars, and arranging the offering to the Most High, the Almighty, he reached out his hand to the cup and poured a libation of the blood of the grape; he poured it out at the foot of the altar, a pleasing odor to the Most High, the King of all. (50: 1–15)*

In ancient society, however, sacrifices and offerings to God were considered not only appropriate but necessary expressions of faith. The word *korban,* or "sacrifice," literally means "draw near" and reveals the purpose of the Temple offerings. They were meant to unite the worshiper with God. By offering sacrifices, a person said thanks to God or sought forgiveness for sins. The drama and beauty of the sacrificial service, along with the music, prayers, and strong odors of incense, created an atmosphere of awe. In presenting a sacrifice, one was giving something important of oneself to God. For the ancients, the smoke of a burning sacrifice on the altar was proof of a person's love and reverence for God and for God's commandments.

Those who misused the ritual sacrifices, however, were severely criticized. When the prophet Isaiah, for example, saw people ignore the poor and sick, cheat, and deal dishonestly with one another but take their offerings to the Jerusalem Temple, he scorned and denounced them. He told them that God did not want their sacrifices because their "hands were stained with crime." (Isaiah 1:11,15) Among ancient Jews, hypocrisy was ridiculed. Sacrifices were not considered a means of removing guilt for wrongdoing.

---

### Acceptable sacrifices

*Let no person say, "I will go and do ugly and immoral things. Then I will bring a bull with much meat and offer it as a sacrifice on the altar, and God will forgive me." God will not have mercy on such a person.* (Leviticus Rabbah 2:12)

*Let a person do good deeds, study Torah, and bring an offering. Then God will have mercy and extend repentance.* (Eliyahu Rabbah, Friedman, editor, p. 36)

---

After the destruction of the Jerusalem Temple by the Romans in 70 C.E., Jews faced the question: "What shall be done with the institution of sacrifices?" The rabbis determined that, since sacrifices were to be offered only at the Jerusalem Temple, Jews would need to wait until the Temple was rebuilt before reintroducing them. Thus the reintroduction of animal sacrifices and offerings is unlikely.

Even before the last sacrifices were being offered in the Temple, *prayer* was already on the way to replacing sacrifice as the most acceptable means of worship for Jews. With the introduction of the synagogue in the third century B.C.E., words of prayer by both individuals and congregations often replaced journeying to Jerusalem. By the time the Temple was destroyed, there were many thousands of synagogues throughout the Land of Israel, with 480 in Jerusalem alone. Many of the prayers that form the basis of Jewish prayer books today were created long before the offering of sacrifices at the Temple ceased.

After the Temple was destroyed, the rabbis included prayers for its revival in the ritual of the synagogue. For example, the traditional version of the *Avodah* prayer of the *Amidah* includes: "Restore the worship [sacrificial] service of Your Temple, and receive in love and favor [the offerings and] the prayers of Israel. . . ." Recalling the "additional sacrifices" offered on Sabbaths and festivals, the rabbis added a special service called *Musaf,* meaning "Additional Service," to the Sabbath and festival celebrations of the synagogue as a way of praying for the day when the Temple would be rebuilt and the sacrifices of animals reintroduced.

In his time, poet-philosopher Yehudah Halevi dreamed of the day when he would awaken in Jerusalem and experience "the Levites' song and sacrificial service." Later, Zionist Rabbi Tzvi Hirsch Kalisher predicted that the Jewish people would be gathered from the four corners of the earth to the Land of Israel, rebuild the Temple, and "offer sacrifices upon the altar of God. . . ."

*Leibowitz*

In her commentary, modern interpreter Nehama Leibowitz explains that the sacrifices are a "positive means of promoting communion with the Divine" and "a symbol and expression of a person's desire to purify himself and become reconciled with God." (B. S. Jacobson, *Meditations on the Torah,* Sinai Publishing, Tel Aviv, 1956, pp. 137–142; Nehama Leibowitz, *Studies in Va-*

*yikra,* World Zionist Organization, Jerusalem, 1980, pp. 18, 22)

Despite the fact that rabbis and Jewish interpreters honored the tradition of Temple sacrifices, even praying for their reintroduction, many believed prayer was superior to sacrifice as a form of worship. They argued that, while the Temple offerings depended upon a particular place and altar, prayer could be offered anywhere and anytime. Prayer consisted of the quiet meditations of the heart or words of the mouth expressed in a whisper, a song, or simply spoken. "Prayer," the rabbis say, "is greater than all the sacrifices." (*Tanchuma, Vayera,* 31b)

It is reported that the leader of the Jewish people at the time of the destruction of the Temple actually counseled his students by telling them not to mourn the fact that they could no longer offer sacrifices. Standing in the ruins of the Temple, Rabbi Yochanan ben Zakkai told his students, "Do not grieve. We have a means of atonement that is equal to sacrifice. It is the doing of kind deeds. For God teaches us, 'I desire mercy, not sacrifices. . . .' " (*Avot de-Rabbi Nathan* 4; Hosea 6:6)

Citing the virtues of prayer as opposed to sacrifices, other rabbis also claimed that prayer was superior. "If the people of Israel say, 'We are poor and have no sacrifices to bring for offering,' God tells them, 'I need only words.' " Furthermore, say the rabbis, "even if they complain that they have no synagogue in their city, God tells them to pray in their fields and, if not there, on their beds and, if not on their beds, then in their hearts." The point is clear. Unlike sacrifices, which depend on an altar, an animal, or a gift, prayer is dependent only upon the hopes and honesty of one's heart. (*Exodus Rabbah, Tetzaveh,* 38:4; *Pesikta de-Rav Kahana* 158a)

---

*What is prayer?*
*Prayer is the heart . . . of significant living. . . .*
*Prayer is a step on which we rise from the self we are to the self we wish to be.*
*Prayer affirms the hope that no reality can crush, the aspiration that can never acknowledge defeat. . . .*

---

*Prayer seeks the power to do wisely, to act generously, to live helpfully. . . .*
*Prayer is the search for silence amidst noise. . . .*
*Prayer takes us beyond the self . . . our prayers are answered . . . when we are challenged to be what we can be. (Rabbi Morris Adler)*

---

 *Rambam (Maimonides)*

In his famous book *Guide for the Perplexed,* Moses Maimonides argues that sacrifices were an early form of worship given to the Jewish people so that they could learn how to serve God without feeling different from all other peoples surrounding them. Slowly, Maimonides says, the people learned that "the sacrificial service is not the primary objective of the commandments but that prayer is a better means of obtaining nearness to God." Agreeing with the early rabbis, Maimonides emphasizes that the superiority of prayer is that "it can be offered everywhere and by every person."

In his study of prayer, Rabbi Abraham Joshua Heschel suggests that "prayer is not a substitute for sacrifice. Prayer *is* sacrifice." By that observation, Heschel means that in true prayer "we try to surrender our vanities, to burn our insolence, to abandon bias, dishonesty, envy." Prayer is the means through which we sacrifice our selfishness and greed and get in touch with our powers for truth, mercy, and love. (*Man's Quest for God: Studies in Prayer and Symbolism,* Scribner, New York, 1954, pp. 70–71)

## PEREK BET: *Defining "Sin" in Jewish Tradition*

*Parashat Vayikra* not only speaks of five different kinds of sacrifices to be offered by the people and their leaders, but it also identifies the reasons for offering sacrifices. Many were presented as gifts to bring the worshiper closer to God and to express thanks for harvests, festivals, personal celebrations, good fortune, healing in time of sickness, or the achievement of peaceful relations between individuals and nations.

Among the many different kinds of sacrifices are those having to do with the "sins" of the people of Israel or of individuals. *Parashat Vayikra* speaks of the *olah* offering and the *chatat* and *asham* sacrifices as means of achieving relief from guilty feelings and forgiveness from God for wrongdoing. In identifying forms of behavior that require offerings at the Temple, the Torah and those who interpret it present us with a unique definition of "sin."

For example, the *olah*, or "burnt offering," the first sacrifice mentioned in our Torah portion, is to be given by all people. The Torah, however, does not provide a reason for the offering. It is Rabbi Simeon ben Yochai, a student of the famous Rabbi Akiba and a leader of the Jewish community in the Land of Israel just after the destruction of the Temple, who teaches that the *olah* offering is given for sinful thoughts and intentions even if they are not carried out. (*Leviticus Rabbah* 7:3)

*Ramban (Nachmanides)*

Nachmanides agrees, explaining that it is natural for human beings to have all kinds of evil thoughts. We think of cheating our neighbors, of twisting the truth to suit our selfish purposes, of secretly taking that which does not belong to us, of committing sexual offenses. Many different thoughts and intentions rise in our minds. For Nachmanides, these "secret thoughts," known only to God, are the first level of "sin." They are the first inclinations that lead to wrongdoing. For that reason, one offers the *olah* as a means of removing any guilt for such reflections or intentions. (Comment on Leviticus 1:4)

**Sinful thoughts**
*Rabbi Bachya ben Asher, author of* Kad ha-Kemach, *commenting on the rabbinic observation that "sinful thoughts are more injurious than the sin itself," says: "It is more difficult to withdraw from sinful thoughts, for habitually*

*thinking about a sin will ultimately lead to its commission." He also notes the opinion of others that "when one plans to commit a sin, one actually prepares oneself to do more than one sin. For example, if one thinks of stealing or robbing, one prepares oneself even to kill in order to accomplish one's desire. . . ." (Charles B. Chavel, translator, Shilo Publishing House, Inc., New York, 1980, p. 276)*

A second kind of "sin" defined in this Torah portion occurs when a person unintentionally breaks the law. Examples of this kind of "sin": one may harvest but forget to leave a portion for the poor and needy; one may neglect paying a worker at the end of the day; or one may accidentally eat a food prohibited by the Torah.

*Hirsch*

Commenting on the seriousness of "unintentional sin," Rabbi Samson Raphael Hirsch writes: "The sinner through error is one who sins from carelessness. In other words, at the moment of omission, that person did not take full care, with whole heart and soul, that the act be in keeping with the Torah and commandments, because the person was not, in the words of the prophet Isaiah [66:2], 'concerned about My word.'" Because one has not been careful and thoughtful, but lackadaisical in carrying out God's commandments, one's actions are considered sinful, and one is required to bring a sacrifice and to offer it in order to gain forgiveness.

Agreeing with Hirsch, Nehama Leibowitz states that "it is no excuse that the sinner had no *evil intention* and that it was *merely* forgetfulness, *just* carelessness and irresponsibility. . . ." She also notes that the Torah clearly includes priests and other leaders in its concern for unintentional sins. Leibowitz argues that "the greater the person, the greater the responsibility. Each negligence, each slip of the mind, each indiscretion, each error borders on deliberate wrongdoing." (*Studies in Vayikra*, pp. 28–29)

> *Sins of a leader*
> *An acknowledged leader must be even more care-ful than ordinary people not to fall into the trap of wrongdoing. Even sins committed uninten-tionally may lead others to do evil, for others are eager to point to such a person as their example when they sin. (Jacob ben Jacob Moses of Lissa)*

In other words, wrongdoings, even those com-mitted in error or by accident, have serious con-sequences. They are not to be whitewashed or treated lightly as if they had no impact on others. Jewish tradition does not permit one to run away from the responsibility for one's actions. The To-rah commands those who unintentionally sin to bring a *chatat,* or "sin offering," to God.

In addition to defining sins committed in thought or by error, the Torah also specifies other wrongdoings for which one must present an *asham,* or "guilt offering." These sins include: (1) withholding evidence from a court by refusing to be a witness; (2) promising to do something, or making an oath, and then failing to keep it; (3) dealing falsely with another person in matters hav-ing to do with deposits, pledges, theft, unfair treat-ment, or lost articles. All of these are considered serious violations of Torah.

Commenting on the sin of withholding evi-dence from a court, Abraham Chill observes that "since justice is the foundation of society, anyone who deliberately impedes justice is thereby guilty of perpetrating an act of injustice. If one could give testimony that would help a court of justice come to a decision but fails to do so, that person has committed a sin." (*The Mitzvot: The Com-mandments and Their Rationale,* Bloch Publishing, New York, 1974, p.150)

Rabbi Hisda asks the question: "What does the Torah mean when it uses the terms unfair treat-ment and theft?" He answers by pointing out that a person must not say to a neighbor, "I have some-thing belonging to you, but I will wait until to-morrow to return it." Hisda defines such behavior as the sin of "unfair treatment." And, if a person says to another, "I have something belonging to you, but I will not return it,"—that, says Hisda, is the sin of "theft." (*Baba Metzia* 111a)

For such wrongdoings, it is not enough for the sinner to bring a sacrifice to the Temple. The To-rah clearly states that the guilty person shall "repay the principal amount and add a fifth part to it" so the injured party will be fully compensated for any losses. Jewish tradition insists on appropriate repayment of stolen property *before* any offerings are acceptable to God.

This first Torah portion of Leviticus offers a significant definition of "sin" in Jewish tradition. It includes wrongdoings that result from thought-lessness and careless error, from accidentally mis-leading others, from deliberately withholding ev-idence, lying, robbing, or treating others unfairly. This definition is important because it demon-strates the high ethical principles that form the basis of Jewish tradition.

## QUESTIONS FOR STUDY AND DISCUSSION

1. Review *Perek Alef.* List the reasons Jewish tra-dition favors prayer over sacrifice. What other reasons would you add to that list? Why?

2. Maimonides and Rabbi Bachya ben Asher ar-gue that sinful thoughts can lead to sinful deeds. Do you agree? Should a person feel guilty for such thoughts? How can prayer lead a person away from such sin?

3. The rabbis raise a significant question of who is responsible in society for sin? Is it the thief or the one who knowingly purchases stolen property? They say that a governor once put to death all those who knowingly had pur-chased stolen goods from thieves. When the people heard what the governor had done, they protested. "You have not acted justly," they told him. So he took them to a field and put out food for animals. The animals came and took the food to their holes in the ground. The next day he took the people to the field and again put out plates of food for the animals. This time, however, while the animals rushed to the food, the governor had his guards cover their holes. When the animals discovered they could not enter their holes, they returned the food to the plates. The governor did this to demonstrate that troubles are due to those who knowingly purchase stolen property (*Leviticus Rabbah* 6:2) Would you agree or disagree with the governor?

# PARASHAT TZAV
## *Leviticus 6:1–8:36*

---

*Parashat Tzav* repeats and enlarges upon the descriptions of the sacrifices already discussed in *Parashat Vayikra*. Included in this portion are details about how the ancient offerings of the *olah, minchah, chatat, asham,* and *zevach shelamim* were performed. We are also given a description of the ordination of Aaron and his sons as priests in the sanctuary and of the dedication of the first sanctuary.

---

## OUR TARGUM

### · 1 ·

Moses, as commanded by God, instructs Aaron and his sons concerning the presentation in the sanctuary of the *olah,* or "burnt offering." The ashes from the offering are to be removed from the altar every morning, and the priests are to keep the fire of the altar burning continually.

### · 2 ·

Aaron and his sons are told to bring a *minchah,* or "meal offering," to present on the altar. Once the offering is presented, the priests spread a handful of the fine flour, together with the oil and frankincense, upon the altar and set it afire. The remains of the offering are to be eaten by the priests.

### · 3 ·

The *chatat,* or "sin offering," for unintentional wrongs is to be slaughtered by the priests. If it is cooked in an earthen pot, the pot is to be broken. If it is cooked in a copper pot, the pot is to be scrubbed clean and rinsed with water. The priests may eat of this sacrifice.

The *asham,* or "guilt offering," is slaughtered, and its blood is poured on all sides of the altar. The priest is to burn all of the animal's fat together with its entrails, kidneys, and parts of its liver. Only the sons of priests may eat of this sacrifice.

### · 4 ·

The *zevach shelamim,* or "sacrifice of well-being or peace," is offered as a gift of thanksgiving. It includes the sacrificial animal, along with unleavened cakes mixed with oil, unleavened wafers spread with oil, and cakes of fine flour with oil

from an ox, sheep, goat, or animals killed by other animals. He also forbids the eating of any blood, warning that a person who eats blood shall be cut off from the people of Israel.

The *zevach shelamim* is offered by individuals for themselves. One part of the sacrifice is to be burned on the altar, another eaten by the priest who offers it, and a third part eaten by the person bringing it.

· 5 ·

In a solemn ceremony before all the people of Israel, Moses ordains Aaron and his sons as priests. They are dressed in beautiful garments and sprinkled with oil. Aaron is given a robe, and the *ephod,* "breastpiece," Urim and Thummim, along with a special headdress are placed upon him.

Afterwards Moses sprinkles oil throughout the sanctuary, upon the altar and all the utensils used for sacrifices, and upon Aaron's head. Sacrifices are then offered by Moses, Aaron, and Aaron's sons. Moses touches the right ears, thumbs, and toes of each priest with some of the sacrificial blood. He then takes parts of the sacrificial animal, along with cakes of unleavened bread, and waves them as an offering to God.

Concluding the ceremony of consecrating Aaron and his sons as priests, Moses commands them to boil the sacrificial animal and eat it at the entrance of the sanctuary. Whatever is left over is to be consumed by fire. They are also told to remain at the entrance of the sanctuary for seven days and nights as a part of their celebration.

mixed in and well soaked. After it is presented to the priest, blood from the sacrificial animal is sprinkled around the altar. The offering is to be eaten the day it is brought to the priest.

If the sacrifice offered is a freewill offering, it may be eaten on either the same day or the day after it is given to the priest. Such an offering may not be eaten by any priest who has been made ritually unclean by touching a dead human body.

Moses commands the people not to eat any fat

## THEMES

*Parashat Tzav* contains two important themes:

1. Finding meaning in obsolete traditions.
2. The holiness of blood.

## PEREK ALEF: *Finding Meaning in Obsolete Traditions*

*Parashat Tzav* presents a detailed description of the sacrifices offered in the first sanctuary of the Jewish people as they wandered through the Sinai desert. Most scholars believe that the description applies also to the sacrifices that were brought to

the Jerusalem Temple after it was built by King Solomon in the tenth century B.C.E.

During the period when thousands of people journeyed to Jerusalem to offer their sacrifices, the Torah's instructions on how the priests were to prepare and receive these sacrifices must have been extremely important. If they were not prepared correctly or offered properly, they were unacceptable. Therefore, knowing and following the directions of the Torah concerning sacrifices was a high priority for both the people and the priests. Studying the details for the presentation of each sacrifice had great importance.

After the Temple was destroyed by the Romans in 70 C.E. and the offering of sacrifices was replaced by prayer, many must have asked: "Do these descriptions and commandments concerning the offering of sacrifices still have any meaning for us? Are they now obsolete? Is there anything for us to learn from these details about the *olah, minchah, chatat, asham,* and *zevach shelamim* offerings?"

For Torah interpreters since the destruction of the Temple, such questions have constantly been asked and imaginatively answered. Sometimes a commentator will find a word or phrase describing a ritual of the sacrifice that calls to mind a significant moral lesson or symbolizes an important truth about human life. At other times, a command about an offering will remind a commentator of another statement or description in the biblical tradition, and, in exploring the meaning of both, new insights are born.

Several examples of finding, or even inventing, meanings from what seems like obsolete and irrelevant descriptions of ancient rituals are presented below.

*Example One:* Rabbi Levi, who lived during the third century, pointed out that the word *olah,* meaning "burnt offering," can also be read and translated as *alah,* meaning "behave boastfully." Therefore, he argued, the Torah's statements "This is the law concerning the *olah.* It shall go up upon its burning place on the altar . . ." can be understood to mean "This is the law concerning the *alah,* the boastful person. He shall be destroyed by fire."

To prove his point, Rabbi Levi cites several examples of insolence or pretentious behavior that were punished by fire. For instance, Noah's generation suffered the Flood; for their injustice and selfishness, however, they were also punished by fire. The people of Sodom and Gomorrah suffered destruction by fire for their cruel treatment of strangers and their snobbish and arrogant behavior toward one another. (Genesis 19:24) Pharaoh was punished by fire because he boastfully questioned God's power, saying: "Who is the God

that I should heed and let Israel go [from Egypt]?" (Exodus 5:2)

By reading the word *alah* for *olah,* Rabbi Levi avoids dealing with a discussion of the "burnt offering" and focuses instead upon the dangers of acting in a boastful, self-centered, and prideful way. The haughty or arrogant person, he declares, will ultimately end up as a burnt sacrifice on his or her own altar. (*Leviticus Rabbah* 7:6)

*Example Two:* Rabbi Menachem M. Schneerson, known as the "Lubavitcher Rebbe" (b.1902), teaches that the sanctuary built by the Jewish people in the desert symbolizes the sanctuary that is inside every Jew. Just as the sanctuary has an inner and outer altar, so each Jew, Schneerson writes, possesses a "surface personality" and an "essential core."

When the Torah says "The fire on the altar shall be kept burning, not to go out . . ." it is referring, not only to the duty of the priest to keep the altar of the sanctuary burning, but also to the way in which one practices Jewish tradition. "It is not a private possession to be cherished subconsciously," argues Rabbi Schneerson. "It must show in the face a person sets towards the world."

Using the symbol of the continually burning fire on the altar, Schneerson stresses that a Jew must be "involved," bringing life and fire to the three aspects of Jewish existence: (1) to the learning of Torah, (2) to prayer, and (3) to the practice of charity.

"Words of Torah," he comments, "should be spoken with fire. . . . They should penetrate every facet of a person's being." In other words, learning must not be dull exercise but a way of filling each person with a desire to practice the wisdom, ethics, and traditions of Torah. One's prayer must be done not as a routine but as an expression of love for God and appreciation of the world created by God. In practicing the mitzvah of *tzadakah,* or "charity," it is not enough to provide money and services for the poor and sick. One must do it "with an inner warmth that manifests itself outwardly," providing an example for others. In all these ways, "the fire on the altar will be kept burning." (*Likutei Sichot,* Vol. I, Lubavitch Foundation, London, 1975–1985, pp. 217–219)

*Example Three:* The Yiddish commentator Jacob ben Isaac Ashkenazi, author of *Tze'enah u-Re'enah,* notes that the Torah commands that the *olah,* or "burnt offering," and the *chatat,* or "sin offering," be sacrificed on the same altar. "Why," he asks, "are these two sacrifices to be made at the same place?"

He answers his own question by declaring that "the Torah teaches us not to embarrass people."

The "burnt offering" is brought by one who is guilty of sinful thoughts. Perhaps that person coveted something belonging to someone else or thought about cheating or stealing from another person. A "sin offering" is a sacrifice brought by someone who has actually committed a wrongdoing.

The Torah, says Jacob ben Isaac Ashkenazi, commands that both should offer their sacrifices in the same place so no one will know the difference between the person who has sinned in thought and the person who has sinned in deed. In this way, embarrassment is avoided. No one can point an accusing finger and say, "There is a thief."

By calling attention to the detail of how the two sacrifices were to be offered, Jacob ben Isaac Ashkenazi emphasizes a significant ethical lesson. It is forbidden to humiliate or shame another person. (*Tze'enah u-Re'enah: The Classic Anthology of Torah Lore and Midrashic Commentary, Tzav,* Miriam Stark Zakon, translator, Mesorah Publications Ltd. in conjunction with Hillel Press, Brooklyn, N.Y., 1983, p. 573)

*Example Four:* Rabbi Meir, a leading teacher in the Land of Israel during the second century, studied the Torah's command about offering sacrifices: "These are the rituals of the burnt offering, the meal offering, the sin offering, the guilt offering, the offering of ordination, and the peace offering." He pointed out that the peace offering is mentioned last and concluded that this was not by accident. By mentioning the *zevach shelamim,* or "peace offering," last, Rabbi Meir taught, the Torah emphasizes the importance of *shalom,* or "peace."

"Great is peace," he told his students. "For the sake [of peace] a person may suffer humiliation."

The story is told of a woman who was fond of listening to Rabbi Meir teach his students. Once, when the rabbi's lesson lasted a long time, she was late in returning to her home. Angrily her husband asked, "Where have you been?" When she told him she had been listening to Rabbi Meir's lesson, he refused to believe her, saying: "I will not allow you into this house until you have spit in Rabbi Meir's face!"

Friends of the couple, who learned what had happened, suggested they go with her for counsel to Rabbi Meir.

When Rabbi Meir heard what happened, he said to the wife, "I have a favor to ask. Since the time you left my lesson, I have developed a serious eye infection that can be cured only with the spital of your mouth. Therefore, please spit in my eye seven times." After the woman had done as Rabbi Meir requested, he told her, "Now go and be reconciled with your husband. Say to him, 'I have spit in Rabbi Meir's eye.'"

After the woman left, Rabbi Meir said to his students, "Great is peace. You may suffer shame to make peace between friends, between a wife and husband." (*Leviticus Rabbah* 9:9)

Rabbi Meir, and other rabbis of his time, taught that "peace is the culmination of all blessings," the most important pursuit for human beings. For the rabbis, the fact that the Torah mentioned the *zevach shelamim,* or "peace-offering," after all the other sacrifices was proof of their claim.

*Parashat Tzav,* with all of its details of the sacrifices offered in the ancient sanctuary and in the Jerusalem Temple, presents Jewish teachers with a crucial challenge. How do you find meaning or relevant messages in obsolete ritual practices?

The challenge is a serious one. And, as we have seen from the examples above, it was answered with creative imagination and innovation. Sometimes in their study of the details of the sacrifices, the commentators suggest a new meaning by altering a word like *olah* to *alah* or by making an analogy between the altars of the sanctuary and those within each human being. Other interpreters suggest lessons by noting the coincidence of two offerings made in the identical place or by calling attention to the order in which the Torah lists the sacrifices.

All of these creative devices of interpretation were used to uncover significant ethical messages to be passed on from generation to generation. No part of the Torah was ever considered obsolete. Through imagination and inventiveness it would yield important lessons. The challenge to commentators was to seek out the meanings of Torah and to reveal its gems.

## PEREK BET: *The Holiness of Blood*

Jewish tradition forbids the eating of blood. *Parashat Tzav* contains the commandment: "And you must not consume any blood, either of bird or of animal, in any of your settlements." (Leviticus 7:26) This prohibition against eating blood also appears in Leviticus 3:17, in 17:14, and later in Deuteronomy 12:23.

---

### Do not eat the blood

*And if any Israelite or any stranger who resides among them hunts down an animal or a bird that may be eaten, he shall pour out its blood and cover it with earth. For the life [soul] of all flesh—its blood is its life. Therefore, I say to the Israelite people: You shall not eat of the blood of any flesh, for the life [soul] of all flesh is its blood. (Leviticus 17:13–14)*

---

The early rabbis who interpreted the Torah's prohibition against eating blood developed a number of methods for slaughtering and removing the blood of animals: The knife used is to be razor sharp and perfectly smooth without any nicks or dents so as to cause as little suffering to the animal as possible. The blood spilled at the moment of slaughter is to be poured on a bed of dust and to be covered with the dust and buried. After the slaughter, the blood is to be removed from the meat by soaking it for a half hour and by salting it for one hour. Then the meat is rinsed and ready for cooking. One may also remove the blood by broiling the meat. (Abraham Chill, *The Mitzvot*, pp. 168–169)

Why this unusual attention to blood? Why does Jewish tradition forbid the eating of blood?

Most commentators agree there are two reasons for the Torah's prohibitions against eating blood. The first has to do with the common use of blood by pagan cults. In pagan ceremonies the blood of animals was eaten in the belief that it would provide strength or healing from sickness. At times

such ceremonies also included the offering of human blood in hope that it would satisfy thirsty demons who, it was believed, might cause harm. Early Jewish tradition rejected such ritual practices as dangerous and misleading.

*Rambam (Maimonides)*

Philosopher and commentator Moses Maimonides discusses the Torah's prohibition against eating blood in his *Guide for the Perplexed*. He explains that pagans believed that, by collecting the blood of animals and placing it in pots and bowls, the spirits would come and dine with them. These spirits would even appear to them in dreams revealing the future or reward them with good luck.

Maimonides argues that the Torah "seeks to cure humanity of such idolatry . . . and to do away with such misconceptions." For that reason, it forbids the eating of blood.

*Ramban (Nachmanides)*

Nachmanides disagrees with Maimonides and offers a second reason for the rule against eating blood. Pointing to the Torah's statement that "the soul of all life is its blood," Nachmanides argues that, while God permits human beings to eat the flesh of other creatures for nourishment and to use the blood of specified creatures for atonement, all blood is forbidden for eating because "all souls belong to God." In other words, one must consider blood as sacred because it contains the soul given by God to all creatures.

Having made the point that human beings are forbidden to eat blood because it is a "sacred container of the soul," Nachmanides adds a curious observation out of the medieval medicine of his times. "It is well known," he writes, "that the food that one takes into the body becomes a part of the flesh." Therefore, if one eats the blood of a lower animal, "the result would be a thickening and coarseness of the human soul . . . thus combining the human soul with the animal soul." (Comments on Leviticus 17:11)

Nachmanides' belief that eating the blood of animals might have the effect of making a person more "animallike," of decreasing human sensitivity, intellect, and powers of understanding, was common in his day. While modern science rejects such a view, there are many vegetarians who maintain that the eating of blood does have psychological significance. They refuse to eat meat, not only because they are opposed to slaughtering animals, but also because they believe that such "slaughter" has a brutalizing effect upon human beings.

> **A vegetarian speaks**
> *Early in my life I came to the conclusion that there was no basic difference between man and animals. If a man has the heart to cut the throat of a chicken or a calf, there's no reason he should not be willing to cut the throat of a man. (Isaac Bashevis Singer)*

*Leibowitz*

According to Nehama Leibowitz, Rabbi Abraham Isaac Kook, the famed Chief Rabbi of the Land of Israel just before the establishment of the Jewish state, held such a view. He taught that the eating of meat was "a temporary dispensation given to humanity, which has not yet reached the stage of overcoming its murderous instincts." For Rabbi Kook, eating meat or blood was a sign of human cruelty, proof that human beings were still primitive. Commenting on Kook's view, Leibowitz writes that the rabbi believed "human beings must slowly be trained to show mercy to their own kind and ultimately to the rest of the animal creation." Refusing to eat blood or meat was a means of furthering such an education in sensitivity and reverence for life. (*Studies in Vayikra,* p.55)

Rabbi Kook's view as presented by Nehama Leibowitz is close to the opinions of Rabbis Sam-

uel H. Dresner and Seymour Siegel in their discussion in *The Jewish Dietary Laws* (Burning Bush Press, New York, 1959). Commenting on the prohibition against eating blood, they write: "There is no clearer visible symbol of life than blood. To spill blood is to bring death. To inject blood is often to save life. The removal of blood . . . *kashrut* (the laws of slaughtering animals for food) teaches is one of the most powerful means of making us constantly aware of the concession and compromise that the whole act of eating meat, in reality, is. Again, it teaches us reverence for life." (p. 29)

The Torah's rule against eating blood because it contains the sacred essence of life—the soul—demonstrates the high value Jewish tradition places upon each human and animal life. When blood is spilled, either at the altar as part of the ritual of atonement or in the process of slaughtering for food, the blood is gathered and buried. It is treated with respect. Through such practices, human beings were to learn that blood is synonymous with life, and life, like blood, is sacred.

## QUESTIONS FOR STUDY AND DISCUSSION

1. Interpreters of Torah sought to find new meanings in ancient and obsolete rituals and even in the language used by the Torah. For example, Rashi notes that the words "And God spoke to Moses, saying, 'Command Aaron and his sons . . .'" (Leviticus 6:1,2) might also be understood as *"Urge* Aaron and his sons. . . ." What is the distinction between "command" and "urge"? Which word do you believe is the more effective in getting something accomplished? Why?

2. Many interpreters of Torah notice that the duties of the priests are very ordinary and menial. The priests clean the altar every morning. They carry the ashes to a special place outside the camp. Some commentators have asked if there is an important lesson here. Could it be that the most important religious deeds are to be found in the most ordinary and even menial tasks? What are some other examples?

3. Author Isaac Bashevis Singer was once asked why he was a vegetarian. He answered, "Because it's good for the animals." Is it also *good* for human beings? For the global environment?

4. Rabbi Joseph H. Hertz stresses that the rule against consuming blood teaches human beings to curb their violent instincts and tames their tendency toward bloodshed. Do you agree? Why?

# PARASHAT SHEMINI
## *Leviticus 9:1–11:47*

---

*Parashat Shemini* opens with Moses' instructions to Aaron and his sons for bringing offerings to the sanctuary as atonement for any sins that they or the people may have committed. Aaron follows Moses' instructions carefully and places the offerings on the sanctuary altar. Afterwards two of Aaron's sons, Nadab and Abihu, decide to bring fire offerings of their own. Because they have brought offerings not commanded by God, they are punished by death. Moses tells Aaron and his other sons, Eleazar and Ithamar, not to mourn for them. Later God tells Moses and Aaron which foods are permitted for eating and which are forbidden to the people of Israel.

---

## OUR TARGUM

### ·1·

Moses tells his brother, Aaron, and Aaron's sons to bring a calf, a ram, a he-goat, and a lamb to the sanctuary for sacrifices. They are to be sin and burnt offerings and an offering of well-being. In offering them, Aaron, his sons, and the entire people are to be forgiven by God for any wrongs they may have done.

Aaron and his sons carefully follow the instructions for offering sacrifices. They slaughter the animals, burn the fat of the sacrifice on the altar, and spill the blood at the base of the altar. Then Aaron lifts his hands toward the people and blesses

them. Afterwards God sends a fire to burn everything they have placed on the altars. When the people see the fire, they fall to the ground in prayer.

### ·2·

Acting independently, without a command from God, two of Aaron's sons, Nadab and Abihu, take pans, place fire and incense upon them, and offer them upon the altar. God sends a fire and destroys Nadab and Abihu, telling Aaron, "Through those near to Me I show Myself holy, and assert My authority before all the people." Hearing God's judgment, Aaron is silent.

Moses commands Aaron and his other sons, Eleazar and Ithamar, neither to bare their heads

nor tear their clothing as signs of mourning for
Nadab and Abihu. "The people of Israel will
mourn their deaths," he counsels. He also tells
them they must drink neither wine nor any other
intoxicant when entering the sanctuary. Their task
is to distinguish between the sacred and the pro-
fane, the clean and the unclean and to teach the
people all the laws that have been given by God
to Moses.

Later Moses criticizes Eleazar and Ithamar for
not eating the sin offering inside the sanctuary as
they had been commanded. Aaron answers his
brother by pointing out that the sin offering had
been presented as he commanded, and the result
had been the death of his two sons, Nadab and
Abihu. "Would it have been different today?
Would such things have happened?" Aaron asks
Moses. Hearing Aaron's painful words and rec-

ognizing the truth of his argument, Moses ap-
proves what had been done.

· 3 ·

Moses and Aaron are told by God to instruct the
Israelites about which foods they are permitted
to eat and which foods are forbidden to them.

They present the following list of permitted
foods: all animals with split hoofs that chew their
cud; all that live in water that have fins and scales;
all locusts, bald locusts, crickets, and grasshoppers.

The following are forbidden foods: camel, da-
man, hare, and swine; the eagle, vulture, black
vulture, kite, falcon, raven, ostrich, nighthawk, sea
gull, hawk, little owl, cormorant, great owl, white
owl, pelican, bustard, stork, heron, hoopoe, and
bat; all animals that walk on their paws; the mole,
mouse, great lizards of every variety, the gecko,

land crocodile, lizard, sand lizard, and chameleon; anything that crawls on its belly or has many legs.

One may not eat or touch the body of an animal that has died of natural causes. If one has such contact, all clothing shall be washed, and the person shall be considered unclean until sundown. If a dead carcass touches any article of wood, cloth, or skin, sack, or any implement, it shall be dipped in water and remain there until sundown. If the implement is made of pottery, it shall be broken.

Any water or food in such an implement is unfit for eating or drinking. Should the carcass be found near a spring or cistern, the water there shall be considered fit for drinking; if it is found on seed grain, the seed is considered fit for planting.

Moses tells the people that all these rules concerning permitted and forbidden foods and what is clean and unclean have been given to them that they might be holy before God.

## THEMES

*Parashat Shemini* contains two important themes:

1. The dangers of excess.
2. Eating as a function of "holiness" in Jewish tradition.

## PEREK ALEF: *What Did Nadab and Abihu Do Wrong?*

According to the Torah, Nadab and Abihu, sons of Aaron, each took a fire pan, placed incense upon it, and brought it to the sanctuary altar for an offering. The fire they offered had not been authorized by God nor had they been commanded to bring it to the sanctuary. As a result, they were both put to death.

What did they do to deserve such severe punishment? Were they put to death for offering the wrong kind of fire on the sanctuary altar?

The story of Nadab and Abihu raises issues with which interpreters have struggled for many centuries. Early rabbinical commentators, for example, claim that the two brothers were not punished for offering the wrong kinds of incense or fire. They were condemned for the evil intent that motivated them. Nadab and Abihu, say the rabbis, were ruthlessly ambitious.

Supporting their interpretation, the rabbis creatively invent an imaginary conversation between Nadab and Abihu as they stand with Moses and Aaron at Mount Sinai. "Look at those two old men," they say to each other. "Soon, they will be gone, and we will be the leaders of this community."

According to the rabbis, God warns Nadab and Abihu about the consequences of such ambitions by asking them: "Who will bury whom? Will it be you who will outlive them, or will they outlive you?" The two young men are stunned. After a moment of silence, God tells them: "Your fathers will bury you and go on to lead My people." (*Sifra* on Leviticus 10:1; also *Leviticus Rabbah* 20:10)

From the point of view of the early rabbis, Nadab and Abihu were punished because they plotted to remove Moses and Aaron from their positions of leadership. They appeared at the sanctuary with their own offerings, hoping that the people would be impressed and bring pressure upon Moses and Aaron to transfer their authority to them. Envy and impatience fueled their scheme, say the rabbis, and, in the end, they were punished because of their lust for position and power.

By contrast, Rabbi Levi argues that it was not ambition but arrogance that motivated Nadab and Abihu. Again employing creative imagination, he claims that the two set themselves off from all their peers and bragged that no woman was good enough for them to marry. In fact, says Rabbi Levi, they insensitively took advantage of women's feelings, raising their expectations and hopes for a serious relationship when they had no intention of marriage.

Rabbi Levi claims that they publicly declared: "Our father's brother is king, our mother's brother is a prince, our father is High Priest, and we are both deputy High Priests. What woman is good enough for us?" Because they arrogantly demeaned others, they were punished. (*Leviticus Rabbah* 20:10)

*Rashi*

Rashi agrees but cites other evidence. Basing his interpretation of the behavior of Nadab and Abihu upon a discussion of it in the Talmud, Rashi points out that, rather than following the carefully detailed directions for offering a sacrifice or bringing fire to the sanctuary, they took upon themselves the power of deciding what to offer, how to bring the offering, and when. For disregarding the process and failing to consult with Aaron and Moses about what they planned to do, Nadab and Abihu were punished. Rashi argues that their arrogance led them to believe that they were accountable to no one.

---

**They failed to consult . . .**
*Not only did Nadab and Abihu fail to consult Moses and Aaron about their plan to bring a "foreign fire" into the sanctuary, they also failed to communicate with each other. Instead of discussing the matter in a way that might have led them to speak with the fathers, or others in authority, they acted quickly, without carefully subjecting their ideas to criticism. For not consulting, they suffered serious consequences.* (Leviticus Rabbah *20:8*)

---

Rashbam, Rashi's grandson, bases his view of what Nadab and Abihu did wrong upon the Torah text. He points out that the Torah states "each took his fire pan, put fire in it . . . and they offered before God alien fire, *which God had not commanded them.*" Their sin, Rashbam explains, is that they offered a kind of fire that had not been commanded. That is why the Torah calls it *esh zarah,*

or "alien or foreign fire." In other words, Nadab and Abihu took the law into their own hands.

Rashbam also speculates on why they did so. He explains that Nadab and Abihu were deeply impressed when God appeared in the midst of the fire on the altar after Moses and Aaron offered their sacrifices. Afterwards, he concludes, they assumed that, if they offered "fire," God would once again appear, and they would be given credit by the people for their special powers—powers equal to those of even Moses and Aaron. They, therefore, were willing to take the law into their own hands to improve their reputations and their chances for deposing Moses and Aaron.

Rabbi Morris Adler believes that the story of Nadab and Abihu is filled with symbolism. The "fire" that they brought, says Adler, "burned within them." It was the "fire of ambition," and their death was "the kind of death people bring upon themselves."

Adler writes: "It was a fire of willfulness and hostility. It was a fire of impulse and desire. As they ministered at the altar, they were the victims of their own appetites and greed, whims and ambitions. No fire came from on high to consume them; they were consumed by their own fierce and false ambitions." (*The Voice Still Speaks,* Bloch Publishing Co., New York, 1969, p. 218)

---

**On ambition**
*Ambition is bondage.* (Solomon ibn Gabirol)

*Look for cake, and you lose your bread.* (Yiddish proverb)

*Ambition destroys its possessor.* (Yoma 86b)

*Do not seek greatness for yourself . . . do not crave a seat at royal tables.* (Avot 6:4)

**Requirement for success**
*This is the indispensable requirement for success: you have to want it and want it badly. "You have to have a will to accomplish whatever it is you're setting out to accomplish," says Rita Hauser, who had to overcome formidable barriers of sex discrimination to become one of the leading female attorneys of her generation. "I believe in*

*will. I think the will to succeed, the will to win, the will to overcome adversity is an absolute major force in the success of anybody." (Lester Korn,* The Success Profile, *Fireside, New York, 1988, p. 39)*

In his reflections on Nadab and Abihu, Naphtali Hertz Wessely is much less critical than other commentators. Wessely calls Nadab and Abihu "religious personalities of the highest order," who did not act out of selfish ambition or any other mean purpose. Quite the opposite, says Wessely. The two sons of Aaron were deeply moved by the beauty and meaning of the ritual sacrifices offered by Moses and Aaron. In their enthusiasm and joy "they lost their heads and entered the Holy of Holies to burn incense, something that they had not been commanded to do by Moses."

Their wrongdoing, Wessely argues, was not the deliberate breaking of the law but rather their failure to control their religious enthusiasms. They should not have gone beyond what Moses had commanded. They should have been more humble instead of blindly assuming that whatever they did in the sanctuary would be acceptable. They were punished, says Wessely, because they occupied positions of importance, which they misused in their misguided excitement and zeal. (*Biur,* comment on Leviticus 10)

*Hirsch*

Rabbi Samson R. Hirsch criticizes Nadab and Abihu for similar reasons. He explains that Judaism is a tradition of laws and commandments given to bond the community together as a sacred people. When individuals act out of their own zeal to change or break the law, they end up disrupting community expectations and unity. Nadab and Abihu may have been dedicated priests, as Wessely argues, but they endangered community discipline and trust with their new and "alien" fire.

Hirsch goes on to identify the actions of Nadab and Abihu with modern Reform and Conservative rabbis who make changes in Jewish tradition. He comments: "We can understand that the death of

the priestly youths . . . is the most solemn warning for all future priests (rabbis) . . . against . . . every expression of caprice and every subjective idea of what is right and becoming! Not by fresh inventions, even of God-serving novices (students), but by carrying out that which is ordained by God has the Jewish priest (rabbi) to establish the authenticity of his activities." (Commentary on Leviticus 10:1)

Disturbed by the rising tide of Reform leaders, who called for more flexibility in interpreting the meaning of Torah and Jewish law and for changes in the law to make it more relevant to modern Jewish experience, Hirsch condemns "reformers" for bringing "alien fire" into the sanctuary. He identifies them as the Nadabs and Abihus of his time.

Most Reform and Conservative Jewish leaders would defend themselves by pointing out that Jewish law has never been static, inflexible, or resistant to change. In every generation, Jews have sought to shape the laws of Torah to meet contemporary needs. Jewish practice is dynamic, always evolving to meet new circumstances and situations. Instead of being Nadabs and Abihus, "reformers" view themselves as carrying on the Torah traditions of Akiba, Hillel, Maimonides, and Rashi by reverently reinterpreting and expanding the meanings and relevance of Torah.

Having surveyed a variety of observations, we are left to decide why Nadab and Abihu were punished. Was it ruthless ambition, arrogance, insensitivity, or the failure to consult others and to honor elders? Was it youthful zeal, blind faith, or the failure to realize the dangers in changing rituals and practices of a community? As we have seen, Jewish commentators see in this sad tale significant ethical and social lessons that continue to challenge Torah interpreters today.

## PEREK BET: *Different Views on Kashrut—the Jewish Art of Eating*

As we have already noted in our discussion of the Torah's laws against the eating of blood (see *Parashat Tzav, Perek Bet*), Jewish tradition links "holiness" with "diet." *Parashat Shemini* presents a list of foods that are permitted for eating and a list of foods that are forbidden. These lists, together with the prohibition against eating blood, form the basis for *kashrut*, or "laws relating to approved Jewish diet."

When we refer to a food as *kosher* (from the Hebrew *kasher*, meaning "proper" or "fit"), we mean any food fit for eating according to Jewish law. The term *terefah* (from the Hebrew *toraf*, meaning "torn to pieces") describes any food unfit for consumption or any utensil that may have become contaminated and is, therefore, unfit for use in the preparation or eating of food.

The Torah permits the eating of all animals with cloven hoofs that chew the cud. The pig is not permitted because it does not chew the cud. All fish with fins and scales may be eaten. Shark and shrimp are not permitted because they have no scales. Some rabbinic authorities permit the eating of sturgeon and swordfish while others do not. There are twenty-four kinds of fowl permitted for eating. They are not birds of prey; all of them have one toe larger than the others; they have a crop and a gizzard with an inner lining that can easily be removed. The Torah also permits the eating of locusts as long as they have four wings, feet, and jointed legs.

All "creeping things," including the weasel, mouse, "great lizard," gecko, land crocodile, lizard, sand lizard, and chameleon, are forbidden foods. So are snakes, scorpions, worms, and insects. The Torah also forbids the eating of any foods that have been contaminated by contact with prohibited animals, carcasses, or decomposed foods. (See Abraham Chill, *The Mitzvot*, pp. 173–180.)

*Kashrut* also includes the separation of all milk and meat products as well as utensils used in their preparation or serving. The Torah forbids "boiling a kid in its mother's milk." (See Exodus 23:19; 34:26; and Deuteronomy 14:21.) To make certain that this prohibition was observed, the rabbis of the *Mishnah* forbade the mixing of all milk and meat. They also designated a waiting period of six hours between eating meat and milk and a waiting period of three hours between milk and meat. (Some authorities say that one hour between milk and meat is permissible.) (See Abraham Chill, *The Mitzvot*, pp. 113–115.)

---

> **Kosher terms**
> *What is referred to as* milchik *in Yiddish,* de'lehe *in Ladino, and* chalavi *in Hebrew is any food containing a dairy product.* Fleishik *in Yiddish,* de'carne *in Ladino, and* besari *in Hebrew is any food product derived from a meat substance.* Pareve *is a neutral food, containing neither meat nor milk products, which can be eaten with either meat or milk foods.*

What explanation is given for this emphasis upon diet in Jewish tradition? Why does the Torah, and subsequent Jewish law, place such importance upon *kashrut* or the art of eating?

Rabbi Bernard J. Bamberger notes in his commentary to Leviticus that "most peoples have some food taboos." Americans, for example, do not eat horse meat. Buddhists avoid all animal food. Hindus look upon the cow as sacred and do not eat beef. Studies of ancient cultures in Syria and Mesopotamia also reveal dietary codes reflecting an understanding of what might be considered "unhealthy" and "healthy" foods. (See *The Torah: A Modern Commentary*, Union of American Hebrew Congregations, New York, 1981, pp. 808–813.)

Rambam (*Maimonides*)

Physician and commentator Moses Maimonides believed that "food that is forbidden by the laws of Torah is unfit for human consumption." Quoting the rabbis of the Talmud, he writes, "The mouth of the pig is as dirty as dung itself." Regarding the prohibited fat of the intestine, Maimonides comments that "it makes us full, interrupts the digestion, and produces cold and thick blood." As for mixing meat and milk, he says that the result "is undoubtedly gross food and makes the person overfull." (*Guide for the Perplexed* 3:48)

The author of *Sefer ha-Hinuch* (possibly Aharon Halevi) agrees with Maimonides' medical approach. He argues that "our perfect Torah separated us from harmful factors. This is the common-sense reason for the Torah's dietary prohibitions. If the harmful character of some of these forbidden foods is unknown to us or to medical science, do not be puzzled since the True Physician (God) who warned us regarding them is wiser than us about them." (#73)

Many interpreters of Torah disagree with Maimonides and the author of *Sefer ha-Hinuch*. Speaking for them, Isaac Arama strongly denounces any hygienic justifications of the Torah's laws. "We would do well," he warns, "to bear in mind that the dietary laws are not, as some have asserted, motivated by medical considerations. God forbid! Were that so, the Torah would be denigrated to the status of a minor medical study and worse than that."

Arama feared that, if the Torah's laws about forbidden foods were reduced to medical suggestions, with the discovery of a medical cure for the harm caused by a particular food, there would be no further reason for the Torah prohibition to be observed. The effect would make the Torah "superfluous." Afraid of such a conclusion, Arama argues that the Torah is not a medical text. Its purpose, he says, is to teach us how to live a life of "holiness."

Most interpreters would agree with Arama, pointing out that a medical or dietary justification for the laws of *kashrut* is indefensible. While some laws make sense in terms of hygiene, the Torah also forbids the eating of many foods that present no danger at all to human beings. (Crab, scallops, shrimp, catfish, shark, swordfish, pork, to mention a few.) Furthermore, the separation of milk and meat products does not seem to be justified by any dietary or medical consideration.

*Abravanel*

For these reasons, Abravanel, agreeing with Arama, concludes that "the Torah did not come to take the place of a medical handbook but to protect our spiritual health." He declares that foods forbidden by the Torah and by the rabbis who developed the dietary laws of Jewish tradition "poison the pure and intellectual soul, clogging the human temperament, demoralizing the character, promoting an unclean spirit, defiling in thought and deed, driving out the pure and holy spirit. . . ." In other words, they bring spiritual trouble—disaster—to those who consume them!

Unfortunately, Abravanel never explains how the forbidden foods of the Torah lead to such moral and intellectual corruption. However, other interpreters make a connection between the dietary laws and "spiritual health."

The philosopher Philo explains that the dietary laws teach human beings to control their bodily appetites. For instance, the law permitting the eating only of animals that have divided hoofs and chew their cud contains a special message: It teaches that a person will reach true wisdom only by learning to divide and distinguish various ideas from one another and by "chewing over" the facts and concepts that may have been gained through study. (*The Special Laws*, IV, 97f.)

A chasidic teacher, Levi Isaac of Berdichev, also offers an interpretation for the laws of *kashrut* that pertains to "spiritual health." He points out that the laws concerning permitted and forbidden foods have to do with what one allows to enter the mouth. If there is no discipline concerning what one eats, if one is careless about consuming forbidden foods, it is likely that one may also be insensitive and careless about what one says, about slandering and lying, about what comes out of the mouth. *Kashrut*, for Levi Isaac, is not only about food; it is also meant to help us keep our mouths clean and pure from harmful talk.

David Blumenthal elaborates on Levi Isaac's observation. "Keeping kosher is a way of preparing oneself to receive the word of God. It is a way of cultivating the bodily habits that will make one a fit receptacle for the Divine Presence." In other words, observing the dietary laws sensitizes one to all the other laws of Torah. It leads to the observance of them, and [it] leads one to be more open to the spiritual message of Judaism. (*God at the Center*, Harper and Row Publishers, Inc., San Francisco, 1987, pp. 60–82)

*Steinsaltz*

Rabbi Adin Steinsaltz makes a similar observation. He argues that all the laws pertaining to *kashrut* "are based on the principle that a man cannot live a higher, nobler life of the spirit without having the body undergo some suitable preparation for it." For Steinsaltz body and soul are connected. What a person eats influences feelings, responses, and readiness to unite with influences of good or evil in the world. Observing the dietary laws, says Steinsaltz, makes one more sensitive to holiness and to the tasks of bringing "all things in the world to the state of *Tikkun* or perfection. . . ." (*The Thirteen Petalled Rose*, Basic Books, New York, 1980, pp. 163–165)

*Luzzatto*

In contrast to those who argue that the laws of *kashrut* protect and promote "spiritual health," other commentators argue that they are a means of separating Jews from non-Jews. Samuel David Luzzatto observes that "every Jew must be set apart in laws and ways of life from other nations so as not to imitate their behavior . . . the laws we observe make us remember at every moment the God who commanded them. . . . The numerous mitzvot and laws of our Torah accustom human beings to exercise self-control. . . ." Luzzatto's point is clear. The dietary laws are a way of preventing Jews from abandoning their faith by falling into the imitation of non-Jewish customs. Since eating is a constant activity, a natural process, observing *kashrut* will become a constant reminder of the unique values, traditions, and obligations of Jewish living.

Mordecai M. Kaplan agrees with Luzzatto but extends his conclusions about the power of the dietary laws to the preservation of the Jewish people. Kaplan explains that the purpose of *kashrut* is to make "the people of Israel aware of its dedication to God as a priestly or holy people." However, argues Kaplan, that purpose has expanded over the centuries. "*Kashrut* has contributed to the perpetuation of the Jewish people and the retention of its way of life."

In other words, the dietary laws regulating what a Jew shall and shall not eat are a means of preserving Jewish identity and Jewish loyalty. *Kashrut*, Kaplan concludes, "is particularly effective in lending Jewish atmosphere to the home, which, in the Diaspora, is our last-ditch defense against the inroads of assimilation." In Kaplan's view, the benefit of *kashrut* is neither medical nor symbolic. *Kashrut* is an effective means of guaranteeing Jewish survival.

Milton Steinberg expands Kaplan's argument. The dietary laws, he says, have "high survival-value for the Jewish group, serving as a reminder to Jews of their identity and as a deterrent to their being swallowed up by the non-Jewish world. Judaism, like all minority faiths, stands constantly in the peril of being absorbed into oblivion. Only on a foundation of preservative group practices can it persevere in its higher aims." The dietary laws of Judaism are, therefore, a means to an end. Observance of them preserves the Jewish people against assimilation so that it can pursue its task of enriching the world through its ethical and spiritual values. (*Basic Judaism*, Harcourt Brace, New York, 1947, pp. 117–118)

As we have seen, the Jewish view of diet differs from that of other cultures. While the Torah forbids some foods and allows others, the dietary laws are not based upon hygienic or medical considerations. Many of the foods that are considered "abominable," or *terefah*, in the Jewish diet are not only considered safe for eating but are even considered staples in other peoples' diets. The laws of *kashrut*, according to most of our commentators, excepting Maimonides, are meant not to guard Jews from poisonous foods but to serve as a means through which the Jewish people attains *kedushah*, or "holiness," "separation," and "uniqueness."

# QUESTIONS FOR STUDY AND DISCUSSION

1. Aaron's reaction to the death of his sons, Nadab and Abihu, is silence. What do you sup-

pose he was thinking? Which of the interpretations we have noted would be closest to his? Why?

2. Rashi and other commentators fault Nadab and Abihu for not consulting before bringing their offering to the sanctuary. Why are they so harsh on the sons of Aaron for not seeking the approval of Moses? What is so wrong about acting independently, spontaneously, and enthusiastically?

3. Author Gail Sheehy observes: "The new young men do not want to work hard. They demand more time for personal growth than for any other purpose in life. They dream of achieving the perfectly balanced life in which there is time for love and leisure and children and personal expression and playing lots of tennis. Their new happiness formula is expressed in a startling shift of values. Highest on the list of personal qualities these young men consider important is 'being loving.' Dismissed to the bottom of the list of qualities they care to cultivate are 'being ambitious' and 'being able to lead effectively.' " (*Pathfinders,* William Morrow, New York, 1981, p. 42) How would you describe yourself and your parents in terms of such a "happiness formula"?

4. A question is raised about whether or not garfish is considered *kosher.* It has microscopic scales and a split tail, which would argue for its acceptance. Modern rabbinic scholars have rejected the garfish as *kosher,* however, because its scales are not "visible to the naked eye." Given the various reasons for the dietary laws by the commentators, why should it matter whether or not one eats garfish?

5. In discussing reasons for observing *kashrut,* the following reasons have been presented: (a) uplifting ("sanctifying") and imposing discipline on eating; (b) identification and solidarity with the worldwide Jewish community; (c) the ethical discipline of avoiding certain foods . . . because of scarcity of food in parts of the world; (d) living by the authority of Jewish law; (e) desire to have all Jews able to eat in your home. (Simeon J. Maslin, editor, *Gates of Mitzvah,* Central Conference of American Rabbis, 1979, p. 132) Which of these reasons makes the best sense to you? Why?

# PARASHAT TAZRIA-METZORA
## *Leviticus 12:1–15:33*

---

*Parashat Tazria-Metzora* is one of seven designated Torah portions that, depending upon the number of Sabbaths in a year, is either read as two separate portions or combined to assure the reading of the entire Torah. While this volume will combine them, it will present an interpretation on each of their most important themes.

*Parashat Tazria* presents the rituals of purification for a woman after childbirth and the methods for diagnosing and treating a variety of skin diseases.

*Parashat Metzora* continues the discussion of skin diseases and the purification rituals for a person cured of them. Attention is given also to the appearance and treatment of fungus or mildew in the home and to the ritual impurity resulting from contact with the discharge of sexual organs.

---

## OUR TARGUM

### · 1 ·

Moses tells the people that after the birth of a son a woman will remain in a state of impurity for thirty-three days, and if she bears a daughter for a period of sixty-six days. Afterwards she will bring a lamb for a burnt offering and a pigeon or turtledove for a sin offering. If, however, she cannot afford a lamb, she shall give the priest of the sanctuary two turtledoves for the offering.

### · 2 ·

When a person notices a swelling, rash, or discoloration that develops into a scaly infection, it must be reported to the priests, who also function as physicians. If, in examining the infected area, the priests notice that the hair within it has turned white and the infection is deeper than the skin, they are to declare the person *tzara'at*, meaning "infected with a serious skin disease." *Tzara'at* may refer to such skin ailments as eczema, psoriasis, impetigo, or leprosy. Such an infected person is considered *tamei*, or "impure."

However, if the infection does not appear

public, that person was to call out, "Unclean! Unclean!" so that others might be protected from infection and impurity.

· 3 ·

The same examination and rules applied to the discovery of an infection, or mold, on garments. After a seven-day period, if the garment was still infected, it was to be either washed or burned.

· 4 ·

Moses also describes the ceremonies for welcoming the cured *tzara'at* back into the community after healing was confirmed by the priests. The cured *tzara'at* is to bathe, shave all the body hair, and wash his or her garments. Special offerings of lambs and birds are then to be presented at the sanctuary. Afterwards the *tzara'at* is pronounced cured and able to reenter the community and participate in all its sacred rituals.

If, however, the person is poor and cannot afford the required offerings, a reduced number is acceptable. The principle followed here is that a person will offer "depending upon his or her means—whichever he or she can afford."

· 5 ·

Moses also instructs the people about what to do if mold or fungus is discovered in the home. In that case, the priests are to quarantine the house for seven days. If the mold remains, they will order either the walls removed or the entire structure destroyed. After seven days, if the mold is gone, repairs are to be made on the home and offerings brought to the sanctuary.

· 6 ·

Regulations concerning the infection of sexual organs are also given to the people. Such infections, like *tzara'at*, make a person unclean. Bedding, clothing, or objects touched by an infected person are to be washed. Anyone who has touched the infected person, or who has used an object touched by that person, shall wash his or her body and clothes. He or she will remain unclean until evening. As with *tzara'at*, the people are told to wait seven days to make sure that the person infected is cured. Similar regulations are followed in the case of the emission of semen by men or

deeper than the skin and the hair of the area has not turned white, the priests are to isolate the person for seven days. At the end of seven days, the person is to undergo another examination. If the discoloration is fading, the priests will pronounce that person cured and clean. Should the area remain infected, the person is to be quarantined for another seven days. Afterwards he or she is to be reexamined and pronounced either impure or clean.

Similar examinations were to be performed for scaly infections, for the appearance of a white discoloration of skin streaked with red, for an infection resulting from a burn by fire, or for an infection on the head or beard. In all these cases, priests were to isolate those infected for seven days and then reexamine them. If the infection had healed, the person was considered clean. If not, the person was pronounced *tzara'at*, or "infected," and, therefore, unclean.

A person declared *tzara'at* and unclean was to wear torn clothes similar to those worn by a person in mourning and was not to wear a head covering. Whenever such an infected person appeared in the discharge of menstrual blood by women, which, in ancient times, were signs of impurity.

Offerings at the sanctuary are to be made to celebrate the end of the impurity.

## THEMES

*Parashat Tazria-Metzora* contains two important themes:

1. Medical-ritual practices and ethics.
2. The sin of slander.

## PEREK ALEF: *Biblical Medicine, Ritual, and Ethics*

*Parashat Tazria-Metzora* presents us with what seems like a discussion of skin diseases and bodily infections. We are told that, upon finding a swelling, rash, or discoloration on the skin that results in a scaly infection, a person is to report the problem to the priest. This is also to be done if a person notices loss of hair, fungus on clothing, or mold on the walls of a home.

All these are signs of *tzara'at,* a variety of skin diseases, and of being considered *tamei,* "unclean" or "impure." The same applies to a person whose sexual organs are infected. In all these situations, waiting periods of healing are prescribed, as are ritual offerings at the sanctuary after one has been cured and pronounced "clean."

In these chapters of Leviticus we have an important view of ancient medicine and ritual. The priest functions not only in his religious role but also as a kind of diagnostician. As modern biblical scholar Baruch A. Levine notes, the priest "combined medical and ritual procedures in safeguarding the purity of the sanctuary and of the Israelite community, which was threatened by the incidence of disease. He instructed the populace and was responsible for enforcing the prescribed procedures." (Baruch A. Levine, editor, *JPS Torah Commentary: Leviticus,* Jewish Publication Society, Philadelphia, 1989, p. 75)

Most Torah interpreters throughout the ages, however, have not considered these chapters about skin infection to be a collection of "medical instructions." Priests prescribe rituals; they do not dispense treatments or medication. Even the use of quarantine regulations shows very little regard for guaranteeing public health. They are more a form of ritual than a means of isolating sick people. For instance, there is no mention of preventing healthy people from contact with the contents of a house where disease has been discovered.

If, as most interpreters suggest, these commandments having to do with infections are not strictly "medical instructions," then what significance did they have to the people of Israel?

The ancients were undoubtedly baffled by skin diseases. Swellings, rashes, boils, and skin discolorations must have frightened and bewildered them. So did molds and fungi on the walls of homes or infections associated with sexual organs. Often they watched these symptoms progress into terminal diseases. Knowing little about the cause or treatment of such infections, they concluded that they must be the result of God's displeasure and that they endangered both the individual infected and the community.

That may explain why those diagnosed with such infections, or those whose homes were discovered with a threatening fungus, were labeled "unclean" and isolated from the rest of the community. In ancient times such people were considered "cursed" by God and "impure." Touching them, or anything that they may have touched, could spread the "curse" to others.

The important matter here, however, was not only looking for signs that the infected person had been cured but guaranteeing the community that the "curse" would not doom everyone. For that reason, priests not only examined the infected person or home, but they also conducted special rituals in the sanctuary celebrating the end of the infection. Their medical-ritual procedures were meant not only to provide some elementary sanitary safety for the community but, more significantly, to save the community from spreading among them what they understood as God's curse.

Because the diagnosis of such infections and the rituals celebrating their conclusion affected everyone in the community, the services of priests had to be accessible and the costs of sanctuary offerings had to be affordable to everyone. Essentially, public need necessitated ethical and economic fairness. If the offerings required by the infected person could not be brought to the sanctuary because they were not affordable, the entire community might suffer a continuing curse.

For that reason, the Torah commands that, if a person is poor and cannot afford to bring birds, lambs, hyssop, cedar wood, crimson stuff, choice flour and oil as offerings for the altar of the sanctuary, "one lamb, one-tenth of a measure of choice flour with oil mixed in, and two turtledoves or pigeons—within his means—" may be acceptably substituted. In this way, the poor were made equal to those who could afford the medical-ritual procedures required. This reduction in the cost of offerings for the poor is mentioned several times in the Torah. (Leviticus 5:7–10; 14:21; 27:8)

The Torah identifies six categories of wrongdoing for which individuals were to bring offerings to the sanctuary: (1) a person who swears he has testimony to give but does not; (2) a person who promises to do a certain thing but does not; (3) a ritually unclean person who takes something forbidden or (4) who enters the sanctuary; (5) a woman in labor who swears that she will never again have intercourse with her husband; and (6) a person who suffers from a skin disease because of slandering others.

For such wrongdoing special offerings were required. Yet, in each situation, the Torah provides against financial discrimination. If the person who sinned is poor and cannot afford the offerings required, special provisions are made. Other less expensive sacrifices are substituted and are acceptable. The guiding principle of Jewish ethics, whether in the area of ritual or medicine, is equal treatment for the poor and rich. Each human being is created in God's image. The offerings of each person, rich or poor, are of equal value to God.

---

**The poor belong to God**
*The poor are called the people of God, as the sages expounded: "If you lend money to any of My people . . ." Who are "My people"? They are the poor, as it is said, "For the Eternal has comforted the people and has compassion upon the*
*poor among them." At times a person who is rich does not pay attention to poor relatives. . . . However, this is not so with God. . . . God cares for the poor. The proof of this is what Isaiah has said: "The Eternal has founded the city of Zion, and in her the poor of God's people take refuge."* (*Bachya ben Asher*, Kad ha-Kemach, *Charles B. Chavel, translator, pp. 533–534*)

 *Hirsch*

In his commentary on Leviticus, Rabbi Samson Raphael Hirsch explains the reason for making these offerings of the poor affordable. The "poverty-stricken and suffering people," he writes, "often presume that they have been forsaken by God's care, abandoned by God." As a result, "they abandon themselves, give themselves up to despair . . . lose their self-respect. . . . They fall because they have given up all thoughts of betterment." In commanding that the offerings be made affordable to the poor, the Torah demonstrates that the poor are as important to God as the rich. They and their offerings are equally sacred and acceptable. God has not forsaken them. (See comments on Leviticus 5:13ff.)

Commenting on charitable gifts of the poor, Rabbi Hillel Silverman draws a parallel to the offerings once given in the sanctuary. "Every Jew is enjoined to contribute offerings according to his or her individual means. The wealthy bring more; the poor bring what they can. In the words of the Talmud: 'But one and the same are the generous and the meager offering, provided that a person's intention and sincerity are directed to God.' [*Berachot* 5b] . . . We should understand that the small gift of the less affluent person may be a far greater sacrifice than the large gift of the wealthy donor. A contribution of time and service given with *kavanah* [enthusiasm] is even more valuable than material gifts." (*From Week to Week*, p. 105)

Jewish tradition seeks to heighten sensitivity to the plight of the poor without ever robbing them of their dignity. Perhaps that explains why the Torah insists on affordable sacrifices for those who must bring sin offerings to the sanctuary but who are impoverished. There was to be no discrimination, no special access by the rich to the priests of the sanctuary who examined for skin diseases and conducted the rituals for declaring a person cured and ready for reentry into the community. Rich and poor were to be treated alike. Their gifts were of equal importance to God.

## PEREK BET: *The Sin of Slandering Others*

As we have already noted, the Torah and its interpreters present neither a medical diagnosis nor treatment for the skin disorders of their times. While the ancient priests examined infections on the body or fungi in the home, they did not prescribe any medicine or therapy for healing. They did determine a period for quarantine, which may have been unrelated to the fear of passing the infection from one person to another. Instead, the isolation of the infected person seems to grow out of a concern for guarding the community against people who were "unclean" or "impure" because of some wrongdoing.

It is for that reason that the offering brought by a person who has been cured of a skin disease, or whose home has been infected, is called a "sin" offering. The rituals of the offerings in the sanctuary are meant to celebrate "purification," the end of being considered unclean. All such wrongdoings that cause infections are forgiven through the sacrifices and offerings brought to the priest at the sanctuary.

Many commentators ask: "What was the wrongdoing or the sin that brought on such serious infections and prompted the emergency procedure of quarantine?"

In answering that question, interpreters focus attention upon the record of major biblical personalities who are said to have been afflicted with *tzara'at*, or "skin disorders."

*Rashi*

Rashi, for example, points out that Moses suffered from a serious skin disease after he complained to God that the people of Israel would

not listen to him. Because he implied that the people refused to follow God's commandments, Moses was punished. The Torah says that "his hand became infected, as white as snow." (See comment on Exodus 4:1–6.)

Earlier rabbinic tradition argues that Miriam, the sister of Moses and Aaron, was stricken with a skin disease because she slandered her brothers by gossiping about their relationships with their wives. "They are busy leading the people and make no time to spend at home," the rabbis accuse her of saying. They also point out that she embarrassed Moses publicly by questioning his marriage to a Cushite woman and by implying that she was as important a prophet as he was. For her gossip, slander, and public accusations, say the rabbis, Miriam was punished with a serious skin infection. (See Numbers 12:1–13; also *Leviticus Rabbah* 16:1.)

*Zugot*

Rabbi Yochanan, quoting Rabbi Yosi ben Zimra, warns that "spreading *leshon ha-rah*—slander, lies, or misinformation—is identical to denying the power of God." God commands honesty and the truth. If a person is dishonest, God's desire is undermined. Such a person, says Rabbi Yochanan, will be punished with skin infections.

---

**The talebearer is a cannibal**
*Teaching the power of gossip to do harm, the Talmud comments that "the gossiper stands in Syria and kills in Rome." (Jerusalem Talmud, Peah 1:1)*

*Have you heard something about someone? Let it die with you. Be of good courage, it will not harm you if it ends with you. (Ben Sira 19:10)*

*Your friend has a friend, and your friend's friend has a friend, so be careful of what you say. (Ketubot 109b)*

> *Where there is no wood, a fire goes out;*
> *Where there is no whisper, a quarrel dies down.*
> *(Proverbs 26:20)*

At another time, Rabbi Samuel bar Nachmeni, quoting Rabbi Yochanan, argues that "the serious skin infections mentioned by the Torah are the result of seven kinds of wrongdoing: slander, bloodshed, perjury, adultery, arrogance, misappropriation, and meanness." Several examples are given: Joab is punished with skin disease because he murders Abner. (IISamuel 3:29) Gehazi is inflicted because he lies to Na'aman. (IIKings 5:23) Pharaoh is penalized because he takes Sarah away from her husband, Abraham. (Genesis 12:17) King Azariah is inflicted with skin disease because he seeks to appropriate the priesthood under his power. (IIChronicles 26:16) For the rabbis, all these examples prove that *tzara'at* is the result of wrongdoing. (*Arachin* 15b–16a)

 *Rambam (Maimonides)*

It should not surprise us that Moses Maimonides agrees. The great physician and Torah interpreter maintains that "*tzara'at* [skin disease] is not a natural phenomenon but rather a sign and wonder for the people of Israel to warn them against *leshon ha-ra*—evil talk."

Obadiah Sforno enlarges upon Maimonides' observation, arguing that the quarantine ordered by the priest is meant to prompt a person to ask God's forgiveness for his or her sins. The quarantine is a time to reconsider one's actions, both the intentional and the unintentional ones. In confronting one's shortcomings, honestly scrutinizing one's treatment of others, there is chance for personal improvement and repentance. In this way the affliction of *tzara'at* leads to isolation, which leads to repentance, which brings about God's forgiveness for wrongdoing and the rehabilitation of each sinful human being. (See comments on Leviticus 14:21.)

 *Leibowitz*

Nehama Leibowitz extends Sforno's logic in a different way. She quotes the Talmud's observation that "the house affected by *tzara'at* . . . exists for the purpose of education." In other words, she says that "the plague teaches us that society should take notice of the first sign of misconduct, however small. Just the same as a disease begins with hardly noticeable symptoms and can be stopped if detected in time, so a moral disease in society can be prevented from spreading if immediate steps are taken. Otherwise it will spread throughout the community." (*Studies in Vayikra*, pp. 137–138)

 *Peli*

Pinchas Peli also links the sin of *leshon ha-ra* to the skin infections and fungus mentioned in our Torah portion. He defines *leshon ha-ra* as "slander, gossip, talebearing, and all the other forms of damage to the individual and society that may be caused by words." The result of such wrongdoing, says Peli, is a "justly deserved punishment—leprosy, an illness that cannot be hidden."

---

*Dangers of the tongue*
*The Book of Proverbs (18:21) teaches: "Death and life are in the hands of the tongue. . . ." One who loves the tongue and uses it to speak words of Torah and commandments will be justly rewarded, but one who speaks slander brings upon himself much sorrow. (Tze'enah u-Re'enah, comment on Leviticus 14:1–2)*

*A person may think, "Of what importance are my words? A word has no substance, neither can it be seen or touched. . . ." It is true that words have no substance and cannot be seen, but, like the wind, they can cause entire worlds to crash. (A.Z. Friedman, Wellsprings of Torah, 2 vols., Judaica Press, New York, 1969, p. 234)*

> *Eleazar Ha-Kappar taught: "If you slander others, you will also commit other such wrongdoing."* (Derech Eretz, *chap. 7*)

Why is the punishment so harsh? Peli explains: "Jewish tradition sees a lethal weapon in the evil tongue and minces no words in its condemnation. The Talmud equates speaking *leshon ha-ra* with flagrant atheism, with adultery, and with murder. In fact, it is worse than murder since it simultaneously destroys three people: the one who relates the gossip, the one who listens to it, and the one it concerns." (*Torah Today,* B'nai B'rith Books, Washington, D.C., 1987, pp. 127–131)

As we have discovered, most commentators connect the skin infections and the outbreak of fungus on clothing or in homes with the sins of an evil tongue. While today we may reject the connection, seeing no medical evidence between such afflictions and what people say or do, Torah interpreters still leave us with much to consider.

The spread of lies, gossip, slander, character assassination, derogatory statements, and fraudulent stories can infect society and destroy human lives. Drawing a parallel to the spread of contagious and dangerous disease, the commentators warn about the damage such evil talk can bring to individuals and society. Learning to quarantine such evil and to cure ourselves from the temptations of *leshon ha-ra* are still significant challenges today.

## QUESTIONS FOR STUDY AND DISCUSSION

1. The Torah teaches that there must be no financial discrimination between rich and poor when it comes to the purchase of offerings for sacrifice in the Temple. The offerings must be affordable to all for the dignity of every human soul is precious to God. How would you extend this ethical principle to synagogue membership and to the cost of health care, hospital insurance, and education?

2. The *Zohar Hadash* teaches that "if a person be in debt to God because of his or her sins, God does not consider it a debt because poverty often misleads a person's powers for reasoning." (Comment on Leviticus 49) Is this so? How may such an argument justify accepting less from the poor by way of an offering for wrongdoing?

3. Rabbi Yannai told of a peddler who went from town to town crying out: "Who wants to purchase the secret of guaranteeing a long and happy life?" When he challenged the peddler to prove that he possessed such a secret, the peddler opened a Hebrew Bible to the Book of Psalms. He then pointed to the words: "Guard your tongue from evil, your lips from deceitful speech. . . ." (34:14; *Leviticus Rabbah* 16:2) Compare Rabbi Yannai's lesson to the dangers of slander emphasized by other Jewish commentators.

4. The Talmud asks the question: "Why does the sin offering of those with skin diseases consist of birds?" In answer, we are told: "Because the sin of such persons is gossip. They are chirping all the time. Therefore, their offering must remind them of their wrongdoing—warn them of how dangerous it is to engage in gossip." (*Arachin* 16a) Why do the teachers of Jewish ethics consider gossip and slander such serious offenses?

# PARASHAT ACHARE MOT-KEDOSHIM
## *Leviticus 16:1–20:27*

*Parashat Achare Mot-Kedoshim* is one of seven designated Torah portions that, depending upon the number of Sabbaths in a year, is either read as two separate portions or combined to assure the reading of the entire Torah. While this volume will combine them, it will present an interpretation on each of their most important themes.

*Parashat Achare Mot,* which means "after the death of," recalls the death of Nadab and Abihu, Aaron's sons. It describes the rituals for the sin offerings that Aaron is to present in the sanctuary for himself and the people. Mention is made of Yom Kippur, or "Day of Atonement." Laws regarding forbidden sexual relations are also presented.

*Parashat Kedoshim,* which means "holiness," lists those ritual and ethical laws that, if followed, will make the Jewish people a "holy" people.

## OUR TARGUM

### · 1 ·

Parashat Achare Mot begins by referring briefly to the death of Aaron's sons, Nadab and Abihu, who had entered the sanctuary without permission and with foreign fire for the altar. God instructs Moses to tell Aaron that he alone is permitted to enter the inner sanctuary, the Holy of Holies. When he enters, he is to dress with special linen garments and to bring a sin offering for himself, his household, and for all the people of Israel.

For himself, he is to bring a bull; for the people, two he-goats. Standing at the entrance of the sanctuary, he is to mark one of the goats "for God," and the other "for Azazel," as the "scapegoat" for the failings, mistakes, and errors of the people.

Afterwards Aaron slaughters the bull and the he-goat marked "for God," offering them upon the altar and sprinkling their blood around the altar as a means of asking God to forgive the people for their sins. When that ritual is concluded, the he-goat marked "for Azazel" is brought to Aaron. He places his hands upon it and confesses all the wrongdoing of the people. The goat is then sent off into the wilderness, where it is set free to wan-

der and to die, thereby bringing forgiveness for the people's sins.

## · 2 ·

The people are commanded to observe Yom Kippur, a "Day of Atonement." It is to be a day of fasting and complete rest, where no work is done and where the people seek forgiveness for all their sins.

## · 3 ·

Chapters 17–26 of Leviticus are known as the "Holiness Code." They contain the ritual and ethical practices that one must carry out to live a sacred or holy Jewish life.

Moses warns the people against offering any sacrifices outside the sanctuary or to any other gods. They are told that they may neither drink the blood of animals nor eat the flesh of animals killed by other animals.

## · 4 ·

Moses condemns the sexual practices of surrounding peoples and tells the Israelites they must follow God's commandments regarding family purity. These commandments include rules against debasing and shaming oneself or others by removing one's clothing or by having sexual intercourse outside of marriage or with animals. Such acts are abhorrent and defile the people of Israel.

## · 5 ·

*Parashat Kedoshim* continues the "Holiness Code" with God's commandment to the people of Israel. They are told: "You shall be holy, for I, the Lord your God, am holy." Echoing the laws given at Mount Sinai, the people are told to (1) honor their parents, (2) observe the Sabbaths and festivals, (3) refrain from worshiping idols, (4) offer sacrifices acceptably, and (5) leave corners of the field and parts of the vineyard for the poor.

They are also commanded *not to* (6) steal, (7) deal deceitfully, (8) swear falsely in God's name, (9) defraud others, (10) commit robbery, (11) keep the wages of laborers overnight, (12) insult the deaf, (13) place a stumbling block before the blind, (14) render unfair decisions in court, (15) favor the poor or rich in court decisions, (16) pass on rumors or stories about others, (17) profit from the difficulties of others, (18) hate others, (19) suffer guilt for truthfully warning others about the consequences of otheir actions, (20) take vengeance, and (21) bear a grudge.

In conclusion Moses tells them: (22) "Love your neighbor as yourself."

### ·6·

To these commandments are added others: people must not allow their animals to mate with different kinds of animals; they must not plant a field with two different kinds of seed; they must not wear garments made of two different kinds of material.

The people are presented with regulations for planting fruit trees. They are told they may eat the fruits of these trees only after five years. The people are also forbidden to eat blood, to practice magic or soothsaying, to shave off the side-growth of the beard, to cut the flesh as a way of mourning the dead, or to turn to ghosts, spirits, or to the cult of Moloch, which practiced child sacrifice. In addition, a man who has sexual relations with a slave is to pay damages to her.

The people are also instructed to show honor to the aging and love to the stranger, "for you were strangers in the land of Egypt." They are also warned against using false weights and measures and insulting parents.

### ·7·

Several laws are given regarding family relationships. Adultery, homosexuality, sexual relations with animals, and marriage to siblings, half-sisters and brothers, or former in-laws are prohibited, as are sexual relations with aunts or uncles.

The Israelites are promised that, if they observe all these commandments, they will be set apart from all nations as "holy." They will be God's people.

## THEMES

*Parashat Achare Mot-Kedoshim* contains three important themes:

1. Yom Kippur and the "scapegoat."

2. "Holiness" in Jewish tradition.

3. "Loving" others.

## PEREK ALEF: *Seeking Meaning for the Strange Ritual of the Scapegoat*

Yom Kippur, or "Day of Atonement," has been called "the climax and crown of the Jewish religious year." Through twenty-four hours of fasting and prayer, Jews are challenged to review the ethical and spiritual standards by which they live and to reaffirm their commitment to carry out the mitzvot, or "commandments," of their faith. In defining the message of Yom Kippur, Rabbi Bernard B. Bamberger writes that "it speaks to each human being and seeks to bring each person into harmony with others and with God."

The origins of Yom Kippur are shrouded in mystery. There are, however, some fascinating traditions associated with the sacred day that help us understand its popularity among the ancient Israelites. One of the most significant and baffling of these is the ceremony of the "scapegoat."

---

*Defining "scapegoat":*
*The term "scapegoat" was apparently coined by William Tyndale, the first great English Bible translator. Thereafter, it came to be used for a person, animal, or object to which the impurity or guilt of a community was formally transferred and then removed . . . in common usage today, a scapegoat is someone whom people blame for*

> *their own misfortunes, and even for their faults and sins. . . ." (Bernard J. Bamberger, The Torah: A Modern Commentary, p. 860)*

As described in the Torah, Aaron is to take two he-goats from the Israelite community as a sin offering. After he has slaughtered a bull as a sin offering for himself and his household, he is to bring the two he-goats to the entrance of the sanctuary. There he is to cast lots upon the two he-goats, designating one "for God" and the other "for Azazel." The one "for God" is to be slaughtered as a sin offering on the altar of the sanctuary. Aaron is then to place his hands upon the head of the other marked "for Azazel" and to confess all the transgressions of the Israelites upon it. Afterwards the goat is to be sent off to wander and die in the wilderness. (See Leviticus 16.)

According to the *Mishnah,* the ritual of taking the scapegoat from the Jerusalem Temple into the wilderness began as a very important ceremony, but later it became a cause for great commotion, even embarrassment. People would stand along the path and ridicule the ceremony. Some would point a finger at the goat marked "for Azazel," upon which the High Priest had confessed Israel's sins, and mockingly remark: "Such a tiny scapegoat for such a huge load of sins!" (*Yoma* 6:4)

As we may imagine, many interpreters have asked: What is the meaning of this strange ceremony? How does it relate to the religious significance of Yom Kippur?

### Ibn Ezra

Commentator ibn Ezra refers to the ritual of the scapegoat marked "for Azazel" as a "mystery." He suggests that it may be connected with a pagan religious practice of offerings to "goat-demons," which were prohibited by the Torah. Such sacrifices may have been gifts to a god many believed ruled the wilderness and was a power for bringing evil into the world. (See Leviticus 17:7.) The scapegoat was offered to protect people from evil influences.

If ibn Ezra is correct, why would Jews have used a ritual that seems to mimic pagan practices forbidden by the laws of Torah? Modern interpreter Baruch A. Levine explains that the ritual of the he-goat "for Azazel" was not considered a gift to a pagan god. Nor was it seen as a pagan rite. Instead, the scapegoat marked "for Azazel" was a dramatic means through which the Jewish people rejected the influences and temptations of evil symbolized by Azazel.

Levine argues that the sanctuary ceremony was "based on an awareness that, even in a world ruled by God, evil forces were at work—forces that had to be destroyed if God's earthly home . . . was not to be defiled."

In transferring all the sins of the people to the scapegoat and then sending it out into the wilderness marked "for Azazel," ancient Jews believed they were forcing "the iniquities of the people back on Azazel." In a way, Levine concludes, they created a "boomerang effect," returning evil influence "back to its point of departure, to the wilderness!" In doing so, they demonstrated that only God had power in their lives and that they had defeated the symbol of evil—Azazel. (*JPS Torah Commentary: Leviticus,* pp. 250–253)

Levine admits that "this entire complex of rituals seems to be predicated on magical perceptions" and that his interpretation is "unacceptable to many modern students of the Bible, as it was to certain traditional schools."

### Rambam (Maimonides)

One of those commentators is Moses Maimonides, who rejects any identification of the scapegoat with powers or angels of evil. He declares, "It is not a sacrifice to Azazel, God forbid." Instead of being a ritual with magical powers, says Maimonides, the scapegoat ceremony is an "active allegory" meant "to impress the mind of the sinner that his sins must lead him to a wasteland." When those who have broken the laws of Torah see that their sins are placed upon the he-goat and sent out into the wilderness, it is hoped that they will "break with their sins . . . distance themselves from them, and turn back to God in sincere repentance." (*Guide for the Perplexed* 3:46)

*Abravanel*

Abravanel also suggests a symbolic interpretation for the ritual of the scapegoat. He believes that the two he-goats, one marked "for God," the other marked "for Azazel," are to remind Jews of the twin brothers Esau and Jacob. Esau, like the he-goat marked "for Azazel," wandered into the wilderness away from his people, its laws, and its traditions. Jacob, like the he-goat marked "for God," lived a life devoted to God's service. According to Abravanel, when Aaron, and the High Priests after him, cast lots to decide which of the two he-goats would be marked "for God" or "for Azazel," Jews were to be reminded that they had a significant free choice to make. They could live like Jacob or Esau, "for God" or "for Azazel." (See commentary on Leviticus 16.)

*Hirsch*

**The meaning of casting lots**
*Rabbi Samson Raphael Hirsch sees in the ceremony of deciding which goat will be "for God" and which "for Azazel" a symbol of the choice each Jew makes on Yom Kippur. "We can decide* for God, *gathering together all the powers of resistance we have been given to resist everything that would tear us away from our vocation to be near to God. . . . Or we can decide* for Azazel

*and uphold, unmastered, our selfish life of desires, and . . . give ourselves over to the uncontrolled might of sensuality. . . ." (Comment on Leviticus 16:10)*

Rabbi Hillel Silverman calls attention to the fact that, according to the Talmud, the two he-goats "must be identical in size, appearance, and value." In this, he contends, is an important lesson. The two goats symbolize what we are willing to give for our own pleasure and enjoyment (for Azazel) and what we are willing to give for the welfare and security of others (for God).

The Talmud insists, says Silverman, that the two goats be identical in size, appearance, and value in order to teach the lesson that "all we devote to personal pleasure and self-aggrandizement (for Azazel) goes 'into the wilderness,' unless we also sacrifice for the Lord and 'make atonement.'" (*From Week to Week*, pp. 108–109)

In other words, the ancient ritual is not just about the "scapegoat," but it is about what is done to both he-goats. One of them ends up as a sacred sacrifice "for God," symbolizing our generosity to others and loyalty to God; the other, "for Azazel," is sent off to wander and die in the wilderness, a sign that serving only our selfish pleasures and pride is a waste of our precious potentials. It is like wasting them in the wilderness. The ritual for both he-goats on Yom Kippur is a reminder of the delicate balance, between caring about oneself and about others, that each person is challenged to achieve.

While its origins are clouded in mystery, the ceremony of the two he-goats continued until the destruction of the Temple in 70 C.E. Interest in uncovering its meaning and connection to Yom Kippur, however, has not ceased. Was it a magical way of ridding the people of Israel of its sins? Was the scapegoat, marked "for Azazel," actually sent out into the wilderness as a sacrifice to a demon or god of evil? Is the scapegoat ceremony a symbol of the various spiritual and ethical choices Jews must make on each Yom Kippur?

Perhaps, in the case of this ancient tradition of the scapegoat, we have an example where all the interpretations provided through the centuries may be correct!

## PEREK BET: *Defining "Holiness" in Jewish Tradition*

*Parashat Kedoshim* begins with God's command to the Jewish people: "You shall be holy (*kedoshim*), for I, the Lord your God, am holy (*kadosh*)." (Leviticus 19:2)

Many Torah interpreters ask what such a commandment means. Does it have to do with a special state of ritual purity? Since it is stated in the midst of a description of rituals associated with the ancient sanctuary, can it have to do with being qualified to enter the sanctuary? Is the commandment to "be holy" possible or practical? Is it realistic to expect a human being to "be holy" as God is "holy"?

Three of the oldest interpretations of the commandment to "be holy" provide some valuable answers to such questions. Rabbi Hiyya, who lived in Israel during the third century, stresses that Moses was told to present the commandment, "You shall be holy, for I, the Lord your God, am holy," to *the whole Israelite community*." The commandment was given not to a few pious priests or individuals but rather to the entire community. Achieving the state of holiness, therefore, is not something done by one person or a small group of persons but rather by the whole people.

Rabbi Levi, who taught with Rabbi Hiyya, emphasizes that the commandment to "be holy" and the section of Torah following it were presented directly to the people because "the Ten Commandments are contained in it." Rabbi Levi may be hinting that the way to holiness is through observance of all the commandments listed in this section of Torah. Seeing a parallel between the contents of the Ten Commandments given to Moses on Mount Sinai and the mitzvot presented in these chapters of Leviticus, Levi concludes that God not only commanded the people to "be holy" but stressed the particular moral way of life that would demonstrate that they were a distinct people. (*Leviticus Rabbah* 24)

The *Sifra*, a fourth-century commentary on Leviticus, echos Rabbi Levi's view. It interprets the words *kedoshim tiheyu* ("you shall be holy") as *perushim tiheyu* ("you shall be separate"). Some scholars say this is a reference to the Pharisees, who were known by the Hebrew name *Perushim*

and who taught that Jews achieved "holiness," or a special status of honor by God, if they carefully observed all the commandments.

Other interpreters argue that the authors of the *Sifra* meant to emphasize the unique responsibility of Jews to become a "kingdom of priests and a *goy kodesh,* or 'holy nation.' " They believed that, by living a Jewish life through carrying out the commandments of Torah, Jews were to be different from other nations, religions, and peoples. By interpreting the word *kedoshim* as *perushim*, the *Sifra*'s authors contend that the words "be holy" mean "be different, unique, separate from the ways of others. Be distinct in your moral and ritual way of life."

Does this mean that Jews are to withdraw from the societies in which they live or from contact with people of other religions and national origins? Modern philosopher Martin Buber says no. He writes: "Israel must, in imitating God by being a holy nation, similarly not withdraw from the world of the nations but rather radiate a positive influence on them through every aspect of Jewish living." For Buber being *kadosh,* or "different, unique," does not mean retreating from contact with other religious and national groups. Instead, it is a special goal and responsibility. It means that the Jewish people must achieve an ethical and spiritual excellence that can enrich and "influence" all other peoples. (*Darko shel Mikra,* p. 96)

Yet what is the source of that positive "influence"? What may Buber mean by "every aspect of Jewish living"?

Surveying the commandments clustered around the words "Be holy, for I, the Lord your God, am holy" provides a significant answer. Taken together they add up to a definition of "holiness" in Jewish tradition. Nearly "every aspect of Jewish living" is noted. Chapters 17–26 of Leviticus, which have become known to biblical scholars as the "Holiness Code," contain commandments that deal not only with the Sabbath, the festivals, and the different sacrifices to be offered at the sanctuary but also include commandments regulating the moral life of the Jewish community.

The list of ethical commandments encompasses nearly every aspect of human relationships. According to these commandments, Jewish morality forbids: exposure of nakedness, incest, infidelity by husband or wife, idolatry or the worship of other gods, declaring false oaths, stealing, dealing deceitfully or falsely, defrauding another, retaining a worker's wage overnight, insulting the deaf, misleading the blind, rendering unfair decisions, favoring the poor in a dispute, showing partiality to the rich in a dispute, dealing dishonestly in business, profiting by taking advantage of others' misfortune, carrying grudges, spreading hatred, taking vengeance, practicing divination, soothsaying, or turning to ghosts and spirits. On the positive side, Jewish ethics command: reverence for parents, leaving the corners of the field and some of the fruit of the vineyard for the poor and stranger, judging all people fairly, warning others who are about to commit a wrong doing, and loving others as you love yourself.

What emerges in this Torah definition of "holiness" is a unique combination of both ethical and ritual demands. When the people are commanded "Be holy," they are actually being challenged with a unique combination of moral and spiritual obligations. God demands that they live by these practices and shape their relationships and community with them. In so doing, they will become a "kingdom of priests and a holy nation." As a model of holiness, they will also inspire or, to use Martin Buber's phrase, "radiate a positive influence on them."

---

**To be holy**
*Rabbi Chaim Sofer comments that "to be holy" . . . means "not merely in the privacy of your home and ashamed of your faith in public. Be not, as the assimilationists put it, 'A Jew at home and a man outside.' Be holy 'in the community,' in public, out in the open, in society. Among your own people or in the midst of strangers, wherever you may find yourself, never be ashamed of your character and sanctity as a Jew."* (Divre Sha'are Chaim)

*Rabbi Aha explained the meaning of "be holy" by quoting the opinion of Rabbi Tanhum, the son of Rabbi Hiyyah: "If a person can protest a wrongdoing of another and does not, or if he can help support students of Torah and does not, such a person is not considered holy. But, if a person*

*does protest the wrongdoing of others and does support students of Torah, that person attains to holiness."* (Leviticus Rabbah *15:1*)

*The idea of holiness implies that what we do and what we make of our lives matters not only to us as individuals, not only to society, but to the entire cosmos. A divine purpose runs through all existence. We can ally ourselves to it or oppose it—or, perhaps, worse, we can ignore it.* (Bernard J. Bamberger, The Torah: A Modern Commentary, *pp. 891–892*)

---

The rabbis of the Talmud emphasize that each Jew has the power to add to the achievement of holiness by the people of Israel. They speak of the "influence" of those who study Torah, calling attention to two types of students. One type studies Torah, generously supports scholars, speaks kindly to others, and is honest and honorable in all business dealings. Of such a person, people say: "Such and such studies Torah. His father and his teacher deserve to be proud of him, for his deeds reflect honor upon his tradition." The other type of person studies Torah but is dishonest, unkind, and selfish. So others say: "He learns Torah, but his deeds are corrupt and objectionable. He brings dishonor to his people, to the Torah, and to God." (*Yoma* 86a)

Clearly, the rabbis of the Talmud are concerned with the reputation of the Torah and of the Jewish people. If one lives by the commandment "Be holy" and carries out the laws that define "holiness," then the people of Israel are strengthened in their responsibility to be a model of moral decency and an influence for good among all peoples. For the rabbis of the Talmud, to "be holy" means that every Jew must ask: "What are the consequences of my decisions, choices, words, and promises? Will they improve the world in which I live? Will they reflect credit upon my people, upon the Torah, and upon God?"

---

**Achieving holiness**
*To say that God is "holy" is similar to saying that He is great, powerful, merciful, just, wise. . . . In order to achieve a holiness of the kind associated with God . . . Israel would have to*

*observe His laws and commandments. The way to holiness, in other words, was for Israelites, individually and collectively, to emulate God's attributes. . . . God shows the way and Israel follows. (Baruch A. Levine, JPS Torah Commentary: Leviticus, p. 256)*

*Ramban (Nachmanides)*

Such questions may have been on the mind of Nachmanides as he thought about the meaning of the words "You shall be holy, for I, the Lord your God, am holy." In his discussion of the commandment he raises a significant point. He argues that one can carry out the commandments but also be a selfish, mean, and corrupt human being. "A person," he comments, "can be a scoundrel with the full permission of the Torah."

Proving his point, Nachmanides says a person can follow all the sexual laws mentioned in the Torah but take advantage of his own wife in satisfying his uncontrolled passions. Or a person can drink too much, eat excessively, carelessly use obscenities, or speak derisively about others. In business dealings a person can uphold the law of not wronging another but still cheat others by being unwilling to reach fair compromises.

Nachmanides believes that, because one can always find loopholes in the Torah law, people will take advantage of it. That is why the Torah not only provides a long list of commandments dealing with every aspect of ethical and ritual life but also contains the "general command" to "be holy," reminding us "to separate ourselves from those things that are permitted but that we can do without . . . from unnecessary and ugly things." To "be holy," as Nachmanides interprets it, is to refuse to take advantage of legal loopholes or overindulge in matters permitted by the Torah. (See commentary on Leviticus 19:2.)

While interpreted in a variety of ways, the words "You shall be holy, for I, the Lord your God, am holy" have been a constant challenge to the Jewish people. In some ages they influenced Jews to separate themselves from other cultures and peoples. At other times they were understood as a reminder that the highest aim of Jewish living is to reach

a "holiness" that reflects honor upon God, Torah, and the Jewish people. Today the ancient words continue to demand new interpretations and new standards for defining what is *kadosh,* or "holy," in Jewish tradition.

## PEREK GIMEL: *Can We Love Others as Ourselves?*

*Parashat Kedoshim* contains one of the most quoted of all commandments within the Torah: "Love your neighbor as yourself." (Leviticus 19:18)

What does this statement mean? Can "love" be *commanded?* Is it possible for human beings to love others, especially outside their families, with the same level of interest and commitment that they have for themselves? What about those who come to harm us or who treat us unjustly? Can we be expected to love them as we love ourselves?

*Zugot*

One of the earliest explanations of the Torah's commandment comes in the form of a story told about Rabbi Hillel, a popular teacher of the first century B.C.E. Once a non-Jew challenged him with the promise: "I will convert to Judaism if you can teach me the whole Torah while I stand on one foot." Rabbi Hillel's response was immediate. "What is hateful to you do not do to your neighbor. That is the whole Torah. The rest is commentary. Now go and learn it." (*Shabbat* 31a)

It is obvious that Hillel preferred stating the Torah's positive commandment to "love your neighbor as yourself" in a negative way. On other occasions, Hillel also deliberately chose a negative formulation instead of a positive one. For example, he taught: "If I am not for myself, who will be for me? If I care only for myself, what am I? And, if not now, when?" (*Avot* 1:14) He also taught: "Do not separate yourself from the community. Do not be certain of yourself until the day of your death. Do not judge your neighbor until you have stood in his place. Do not say:

'When I have leisure time, I will study.' You may never have leisure time." (*Avot* 2:5)

From Hillel's statements we might conclude that he transposed the positive commandment about loving one's neighbor into a negative formulation because he was convinced that it was easier to understand. We can identify what hurts and harms us. We can say what brings us pain. Hillel's statement counsels that "loving our neighbors as ourselves" means asking, "If my neighbor did to me what I am thinking of saying or doing to him, would it hurt or harm me?" If the answer is "it would bring pain or harm," then it must be avoided.

But what if my tastes are different from my neighbor's? What if my neighbor is hurt by matters or statements that simply do not affect me at all? Is it fair to make judgments about what is hurtful or enjoyable to others from my own narrow perspective? Is it not true that "one person's meat is another person's poison"?

We are told that, when Rabbi Akiba, who considered himself a student of Rabbi Hillel, suggested that the commandment "Love your neighbor as yourself" was "the greatest principle of the Torah," his colleague ben Azzai disagreed. Ben Azzai argued that the teaching "God created man in the likeness of God" (Genesis 5:1) was a more important principle.

Ben Azzai's view is that people cannot use their own feelings or attitudes as a basis for deciding how to treat others. Preferences, tastes, and perceptions of what brings happiness and what brings pain are very different. Some people are careless about their property; others are not. Because a person may not consider a remark insulting does not mean that another will agree. "You should not say," ben Azzai explains, " 'Since I am hated, let my neighbor be similarly hated or, since I am in trouble, let my neighbor be similarly in trouble.' You should remember that both you and your neighbor were created in the likeness of God." In other words, we are to treat others with respect and love, not because we are commanded to do so, nor because we understand their feelings, tastes, or reactions to be like our own. We are to respect the rights, dignity, and feelings of others because, like us, they were created in God's likeness. (*Genesis Rabbah* 24)

> **Why should we love our neighbor?**
> *Commenting on the commandment "Love your neighbor as yourself: I am the Lord," ibn Ezra explains that one is responsible to love other human beings because the one God has created all of them. (See Leviticus 19:18.)*

Moses Maimonides also seeks to clarify what the Torah means when it commands "Love your neighbor as yourself." What is meant, says Maimonides, is that "you should love your neighbor with all the qualities and modes of love with which you love yourself." In other words, "the quality and nature of our love must be of the highest category—parallel to that which we employ in promoting our own welfare."

Maimonides, however, realizes the difficulty of the challenge of loving others. Therefore, he suggests it may not always be possible for human beings to provide an equal quantity of concern for the welfare of others. Love and concern, he counsels, are expressed in varying intensities "depending upon the circumstances." There are times when promoting the welfare of others may clash with what we believe is in our own best interest and welfare. In such cases, Maimonides suggests that the intensity and quantity of our love may be compromised. "The Torah," Maimonides concludes, "does not command the extent of our love but rather the genuine character of it."

As to the character of our love, Maimonides is quite specific. Loving your neighbor as you love yourself means visiting the sick, comforting mourners, joining a funeral procession, celebrating the marriage ceremony with bride and groom, offering hospitality, caring for the dead, or delivering a eulogy. Concluding his list of examples, Maimonides writes: "All the things that you would want others to do for you—do for your brothers and sisters." (*Mishneh Torah, Hilchot Evel 14:1*)

Like Maimonides, Nachmanides also senses that "loving" another person with the same intensity and quantity of concern that one has for oneself is not possible. He bluntly declares that "human beings cannot be expected to love their neighbors as they love their own souls." What the

Torah means by the command to "love your neighbor as you love yourself," Nachmanides argues, is that people should "wish their neighbors well in all things, just as they wish success for themselves."

Nachmanides maintains that "even if a person wishes another well in everything, in wealth, honor, learning, and wisdom, he will not want him to be absolutely equal with him. He will want to be superior to him in some ways." The Torah recognizes this truth about human beings. That is why, says Nachmanides, "the Torah condemns this form of selfishness." We are commanded "to love your neighbor as yourself" so that "we will learn to wish others success in all things, just as we wish well for ourselves—and to do so without reservations." (See discussion on Leviticus 19:18.)

*Malbim*

Rabbi Meir Lev ben Yechiel Michael, known as Malbim, disagrees with both Maimonides and Nachmanides. He argues that the matter of loving one's neighbor is not an expression of feelings or wishing others "success in all things." Instead, the commandment has to do with how one behaves toward others, with actions and not with thoughts.

Drawing upon Hillel's negative teaching and upon the philosophical writings of a contemporary, German philosopher Immanuel Kant (1724–1804), Malbim says that a person should not just wish for his neighbor what he wants for himself, namely, "advantage and protection from harm. He should endeavor to do everything that is to the advantage of his neighbor, whether in terms of bodily health or success in business . . . and it goes without saying that he should not be responsible for doing anything to his neighbor that he would not wish to be done to him. . . . For instance, if a person is prepared to harm his neighbor for the sake of his own advantage, he should ask himself whether he would wish this kind of conduct to become a universal rule." A person would say to himself: "Do I want to live

in a world where everyone is free to do what I am about to do?" (See discussion on Leviticus 19:18.)

*Peli*

### Loving is also forgiving
*Basing his observation on one first created by the Ba'al Shem Tov, Pinchas Peli writes: "It does not take much effort to love good people, nice people. The test of the fulfillment of the commandment is in loving those who are not as good and lovable in one's eyes. 'Love your fellow human—as yourself,' as you accept yourself with all your faults and shortcomings, accept others the same way." (Torah Today, p. 141)*

### Loving without qualifications
*Simcha Zissel Ziv, a teacher of the Musar, or "Ethical," movement of Judaism, writes: "The Torah demands that we promote the best interests of others. This cannot be accomplished by repressing our hatred or our rejection of them, nor by summoning up our love as a duty. Such endeavors will never bring genuine love. We simply have to love human beings as we love ourselves. We do not love ourselves because we are human beings, but our self-love comes to us naturally, without calculations, without qualifications and reservations, without any aims and ends. We never hear anybody say: 'I have already fulfilled my obligation towards myself!'—We must love others the same way, naturally and spontaneously, joyously and creatively, without set limits, purposes, or rationalizations." (As found in B.S. Jacobson,* Meditations on the Torah, *pp. 180–181)*

This idea that love for oneself and love for others are mutually connected forms the basis of modern psychologist Erich Fromm's classic work *The Art of Loving* (Harper and Row, New York, 1974). Stressing the importance of "self-love," Fromm writes, "The idea expressed in the biblical 'Love your neighbor as yourself!' implies that respect for one's own integrity and uniqueness, love for and understanding of one's own self, cannot be separated from respect and love and understanding for another individual. The love for my own self is inseparably connected with the love for any other being."

Fromm explains that "love is an activity . . . it is primarily *giving*, not receiving." In the act of giving, we do not lose, sacrifice, or "give up" that which is precious to us. Instead, giving allows us to experience our power, our vitality. "In giving," Fromm observes, "I experience my strength, my wealth, my power. This experience of heightened vitality and potency fills me with joy. I experience myself as overflowing, spending, alive. . . . Giving is more joyous than receiving . . . because in the act of giving lies the expression of my aliveness."

In defining "genuine love" as "giving," Fromm stresses that one must learn to give to oneself even before giving to others. "Love of others and love of ourselves are not alternatives. . . . Love, in principle, *is indivisible as far as the connection between 'objects' and one's own self is concerned.* Genuine love," Fromm writes, "is an expression of productiveness and implies care, respect, responsibility, and knowledge (of one's self and others). . . . It is an active striving for the growth and happiness of the loved person, rooted in one's own capacity to love. . . . If," Fromm warns, "an individual is able to love productively, he loves himself too; if he can love *only* others, he cannot love at all."

The Torah's command to "love your neighbor as yourself" continues to provoke significant questions about the meaning of love. Despite the various opinions and definitions, however, it is clear that Jewish tradition challenges us to love ourselves by striving for self-understanding, respect, and a sense of our powers for giving and to transform our love of self into a generous love for others. (pp. 18–19, 48–53)

# QUESTIONS FOR STUDY AND DISCUSSION

1. Compare the various interpretations given for the "scapegoat." Which makes the most sense? Why?

2. Jews have often been the target for hatred, the "scapegoat" for the frustrations, anger, and disappointments of others. Rabbi Milton Steinberg suggests that only Jews who are knowledgeable and proud of the "positive healthful values" of their tradition will not be "invaded by self-contempt." Such Jews would not be affected by the hatred of those who would try to make them scapegoats. Do you agree? Why?

3. How would you define "holiness" in Jewish tradition? What are its elements? What must the individual Jew do to achieve "holiness"? What must the Jewish people do?

4. Is it realistic to expect that human beings can really fulfill the commandment "Love your neighbor as yourself"? Do you agree or disagree with Erich Fromm that, unless you love yourself, you cannot really love your neighbor?

5. Rabbi Leo Baeck notes the talmudic teaching that "the person who withholds love from another is like one who rejects the service of God." Baeck comments: "To place oneself in the position of our neighbor, to understand his hope and his yearning, to grasp the needs of his heart is the presupposition of all neighborly love, the outcome of our 'knowledge' of his soul." (*The Essence of Judaism,* Schocken Books, New York, 1948, pp. 211–212) How would you compare Baeck's observations with those of Hillel, Maimonides, Nachmanides, and Malbim?

# PARASHAT EMOR
## *Leviticus 21:1–24:23*

---

*Parashat Emor* presents the laws regulating the lives of priests, who presided over the sanctuary and its sacrifices. Mention is made of the donations and offerings that are acceptable for the sanctuary. This portion also includes a calendar of celebration, including the Sabbath, Pesach, Shavuot, Rosh Hashanah, Yom Kippur, and Sukot. It concludes with the laws dealing with profanity, murder, and the maiming of others.

---

## OUR TARGUM

### ·1·

Rules concerning the holiness of priests are presented to Aaron and his sons. They are not to touch a dead body except that of an immediate relative. They are not to shave their heads or the side-growth of their beards, or deliberately cut their skin to leave marks upon it. Neither are they allowed to marry divorced women. Only one without any physical impediment can become a priest.

A priest who has a skin disease, has touched a dead body, or has had a sexual emission is considered unclean and may not officiate in the sanctuary, nor may he take donations or offerings from the people. After sunset he is to be declared clean, and he can eat once again from the donations and offerings. Lay people, except those belonging to the priests, may not eat from the donations or offerings.

All offerings, whether donated by Israelites or non-Israelites, are acceptable in the sanctuary. However, any blemished or contaminated offering is to be rejected by the priests.

Moses reminds the people that the purpose of "faithfully" observing all these commandments is to "sanctify God," to demonstrate their love and loyalty to God.

### ·2·

Moses continues by presenting the people with the *moadei Adonai*, the "sacred times or occasions [festivals] of God" that they are to observe.

The Sabbath is to be celebrated every seventh day as a time of complete rest—a day of no work.

On the evening of the fourteenth day of the first month (Nisan) and for the next seven days,

Pesach is to be celebrated. The first and last days are to be treated as sacred occasions during which work is prohibited.

Seven weeks are to be counted from the first day of Pesach until the festival of Shavuot, or "Weeks." Special offerings of grain, two bread loaves, choice flour, one bull, two rams, and seven unblemished lambs are to be brought to the priests for offerings on the fiftieth day. It is to be observed as a sacred occasion, a day of no work.

In the midst of presenting the sacred calendar of celebration, Moses reminds the people that, when they reap their harvests, they must leave the edges of the field and the gleanings of the harvest for the poor and the stranger.

He then tells the people that the first day of the seventh month (Tishri) is to be celebrated with loud blasts of a horn and is to be a sacred day of no work.

Ten days later they are to observe Yom Kippur, a sacred day of no work, of "self-denial" and fasting. It is to be a day of complete rest from evening to evening.

For seven days from the fifteenth day of the seventh month (Tishri), the festival of Sukot, or "Booths," is to be celebrated. The people are to build booths and, during the festival, reside in them as a reminder that the Israelites lived in booths when they were freed from Egyptian slavery. On the first day of the festival the people are to bring the fruit of the hadar tree, the *etrog*, or "citron"; branches of palm trees, the *lulav;* boughs of leafy trees, myrtle; and branches of willow to the sanctuary. The first and eighth days of the celebration are rest days of no work. Burnt offerings, meal offerings, sacrifices, and libations are to be brought to the sanctuary.

· 3 ·

The Israelites are also told, as they were in Exodus 27:20–21 (see *Parashat Tetzaveh*), to bring clear oil of beaten olives to fuel continually the lamps of the sanctuary.

They are also instructed to bake twelve loaves and place them in the sanctuary along with pure frankincense as a token offering for the bread. Afterwards the priests are to eat the loaves.

### ·4·

Moses reports an argument between an Israelite man and another man whose mother was an Israelite and whose father was Egyptian. The man, whose Israelite mother was a woman named Shelomith daughter of Dibri of the tribe of Dan, profaned God's name and was placed in custody.

Moses orders him to be taken outside the camp and to be stoned to death, declaring that whoever profanes God's name shall be punished with death.

He also declares that, if one person murders another, he shall be put to death. If one causes bodily harm to another, then the same will be done to him or her as punishment. In other words, declares Moses, "fracture for fracture, eye for eye, tooth for tooth." Furthermore, whoever takes the life of an animal shall make restitution for it. In all these matters, Moses tells the people, Israelites and non-Israelites shall be treated with the same standard of justice.

## THEMES

*Parashat Emor* contains two important themes:

1. The evolution and meaning of the three festivals: Pesach, Shavuot, and Sukot.
2. Eye for eye: Retribution or compensation?

## PEREK ALEF: *The Jewish Festivals: Pesach, Shavuot, and Sukot*

Rabbi Abraham Joshua Heschel observed that "Judaism is a *religion of time* aiming at *the sanctification of time.* Unlike the space-minded man to whom time is unvaried . . . homogeneous, to whom all hours are alike . . . the Bible senses the diversified character of time . . . Judaism teaches us . . . to be attached to sacred events, to learn how to consecrate sanctuaries that emerge from the magnificent stream of a year." (*The Sabbath: Its Meaning for Modern Man,* Farrar, Straus and Giroux, New York, 1951, p. 8)

*Parashat Emor* contains the calendar of sacred celebrations through which Jews have sanctified time, setting aside days for uplifting, enjoying, and sharing the meanings of human existence. Chapter 23 of Leviticus describes the weekly Sabbath, Rosh Hashanah (known within the Torah as "the first day of the seventh month" and "the day of blowing of the horn"), and Yom Kippur, as well as the three festivals of Pesach, Shavuot, and Sukot.

Both Pesach and Sukot begin on the evening of the fourteenth day of the month, at the time of the full moon, and both festivals are seven days in length. According to the Torah, the first and last days of these festivals are observed like the Sabbath: from sundown to sundown, with no work. Shavuot is also a no-work day but is celebrated on the fiftieth day after the beginning of Pesach.

---

### The Jewish calendar
*The Jewish calendar consists of 12 months with a little more than 29½ days in each month. It is a lunar calendar with each month beginning at the time of a new moon. An entire year consists of about 354⅓ days, 11 days less than the 365¼ days of the solar calendar year. As a result, every few years, an extra month is added to the Jewish calendar to make a leap year and to keep accurate the adjustment of the months to the season. This extra month is known as* Adar Sheni, *or* Adar II.

### Months and celebrations
*The Jewish calendar begins in the spring. The first month of the year is Nisan.*

| Nisan | 15–22 | —Pesach |
|---|---|---|
| | 2 | —Yom ha-Shoah |
| Iyar | 5 | —Yom ha-Atzmaut |
| | 18 | —Lag ba-Omer |
| Sivan | 6–7 | —Shavuot |
| Tamuz | 17 | —Fast Day |
| Av | 9 | —Fast Day |
| Elul | | |

| *Tishri*  | *1*     | —*Rosh Hashanah*   |
|-----------|---------|--------------------|
|           | *3*     | —*Fast Day*        |
|           | *10*    | —*Yom Kippur*      |
|           | *15–21* | —*Sukot*           |
|           | *22*    | —*Shemini Atzeret* |
|           | *23*    | —*Simchat Torah*   |
| *Cheshvan*|         |                    |
| *Kislev 25—Tevet 2* | |                   |
|           |         | —*Chanukah*        |
| *Tevet*   |         |                    |
| *Shevat*  | *15*    | —*Tu Bishvat*      |
| *Adar*    | *13*    | —*Fast Day*        |
|           | *14*    | —*Purim*           |

Just as Jewish commentators have seriously questioned the motives of biblical personalities and the reasons for the Torah's laws and commandments, they have also focused upon the meanings and evolution of Jewish holy days. What makes them "holy"? How are they unique? What do they contribute to our human quest for purpose and fulfillment?

### Probing the meaning of Pesach

There are several descriptions of Pesach within the Torah. The one found in *Parashat Emor* indicates that the celebration begins on the evening of the fourteenth day of the first month of the year and is to last seven days. The first and last days are to be celebrated, like the Sabbath, as rest days. No work is to be done on them. At the evening celebration on the fourteenth of the month, a *Pesach offering to God* is to be presented. On the fifteenth, the people are to celebrate *Chag ha-Matzot,* or "Festival of Unleavened Bread." In addition, Chapter 23 of Leviticus informs us that *matzah,* or "unleavened bread," is to be eaten by the people for the seven days of the celebration, and offerings are to be brought to the sanctuary.

Other sections of the Torah offer more information about the early Pesach festival. For example, just before the tenth and last plague is sent upon the Egyptians, Moses and Aaron are told that "this month" (the spring month of Nisan) will mark the beginning of the calendar year, in other words, the "new year." On the tenth day of the month, the head of the household will pick a lamb to be set aside until the evening of the four-

teenth day. At twilight, the lamb will be slaughtered, its blood painted on the doorpost of each Israelite house, and its flesh roasted and eaten together with *matzah* and *merorim,* or "bitter herbs." Everything not eaten is to be destroyed by fire before dawn.

We are also informed that the head of each family is to wear a cloth around his loins and sandals on his feet, and he is to hold a staff in his hand. His special costume will make him look as if he were leaving on a journey. All these observances will stimulate children to ask: "What is the meaning of this ritual?" According to the Torah, he is to explain his strange costume to them by saying: "It is the *pesach* sacrifice to the Lord, because God passed over the houses of the Israelites in Egypt when God smote [killed] the Egyptian [firstborn], but saved our houses." (Exodus 12:1–27; also Deuteronomy 16)

This early description of ceremonies on the first night of Pesach contains some of the elements that are today part of the festival's *seder* ceremony. They include the *matzah, maror,* special meal, gathering of family, and the questions asked by the young people. While the *seder* ceremony did not evolve until the second century C.E., it is clear from the beginning that Pesach commemorates the liberation of the Jewish people from Egyptian slavery. It is a reminder of how God saved their "houses" and their firstborn and rescued them from oppression. The significance of freedom was to be dramatized at the beginning of each year, and it was to be taught to all the children.

Many centuries later, Jews in the Land of Israel journeyed, at Pesach time, to Jerusalem. The heads of each household would slaughter the *pesach* sacrifice, prepare it for roasting, and then take it to a place where the family group would eat it. By the time of Hillel and Shammai (first century B.C.E.), the Pesach meal had evolved into an elaborate banquet with a special *seder,* or "order," to it. The festivities included four cups of wine; the blessings for the wine; the eating of *matzah, maror, charoset* (a mixture of chopped nuts, apples, wine, and honey); the asking of questions by the children; mention of the *afikoman* (entertainment after dessert); the retelling of the liberation from Egypt; and the singing of Psalms 113–118. (*Mishnah, Pesachim* 5, 10)

The importance of the Pesach celebration is, however, not lost in the festivities of the banquet. The leader reminds the family group of its origins. He tells the group, "My father was a fugitive Aramean . . ." and he concludes the reflection upon its history with "the Lord freed us from Egypt. . . ." After explaining the symbols of the *pesach, matzah* and *maror,* he quotes the words of Rabban Gamaliel: "In every generation a person is obligated to see himself [herself] as if he [she] went forth from Egypt."

While the first *haggadah,* or "narration" of the Exodus, does not emerge until the ninth century in Babylonia, nearly all elements of the *seder* ceremony were already known. Rav Amram, who edited the first *haggadah,* however, adds some important innovations of his own. Building upon discussions and decisions of teachers in the great Babylonian academies, he introduces the *Kiddush,* or "ceremonial blessing for the wine," at the Pesach meal, organizes the Four Questions asked by the children at the *seder,* and includes a section describing four different kinds of participants at the *seder* meal.

In Rav Amram's *Haggadah,* the *seder* has become a "family learn-in," a time for recalling and discussing Jewish history and the miracle of freedom from Egyptian oppression. Referring to an all-night Pesach discussion in the town of Lod among Rabbi Eliezer, Rabbi Joshua, Rabbi Eleazar ben Azariah, Rabbi Akiba, and Rabbi Tarfon, Rav Amram's *Haggadah,* and all others after it, suggests a model for celebration. The Pesach *seder* is for bringing family and friends together. It is for bonding Jews to their history and to one another. Its discussion emphasizes all the difficult questions we ask about freedom, and its prayers offer thanks to God for liberating the Jewish people from Egyptian slavery.

In the gradual evolution of Pesach one sees how Jewish rituals and ceremonies have changed to meet new circumstances, needs, and tastes throughout the centuries. From sharing an all-night sacrifice and meal to the development of an elaborate banquet with a carefully written script, Pesach has become one of the most popular festivals of the Jewish year. Yet its powerful message and pupose have not been lost. Pesach remains the Jewish people's great celebration of freedom.

## Probing the meaning of Shavuot

Just as the rituals of Pesach changed through the centuries, so did the celebration of the festival of Shavuot. What began as a harvest festival of rest and sacrifices on the fiftieth day after the first day of Pesach evolved through the centuries into *Zeman Matan Toratenu,* or "Season [Festival] of the Giving of Our Torah."

How and why did such a transformation take place?

Within the Torah, Shavuot is also known as *Chag ha-Katzir,* or "Harvest Festival" (Exodus 23:16), and as *Yom ha-Bikkurim,* or "Day of the First Fruits of the Harvest" (Numbers 28:26). *Shavuot* means "weeks" and refers to the span of seven weeks stretching from Pesach at the beginning of the barley harvest in the Land of Israel to the beginning of the wheat harvest. For the ancients, the fifty-day countdown was a journey from one harvest to the next.

On the fiftieth day the Israelites celebrated by bringing two loaves of bread, seven yearling lambs, one bull, and two rams with their meal offerings and libations to the sanctuary. These, along with one he-goat as a sin offering and two yearling lambs as a sacrifice of well-being, were presented to the priests. The festival was observed as a Sabbath and as a day of thanksgiving for a bountiful harvest. All forms of work were prohibited.

The *Mishnah* contains a description of how offerings were made at the Jerusalem sanctuary. When the Israelite entered, he would stand before a priest and declare: "My father was a fugitive Aramean. He went down to Egypt with meager numbers and sojourned there; but there he became a great and very populous nation. The Egyptians dealt harshly with us and oppressed us; they imposed heavy labor upon us. We cried to the Lord, the God of our ancestors, and the Lord heard our plea and saw our plight, our misery, and our oppression. The Lord freed us from Egypt by a mighty hand, by an outstretched arm and awesome power, and by signs and portents. God brought us to this place and gave us this land, a land flowing with milk and honey. Wherefore I now bring the first fruits of the soil that You, O Lord, have given me." (*Mishnah, Bikkurim* 3:2–5; also Deuteronomy 26:5–10)

As we have already noted, the words "My father was a fugitive Aramean . . ." are also used at the beginning of the Pesach *haggadah*'s narration about Jewish history. Here again on Shavuot the prayer expresses the individual's relationship to the slavery and liberation of the Jewish people. When reciting the story of oppression and freedom, one relives it, becomes part of it. By connecting thanksgiving for the harvest with gratefulness to God for liberty, the ancient Jew celebrated the fruits of the past and hope for the future.

Shavuot merged Jewish identity into a sacred partnership with the God of freedom and the harvest. The same God who liberates the seed from the darkness of earth to bloom in the bright sun and yield its fruit also liberates the Jewish people from oppression. For the ancients, Shavuot, like Pesach, was a time of rebirth, harvest, awakening, and liberation.

So how did this festival later emerge as *Zeman Matan Toratenu*, or "Festival of the Giving of Our Torah"?

No one can be sure. There are, as we may imagine, many theories. For instance, the rabbis of the Talmud point out that the Israelites arrived at Mount Sinai "on the third new moon" after their Exodus from Egypt. There they camped for three days and spent another three days creating boundaries around the mountain. That brought the date to the sixth of Sivan, fifty days after the beginning of Pesach. All of which, for the rabbis of the Talmud, proves that Shavuot is also the day on which the Israelites received the Torah at Mount Sinai. (*Shabbat* 86a)

Others, among them many modern scholars, believe that the attachment of the giving of the Torah at Mount Sinai to Shavuot coincides with the emergence of the synagogue and perhaps came after the destruction of the Jerusalem Temple in 70 C.E. With that destruction, pilgrimages to Jerusalem ceased, and the focus of the festival shifted from giving thanks for the harvest to giving thanks for God's revelation, the "harvest" of Torah.

This theory complements the view held by many teachers whose observations were included in the Midrash. For them the journey of the Jewish people from the fleshpots of Egypt led to the glorious moment at Mount Sinai when Moses received the Torah and the people accepted it with the pledge "We will do and we will hear." (Exodus 24:7) Within the newly emerging synagogue with its emphasis on Torah study, the drama of giving thanks for the first fruits was superceded on Shavuot by the drama of giving thanks for God's gift of Torah.

However—and whenever—the decision was made by the rabbis to recast Shavuot as *Zeman Matan Toratenu*, or the "Festival of the Giving of Our Torah," they made their intentions clear when they selected the Torah portion to be read on the festival. Rather than choosing a selection of Torah that describes the celebration of first fruits at the sanctuary, they designated Exodus 19:1–8 and 20:1–14, describing the arrival of the Israelites at Mount Sinai and containing the Ten Commandments. Clearly for them, the journey of liberation from bondage led to accepting the ethical and ritual laws of Torah and to the challenge of creating a just and caring society. For the rabbis whose views are recorded in the Midrash, it was the acceptance of the mitzvot, the commandments of Torah, that gave purpose to the Jewish people and justified their existence.

Rabbi Abdimi ben Hama ben Hasa playfully makes this point in his version of what happened at Mount Sinai: He describes God as picking up the mountain and holding it over the heads of the people. They look up at the danger, and God says to them, "If you accept the Torah, you will live. If not, I will bury you under Mount Sinai." Seeing their situation, the people respond with the words of Proverbs 3:18, "It is a tree of life to those who hold on to it. . . ."

Rabbi Abdimi's humor is meant to emphasize the choice for the Jewish people: life, if they choose to embrace the Torah; death, if they do not. In other words, the Torah is the lifeline of the Jew, the reason for Jewish survival. Fulfilling its mitzvot, living by its ethical and ritual standards, is the purpose of Jewish existence.

Shavuot, as *Zeman Matan Toratenu*, celebrates that sacred moment at Mount Sinai when the Jewish people committed themselves and all the generations afterwards to making the Torah a "tree of life." From its early origins as an agricultural thanksgiving day, known as *Chag ha-Katzir*, "Harvest Festival," and *Yom ha-Bikkurim*, "Day of the First Fruits of the Harvest," Shavuot emerges into a festival marking the central role of Torah in Jewish life. On Shavuot, Jews return to Mount Sinai, hear the Ten Commandments, and are reminded that they are partners with God in applying the teachings of Torah to every corner of society and to their personal lives.

### Probing the meaning of Sukot

What we have already discovered about the evolution of Pesach and Shavuot is also true of the seven-day festival of Sukot. Named *Sukot,* from the plural of the Hebrew word *sukah,* or "booth," the week of celebration began as a harvest festival, but its rituals and meanings, like those of Shavuot, have changed and enlarged throughout Jewish history.

Like Pesach, Sukot begins in the middle of a month (Tishri) at a full moon. Its first and last days are sacred no-work Sabbaths. The sacrifices prescribed by the Torah for offering at the sanctuary include a fire offering, burnt and meal offerings, and libations. In addition, on the first day of the festival, the Israelites were to bring a special bouquet consisting of an *etrog,* or "citron," together with palm, myrtle, and willow branches.

Special accommodations were also commanded. The Israelites are to construct *sukot,* or "booths," and they are to eat and sleep in them during the seven days of celebration. Our Torah portion makes clear the purpose of dwelling outside the comforts of one's home. The Israelites are to live in booths for the same reason they are to celebrate Pesach: The Israelites are to celebrate in booths for seven days "in order that future generations may know that I made the Israelite people live in booths when I brought them out of the land of Egypt." (Exodus 23:37–43) The booths are a reminder of their liberation from oppression.

Furthermore, Sukot is also known in the Torah by the terms *he-Chag,* or "the Festival," and *Chag ha-Asif,* or "Festival of Ingathering." As the fall harvest celebration, it was a time of thanksgiving for all the earth's bounty. Yet the festival also focused on the future. Farmers living in ancient times, like those of today, were concerned with adequate rains to guarantee a plentiful harvest in the next season. The uncertainty haunted them. Would the skies fill with rain clouds or would their crops wither and their flocks and herds die beside dry water holes?

Such concerns explain the ancient ceremony of bringing to the sanctuary the Sukot bouquet of the *etrog* and myrtle, willow, and palm branches. During Temple times, we are told that on each day of the holiday a procession would carry water from the Pool of Shiloach in Jerusalem to the Temple sanctuary. There the priests would pour the water onto the altar. The people would then wave their Sukot bouquets and beat them on the ground around the altar. Commenting on this ceremony, the rabbis make it clear that its purpose is to ask God for rains in the coming year. (*Rosh Hashanah* 16:1)

Today such rituals are defined as forms of "sympathetic magic." They imitate the wishes of those who employ them and remind God to fulfill them. In combining the rituals of pouring water on the altar and waving a palm branch, or *lulav* (which makes the sound of cracking thunder and falling rain), together with the myrtle and willow branches (which grow near water), it was hoped that these sounds of water would cause God to give plentiful rain for the next growing season.

If that was the meaning of Sukot rituals to the ancients, what may these rituals mean today? Can the *sukah,* or "booth," be more than a reminder of the booths used by the wandering Israelites? Is the Sukot bouquet more than a quaint form of sympathetic magic or a rite for rain?

In seeking answers for such questions, Torah interpreters have suggested many significant insights. For instance, Rabbi Akiba and a majority of his contemporaries declared that the *sukah* "must have the character of a nonpermanent residence." While one is to enjoy it with family and friends and eat and sleep in it, the roof of the *sukah* must be open to the stars. It is to be decorated with the fruits of the harvest and with *shach,* palm or tree branches, all of which will decay. (*Sukot* 23a; *Yoma* 10b; *Betzah* 30b; *Kitzur Shulchan Aruch* 134–135)

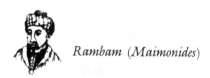

Rambam (*Maimonides*)

According to Maimonides, while beautifying the *sukah* with tapestries, streamers, and the use of special holiday dishes is praiseworthy, one must never make of it a permanent dwelling. (*Mishneh Torah, Sukot* 6)

The temporary nature of the *sukah* may be the key to its deeper meaning. Beyond reminding those celebrating the festival of the booths used by the Israelites after their liberation from Egypt, the *sukah* may also symbolize the nature of human life. This is the meaning Jewish philosopher Philo of Alexandria (20 B.C.E.–40 C.E.) suggests in his discussion of Sukot. He writes that the purpose of the *sukah* is to remind you "in wealth to remember your poverty. When you are popular and highly regarded . . . remember your insignificance. When you are in high office . . . remember that you are a humble citizen. When you enjoy peace . . . recall war. When you are on land . . . remember the storms at sea. When you are surrounded by friends in the city . . . remember those who are lonely and desperate for company." (*The Special Laws* 204, 206–211)

This association of the *sukah* with the fragile and constantly changing nature of human life was quite obviously in the thoughts of the rabbis who chose the Book of Ecclesiastes for reading and study on the Sabbath of Sukot. The message of Ecclesiastes, like the message of the *sukah*, is that life is fragile, constantly changing. There are moments for joy, then sadness; followed by times for laughter, then tears; succeeded by seasons for gathering, then losing; for love, then hatred; for war, then peace. (See Ecclesiastes 3.) Sitting in the temporary *sukah*, which has been built and made beautiful by harvest decorations, one not only senses gratefulness for the bounty of nature but also realizes all the varying seasons of human existence—of how quickly human beings journey from birth to death.

---

*It was the custom of Levi Isaac of Berdichev to invite to his* sukah *simple, unlearned people. Once his students asked him: "Master, why do you ask these people to be here with us each year?" Levi Isaac replied: "In the world to come, when the righteous are sitting at the holy feast in the heavenly* sukah, *I shall come there and seek to be admitted. But they will refuse me. For who am I that I should sit among the great, righteous*

*ones? Then I shall present my case. I will tell them how I invited simple and unlearned persons into my* sukah. *And they will allow me to enter."*

---

According to the mystical text known as the *Zohar*, it is not enough to construct, decorate, and enjoy a *sukah* by eating, sleeping, and studying in it. One must also share it with guests of two different kinds. First, there are seven illustrious Jewish heroes, Abraham, Isaac, Jacob, Joseph, Moses, Aaron, and David, one for each day. However, according to the *Zohar* (*Emor* 23), they will not automatically visit the *sukah*. They will arrive only if those who have built the *sukah* first invite the other category of guests, the poor and needy. In other words, the meaning of the *sukah* is to remind us to share our good fortune with others. It is to be shared with guests—friends, great Jewish leaders of the past, and, above all, with the hungry and homeless.

Regarding the Sukot banquet of the *etrog, lulav*, myrtle, and willow, interpreters suggest a variety of meanings.

Many of the rabbis teaching after the destruction of the Jerusalem Temple explain that the *Arba'ah Minim*, or the "Four Species," symbolize the Jewish people. In one commentary, the *etrog*, which has both taste and odor, is compared to Jews who know Torah and practice good deeds; the *lulav*, which has taste but no odor, is equated with Jews who know Torah but fail to practice good deeds; the myrtle, which has odor but no taste, is likened to those who practice good deeds but know nothing of Torah; the willow, which has neither odor nor taste, is compared to the person who knows no Torah and fails to practice any good deeds. Since they are all Jews, God, the rabbis say, binds them together in a bouquet and says: "Let them atone for one another's failings." (*Leviticus Rabbah* 30)

This use of the Sukot bouquet as a means of teaching God's tolerance and concern for all Jews is also found in another commentary. The author points out that both the *etrog* and *lulav* produce fruit while the myrtle and willow do not. For the Sukot bouquet to be brought into the sanctuary, however, all four kinds must be bound and held together. "Just as the four kinds must be brought together," says the interpreter, "so the people of Israel will not be allowed to return to their land unless they are united." (*Yalkut Shemoni, Emor,* 188a)

What is particularly significant about these interpretations of the Sukot bouquet is not only their concern for Jewish unity but their acceptance of pluralism, of differences, within Jewish life. Each segment of the Jewish people, like each of the Four Species in the Sukot bouquet, has something special to contribute. They depend upon one another. Without respect for differences, people will never reach the Promised Land—the fulfillment of all their hopes and aspirations.

Twentieth-century teacher Rabbi Ya'akov Israel in his book *Knesset Israel* puts the argument for pluralism this way: "When Jewish groups stand apart, each in its place, and each claiming that it alone has justice on its side, and they refuse to listen to one another, then no cure will ever come to the Jewish situation. . . . The Four Species symbolize peace and unity. For just as they differ in taste, odor, and form but are united together, so, too, the different parties of our people must form one alliance and work together for the good of the people."

Underlying this interpretation of the Sukot bouquet is a concern for the future survival of the Jewish people. The insistence of binding all the various segments of the community together, of accepting differences and promoting unity, is seen as the only way of guaranteeing the vitality and future of the community. The bouquet of four kinds held together as an ancient prayer for rain to assure new harvests and survival is transformed into a symbol for holding the people together. Its purpose is to remind all segments of the Jewish community that their future depends upon mutual appreciation, cooperation, and unity.

### A concluding comment about Pesach, Shavuot, and Sukot

Each of the festivals mentioned in *Parashat Emor* continues to play a central role in the celebration of the Jewish people. As we have seen, their ritual expressions have changed and evolved through the centuries. As the people adjusted to new circumstances—from the desert sanctuary to a Temple in Jerusalem; from the destruction of the Temple with its sacrifices to the creation and exclusive use of the synagogue; from living in the Land of Israel to exile and dispersion throughout the world; from pogrom and persecution to lands of safety; from the Holocaust to the birth of the State of Israel—Jewish rituals have taken on new forms, meanings, and significance.

Whether it is the addition of a *haggadah,* or the transformation of Shavuot from a harvest day to a celebration of the giving of the Torah, or the reinterpretation of the Sukot bouquet, each emerging ritual contains traces of its origins. While Jewish tradition has altered its rituals, even abandoned some, it has consistently retained and developed the original themes of the festivals. Pesach has remained the Festival of Freedom, Shavuot a harvest of thanksgiving for the fruits of nature and of Torah, and Sukot a celebration of thanksgiving and concern for the future. The relevance of these ancient themes underscores the continuing importance of these three Jewish festivals.

## PEREK BET: *Eye for an Eye, Tooth for a Tooth: About Lex Talionis*

Three times within the Torah we find a formulation that deals with compensation for physical harm inflicted by one person upon another.

In *Parashat Emor* we are told: "If a man kills any human being, he shall be put to death. One who kills a beast shall make restitution for it: life for life. If anyone maims his fellow, as he has done so shall it be done to him: fracture for fracture, eye for eye, tooth for tooth. The injury he inflicted on another shall be inflicted on him. . . . You shall have one standard for stranger and citizen alike: for I the Lord am your God." (Leviticus 24:17–22)

In Exodus 21:22–25 we are told that, if one is involved in a fight and pushes a pregnant woman causing a miscarriage, the husband of the woman may ask for compensation for the loss of life. However, "if other damage ensues, the penalty shall be life for life, eye for eye, tooth for tooth, hand for hand, foot for foot, burn for burn, wound for wound, bruise for bruise."

A third example of this principle occurs in Deuteronomy 19:18–19, 21. Here the dispute between the two parties is not of a physical nature. It relates to one person's intention to harm another by deliberate falsification of testimony in court. In this situation, the Torah commands the judges to "do to him as he schemed to do to his fellow. . . . Nor must you show pity: life for life, eye for eye, tooth for tooth, hand for hand, foot for foot."

Many interpreters through the centuries have sought to explain what the Torah meant by such a penalty. For example, Robert H. Pfeiffer, a modern biblical critic, suggests that "eye for eye and tooth for tooth . . ." is "the old law of the desert" practiced "among the Israelites who never forgot their desert origin." He explains that " 'life for life' in its absolute form is the principle of the desert law of blood revenge. . . ." In other words, the practice sanctioned by the Torah was physical mutilation as recompense for any physical injury inflicted by others. If an eye was put out, the person responsible for the injury was to lose an eye. This was so with a foot, a tooth, a burn, a fracture, a hand. According to Pfeiffer, blood revenge is what the Torah sanctions. (*Introduction to the Old Testament,* Harper and Brothers, New York, 1941, pp. 219–220)

*Sarna*

Most commentators disagree with Pfeiffer's conclusion. Contemporary scholar Nahum Sarna points out that *lex talionis,* or the "law of retaliation," as it is called in Roman law, is based upon the principle that "the punishment must fit the crime." This concept, which had been a part of Israelite practice even before the people were enslaved in Egypt, was introduced by them into Mesopotamia. It represented a revolutionary idea. Rather than calling for the deliberate physical injury to others as blood revenge, the principle actually created "a law of equivalence." It allowed the injured party to be paid for damages. If an eye was lost, one paid the worth of an eye; if a tooth, the equivalent of a tooth.

Furthermore, not only in this way was the To-

rah revolutionary. Sarna points out that other cultures surrounding the Israelites introduced monetary compensation for physical damages along class lines. In the *Code of Hammurabi* we are told that "if a seignior has knocked out the tooth of a seignior of his own rank, he shall knock out his tooth. If he has knocked out a commoner's tooth, he shall pay one-third mina of silver." (200–201) In other words, within the *Code of Hammurabi,* compensation is dictated by class rank, by one's position in society. Within the Torah, however, the person's class does not apply. No one person's eye or tooth is worth more than that of another. Equal and fair compensation for damages is the right of every person within the society.

Those, like Pfeiffer, who argue that the Torah actually calls for bodily mutilation in retaliation for physical injury miss the point, says Sarna. There is no way of assessing an equivalent mutilation. What if a person only loses part of his sight or partial use of a limb? How would it be possible to enforce the law, to punish with exactly the same injury? Sarna, therefore, concludes that the Torah passages, in reality, refer to "pecuniary compensation." If one injures someone's eye, or foot, or tooth, one must pay the designated worth of that injury.

Most Jewish commentators agree with Sarna. One of the earliest discussions of the matter in the Talmud stresses the importance of financial compensation for physical injuries. Rabbi Simeon ben Yochai teaches that "eye for eye" means "money." He then clarifies his conclusion with a question: "If a blind man maims another by blinding him, how is this considered just or sufficient compensation?" In asking the question, Rabbi Simeon means to reduce to nonsense the notion of physically injuring another as a form of compensation. (*Baba Kamma* 84a) Rabbi Simeon ben Yochai's interpretation of "eye for eye" as fair monetary compensation became the standard interpretation of Jewish tradition.

*Ibn Ezra*

In his commentary on the subject, Abraham ibn Ezra quotes the leader of Babylonian Jewry,

Sa'adia Gaon. Objecting to those who argued that "eye for eye" should be understood literally as justifiable retaliation for physical mutilation, Sa'adia asks: "If a person deprived his fellow of a third of his normal sight by his blow, how can a retaliatory blow be so calculated as to have the same precise results, neither more nor less. . . ?"

Answering his own question, Sa'adia declares that "such an exact reproduction of the effects is even more difficult in the case of a wound or bruise that, if in a dangerous spot, might result in death." It is clear that from Sa'adia's point of view, and from the view of ibn Ezra who quotes him, the Torah's intention was never physical retaliation by mutilation of another but rather some form of equal financial reimbursement. (See discussion of Leviticus 24:17–22.)

Maimonides makes a similar point. "When the Torah uses the words 'as he has maimed a person, so shall it be done to him,' it does not mean the literal inflicting of the identical maiming on the guilty person but merely that, though the latter deserves such maiming, the person who has inflicted the damage pays the monetary equivalent." (*Yad Hazakah, Hilchot Havel u-Mazik* 1, 3–6)

*Leibowitz*

In commenting on Maimonides' argument, Nehama Leibowitz goes one step further in explaining why monetary compensation instead of physical retaliation was preferred by the Torah. She suggests that the body is not an ordinary machine that can be used and discarded. It is sacred because it is the house of the human soul and a gift from God. In other words, says Leibowitz, "a person cannot dispose of his limbs in the same way he can dispose of his goods since his limbs, his entire body, are not under his authority. A person is not master of his body, but God to whom belongs both soul and body is master of them." Thus no person has the right to inflict harm on another person's body or upon his own. When justice demands compensation for damages to another's body, only financial compensation will do. Honoring the body is honoring God. (*Studies in Vayikra*, pp. 245–257)

If Jewish tradition rejects the notion of physical mutilation as retaliation for injury, then how does it assess a "monetary equivalent" for damages that have been done?

Five categories of consideration are used to calculate fair compensation:

First is *nezek,* an assessment of how the permanent physical disability will affect one's future earnings. Here the task is to establish the financial difference between what one could have earned and what one will now earn as a result of the injury. The amount lost must be compensated.

The second category is *tza'ar,* or "pain." One is to be paid the difference between the amount he would have requested for amputating the limb with anaesthesia and the amount he would have asked for without anaesthesia.

Third is *rippui,* or "medical treatment." It is the total amount of medical bills from the time of the injury to the time of a complete recovery.

Fourth is *shevet,* or "loss of earnings." It is calculated on the basis of the injury. If one must remain away from work while healing, then compensation must be given for each day lost. If, however, one's injury will be permanent, compensation is calculated by determining how much a person with such a disability would be paid if employed in his original field of work.

Finally, a person injured is compensated for *boshet,* or the "indignity" suffered. This is calculated by determining the status of the person who caused the damage. If it was a child who brought harm, compensation will be different from damages brought about by an adult. If one was injured by a leader or important person whose anger caused humiliation or embarrassment, compensation must be calculated to take mental anguish into consideration. (A. Chill, *The Mitzvot,* pp. 71–74)

In addition to these five conditions, Jewish tradition also demands that the person who has physically damaged another must ask forgiveness from the injured party. Maimonides puts it this way: "No compensation is complete, no wrong is forgiven until the person who has inflicted the injury requests the victim's forgiveness and has been forgiven."

Maimonides, however, does not leave the matter there. Knowing that the victim may be hurt, angry, and unforgiving, he warns: "It is forbidden for the injured party to be cruel and unforgiving. This is not the Jewish way . . . as soon as the guilty party has sought forgiveness, once or twice, and is sincere and regrets his action, then he must be forgiven. The quicker, the better." (*Yad Ha-zakah, Hilchot Hovevi u-Mazik* 5, 9)

While other ancient Middle Eastern cultures surrounding the early Israelites allowed physical mutilation as a form of retaliation, Jewish tradition introduces the practice of monetary compensation and reconciliation. When the Torah uses the formula "fracture for fracture, eye for eye, tooth for tooth . . ." it means payment for damages. As we have seen, rabbinic tradition refines this principle of equivalent compensation by ruling that payment must take into consideration disability, pain, cost of medical care, loss of earnings, and shame. Not only must the injured party be paid damages, but the person inflicting injury must seek forgiveness.

Regard for the human body as the sacred container of the human soul is at the heart of Jewish ethics. So, too, are guaranteeing equal treatment for damages and good relations between all members of society. Realizing that injury to the body, or the loss of a limb, can never be fully compensated and could spark bloody revenge, Jewish tradition mandates a just form of compensation and reconciliation. In doing so, it advances the cause of justice and the pursuit of peace.

# QUESTIONS FOR STUDY AND DISCUSSION

1. List and discuss the rituals and benefits of the Pesach *seder* ceremony. Which ones are ancient in origin? Which are new, modern? Which are the most important and the least important to you? Why?

2. Some early rabbis suggest that the people of Israel should have received the Torah immediately after their Exodus from Egyptian slavery. Others argue that the people were not ready for its responsibilities. It was only after wandering for seven weeks in the desert that they were prepared to accept the teachings of Torah—and, even then, they abandoned God and built the golden calf. With which of these two views do you agree? Why?

3. Modern Jewish philosopher Abraham Joshua Heschel has written that "the Jewish people without Torah is obsolete." Given the celebration of Shavuot, what may Heschel mean by his bold declaration?

4. Given the differences among Jews on the interpretation of Torah and the practice of Jewish tradition, what lessons may modern Jews learn from the meanings of the Sukot bouquet and festival?

5. A mayor of a city, X, strikes a vocal and critical constituent, Y. Y's arm is broken, and he is unable to work for five months in his profession as a computer expert earning $5,000 a month. According to Jewish tradition, how would you assess the damages? What would you have X pay Y by way of compensation? What would you have X do by way of reconciliation? Consult with insurance experts. What do modern insurance companies cover? What don't they cover? How does this compare with Jewish tradition?

# PARASHAT BEHAR-BECHUKOTAI
## *Leviticus 25:1–27:34*

*Parashat Behar-Bechukotai* is one of seven designated Torah portions that, depending upon the number of Sabbaths in a year, is either read as two separate portions or combined to assure the reading of the entire Torah. While this volume will combine them, it will present an interpretation on each of their most important themes.

*Parashat Behar* presents laws regulating the sabbatical year and the jubilee year. The people are told that for six years they are to sow their fields and prune their vineyards, but, during the seventh year, the land is to be given a complete rest, a Sabbath. Every fiftieth year is to be a jubilee year in which land and vineyards must not be worked and in which liberty will be granted to all Israelites enslaved during the previous forty-nine years. The jubilee year also marks a return of any properties purchased during the previous forty-nine years to the original owner-families who had been given the land at the time the Israelites entered it.

*Parashat Bechukotai* is filled with God's promises to the people if they are loyal and faithfully follow all the commandments and with God's warnings if they disobey. Peace, security, and abundant crops are promised if they are faithful. Misery, suffering, and ruin will come if they spurn God's commandments. The portion also includes brief discussions of the payment of vows and gifts made to the sanctuary.

## OUR TARGUM

### · 1 ·

*P*arashat Behar begins with the commandment prohibiting the sowing or harvesting of lands or the pruning of vineyards during the sabbatical year. The Israelites are forbidden to use the aftergrowth of the harvest or to gather grapes from untrimmed vines during the year of rest. It is permissible, however, to eat whatever the uncultivated land happens to produce during the year of rest.

· 2 ·

After every forty-nine years a jubilee year is to be celebrated. It is to begin with the sounding of a *shofar* on Yom Kippur and with a proclamation of liberty, or release, throughout the land for all its inhabitants.

"Liberty," or "release," meant that all Israelites were to take possession of the original lands given to their ancestors at the time Joshua and the people conquered Canaan.

Given the rule about returning the land to its original owners, the people are told that, when they sell or buy property, they are to deduct for the years since the Jubilee and to charge for only the remaining potential years of productivity. The more years of use, the higher the price; the fewer the years of ownership, the lower the price. The people are taught: "When you sell property to your neighbor, or buy any from your neighbor, you shall not wrong one another." They are also instructed that the land belongs to God, and they are warned, "You are but strangers resident with Me."

· 3 ·

If an Israelite is in trouble and must sell part of his holding, a relative is to help him. If, for financial reasons, one must sell a house in a walled city, one has the right of repurchase for a year. Once the year has passed, the house belongs to the purchaser forever. Houses in villages, however, are classified as "open country" and are to be returned to their original owners at the Jubilee.

The people are instructed that, if brother or sister Israelites are in trouble, they are to be treated as resident aliens. They are not to be charged interest on loans or food. Nor are they to be treated as slaves. While they may work as hired laborers, they must be freed at the Jubilee. The people are told: "For they are My servants, whom I freed from the land of Egypt; they may not give themselves over in servitude. You shall not rule over them ruthlessly; you shall fear your God."

If an Israelite, having had financial troubles, comes under the authority of a resident alien or his family, who have prospered, he may be redeemed by a member of his own family. His price will be computed on the basis of the work years remaining until the Jubilee. Should no family member come along to pay for his release, he and his family will be liberated at the Jubilee.

## ·4·

*Parashat Bechukotai* opens with a promise by God to the Israelites. If they follow all the commandments, they will be rewarded with abundant rains and harvests. They will be secure in their land and enjoy peace. When attacked by enemies, they will be victorious. Parents will enjoy many children, and none of them will know hunger. God will care for them, and they will always walk proudly as free people.

However, if they refuse to follow God's commandments, they will suffer terrible illnesses, lack of harvests, and defeat by their enemies. The skies will be as iron and copper [unproductive]; no fruit trees will yield produce; and wild beasts will destroy them.

Should the people turn away from God and refuse to follow God's commandments, pursuing idolatry and cults, their cities will be laid waste, and they will be scattered among the nations. The land will be given a long Sabbath time with no harvests. Fear of enemies will be so great that the sound of a fluttering leaf will set the people fleeing. Those who survive this desolation will wish they had perished.

When the people have suffered exile and punishment because they failed to observe God's commandments, God will remember the covenant made with them, with Abraham, Isaac, and Jacob. They will not be rejected forever. God will not annul the covenant with them, for it is God who freed them from Egypt to be their God.

## ·5·

This Torah portion and the Book of Leviticus conclude with laws concerning vows, gifts, and payments to the sanctuary.

If a person vows, or promises, to donate the equivalent worth of a human being, he is to use the following scale: for a male from twenty to sixty years of age, fifty shekels of silver, and thirty for a female; for a male from five to twenty years of age, twenty shekels, and ten for a female; for a male from one month to five years of age, five shekels, and three for a female. If the person promising a donation cannot afford it, the priest will make an assessment according to what the person can afford.

For promises of donations of animals, houses, or land, the priest shall make the proper assessment. In the case of land given to the priest, it can be bought back at the time of the Jubilee for an additional twenty percent of the sum. If it is not redeemed, it belongs to the priest. If the land is not actually owned by the person giving it to the sanctuary, it is to be returned to the original owner at the Jubilee.

All tithes, or payments of ten percent of seed, fruit, or the herd, are to be given to the sanctuary. However, one can pay the equivalent value plus one-fifth more and retrieve them for his own use.

## THEMES

*Parashat Behar-Bechukotai* contains three important themes:

1. The sabbatical and jubilee years.
2. Caring for the poor.
3. God's rewards and punishments.

## PEREK ALEF: *Lessons from the Sabbatical and Jubilee Years*

Just as the Torah calls for a Sabbath day of rest for people after every six days of work, it also commands a Sabbath year of rest for the land after every six years of cultivation; it also calls for a *Yovel*, or "Jubilee," a fiftieth year, completing a cycle of seven sabbatical years.

Mention is made of the sabbatical year in Exodus 23:10–11, where the Israelites are instructed not to cultivate their lands, vineyards, or olive groves. During the sabbatical year they are to leave whatever grows for the needy and wild beasts.

Within our Torah portion, the Israelites are told that, while they may not work the land or prune their vineyards or orchards, it is permissible to eat whatever *happens* to grow during the sabbatical year. (Leviticus 25:1–7) In addition to the practice of resting the land, the Torah also commands that all debts are to be cancelled during the seventh year. (Deuteronomy 15:1–3)

During the year of the Jubilee, which is announced by sounding the *shofar* on Yom Kippur, all laws of the sabbatical year are to be observed. In addition, all properties are to be returned to the families who inherited them at the time Joshua led the Israelites into the Land of Israel. To guarantee fairness in land values, all prices of land were calculated on potential usage before the sabbatical when they would revert to their original owners. The Jubilee was also a time when Israelites forced to sell themselves into slavery because of poverty were freed. (Leviticus 25:8–17)

These practices concerning both the sabbatical and jubilee years were adapted and extended by the rabbinic tradition. For example, owners of fields were not allowed to collect and store large amounts of food in their homes because such a practice would deprive the poor. Individuals or families were to take only the amount of fruits and vegetables required for their normal needs. If there was no longer any food available in the fields, owners were commanded to remove all food from their storage places and make it available to the entire community. It was forbidden to buy or sell produce from the field during the sabbatical or jubilee years.

With Alexander the Great's domination of the Middle East (330 B.C.E.), Jews moved from an agriculturally centered economy to an urban economy. Loans of currency were required for business dealings. However, the strict laws of Torah called for a release of all debts by creditors during the sabbatical year. This meant that potential creditors, fearing their loans would never be repaid, refused to make loans available, resulting in a desperate situation for the poor who were unable to secure necessary loans. To solve this unjust situation, Rabbi Hillel created a financial arrangement known as *prosbol*. It allowed for the transfer of debts to the courts, with a guarantee that, even during the sabbatical year, loans would be repaid.

(See Abraham Chill, *The Mitzvot,* pp. 108–111, 297–300, 413–415.)

It is clear from our Torah portion, and from later rabbinic considerations of the commandments having to do with the sabbatical and jubilee years, that much concern was given to easing the plight of those who might suffer during years of no-work, no-production, and the release of debts. The needs of the poor were a primary concern of Jewish tradition. Why, therefore, was the practice of a sabbatical or jubilee year established if it produced hardships for parts of society? What did such years mean to the Israelites and to later generations of Jews?

 *Rashi*

The commentator Rashi suggests that the reason for the sabbatical year is to give the land time to rest, just as the weekly Sabbath allows a human being to seek renewal and revitalization through rest. It is doubtful Rashi understood the process of natural fertilization and regeneration that occurred when the land was fallow for a year. Yet he, like the ancients, must have realized that crops usually grew more plentifully after the land had "rested" during a sabbatical year. For Rashi, the sabbatical and jubilee years, like the Sabbath, provided the land with a required period of reinvigoration. (See commentary on Leviticus 25:2.)

 *Rambam (Maimonides)*

Moses Maimonides clearly understands the relationship between "rest" for the land and its productivity. The sabbatical and jubilee years, he explains, are commanded because "by releasing the land it will become invigorated; by lying fallow and not being worked it will regain its strength."

Maimonides, however, also stresses a social and ethical benefit of the sabbatical and jubilee years. In his discussion of charity, he emphasizes that such sabbatical and jubilee laws as guaranteeing food for the needy, freeing slaves, canceling debts, and returning lands are all meant to teach "sympathy toward others and promote the well-being of all." A significant side of these special years is to encourage and instruct Jews to be generous with those in need, to share their profits and products, and to be just in their business practices. (*Guide for the Perplexed* 3:39)

*Ibn Ezra*

### A parallel to creation

*Abraham ibn Ezra suggests that the seven-year agricultural cycle parallels God's plan for creation. God completes the work of creation in six days, then rests. So, too, the Jew is asked to work the soil. Each year parallels a day of creation. The seasons of summer, fall, winter, and spring parallel the morning and evening hours of each day. And the seventh year is like the weekly Sabbath, a time of no work, a rest period for the fields. (See comment on Leviticus 25.)*

### Not like creation at all

*Rejecting Moses ibn Ezra's argument, the author of* Kelei Yakar, *Ephraim ben Aaron Solomon, says that the purpose of the sabbatical and jubilee years is "to teach us not to think that human beings control the yield of the soil . . . [and] to teach us to trust that God will provide us with adequate crops during the sixth year so that we will be able to subsist during the rest years." The sabbatical and jubilee years are meant as exercises in faith and self-discipline. (See Chill,* The Mitzvot, *p. 110.)*

*Peli*

### Protecting society against evil

*This Sabbath of the land and the jubilee year that comes in its wake are considered by many thinkers to be among the most advanced social reforms in history. They protect society against the evils of feudalism and totalitarianism, as-*

*suring an inherent "liberty to all the inhabitants in the land" and the right of each individual to "return to his home and to his family." (Pinchas Peli,* Torah Today, *pp. 146–148)*

Aharon Halevi, author of *Sefer ha-Hinuch*, also emphasizes the moral significance of the sabbatical and jubilee years. God commands us not to work the land and not to use its fruits, except for the poor, to remind us that the earth does not yield by itself or even by human cultivation. "There is a God who commands it to produce." Furthermore, Halevi says, "There is no nobler generosity than giving without expecting returns." That is the goodness God displays for all human beings to see in the sabbatical and jubilee years. God generously provides food for all, and human beings are to copy God's goodness in their relationships with one another. Just as God grants food during the years of rest, human beings are commanded to leave produce for the needy and hungry, acting out of compassion and generosity.

Concerning the commandments relating to the forgiveness of debts, the freeing of slaves, and the return of all lands to their original owners, Halevi argues that these laws of the sabbatical and jubilee years "mold ethical character." Their purpose is to "impress upon human beings that everything belongs to God, and ultimately everything returns to God and to whomever God wishes to give it."

Such an understanding is meant "to prevent people from stealing their neighbor's land or coveting it in their hearts." If they comprehend that everything belongs to God and will return to God, people are less likely to cheat others or deal unfairly with them in business. Knowing that all lands will be returned to their original owners and all slaves will be released assures security, justice, and liberty in society. (See B.S. Jacobson, *Meditations on the Torah*, pp. 188–189; also Nehama Leibowitz, *Studies in Vayikra*, pp. 260–261.)

### Measuring life by sabbatical years

*Rabbi Morris Silverman suggests that a person's "span of life normally consists of ten sabbatical periods of seven years each. . . ." [After] you have lived twenty-one years, or three sabbatical periods, "instead of saying that you have forty-*

*nine years ahead of you, you should say that you have only seven more sabbatical periods to live. And so you see the days of your life are all too short. You will better appreciate how precious is time when you think of life in terms of sabbatical periods and not of one year at a time." This is what the commandment to observe the sabbatical year teaches us.* (S.Z. Kahana, Heaven on Your Head, *Morris Silverman, editor, Hartmore House, Hartford, 1964, pp. 134–135*)

Modern commentator Baruch A. Levine explains the goal of the jubilee laws regarding the return of lands to the original owners as a means of insuring the Land of Israel for the Jewish people. It was not a matter of morality, theology, or agricultural renewal; it was a matter of politics.

Levine explains that this part of the Torah may have been composed after the Jewish people returned from Babylonian exile in about 420 B.C.E. They had been promised by the Babylonian ruler, Cyrus, that they could repossess the land. In returning after nearly eighty years of exile, they found their holdings in the hands of other Jews and many non-Jews. A crisis faced them. How could they settle the land when it now "belonged" to others?

The jubilee law of returning the land to the original families, who had been given it at the time of Joshua, seemed to settle the issue. God had given the land to the people of Israel, family by family. While it could be sold for use, it could not be sold forever. At each Jubilee it was to revert to the original family. When Jews returned to the Land of Israel from Babylonia, this meant that, at the Jubilee, all lands, whether owned by Jews or non-Jews, were to be returned to their original owners. As Levine says, "The goal was to regain control over the land." In this way rich and poor were equal. Both classes would regain their lands. (*JPS Commentary: Leviticus, pp. 270–274*)

*Leibowitz*

Nehama Leibowitz also provides a social-political meaning for the jubilee laws concerning the return of property to its original owners. However, quoting the arguments of nineteenth-century American thinker Henry George, Leibowitz points out that the Jubilee was "a measure designed to maintain an even distribution of wealth." Moses realized from his experience in Egypt that oppression of the masses came about as a result of a monopoly of land ownership and wealth in the hands of the rich. According to George's view, says Leibowitz, "the Torah . . . intended to prevent the evolving of a landless class and the concentration of power and property in the hands of the few." The guarantee that land would return to its original owners, every fifty years at the Jubilee, was seen as the best means of promoting "justice and equity." (*Studies in Vayikra, pp. 260–261*)

The interpreters of Jewish tradition offer a variety of explanations and meanings for the sabbatical and jubilee years. Yet they all have one thing in common. Each explanation finds within the traditions of resting the land, feeding the hungry, returning the land to its original owners, and liberating the slaves measures of great ethical, political, or spiritual significance. By contrast, the ethical concerns underlying these ancient agricultural and economic laws challenge many of the social, religious, and economic policies and priorities of our own era.

## PEREK BET: *The Mitzvah of Caring for the Poor*

According to Rabbi Assi, who lived and taught during the third century C.E., in Babylonia, the mitzvah of *tzedakah,* or caring for those in need, "is more important than all the other commandments put together." (*Baba Batra* 9a)

What are the origins of such an observation? Where do we find the basis within the Torah for Assi's conclusion about Jewish ethics?

The answer may be found in *Parashat Behar.* Just after the discussion of the sabbatical and jubilee years, the Torah deals with the question of how the poor and needy are to be protected and cared for by the community. Four times the words *ve-chi yamuch achicha,* or "and if your brother [or sister] should be reduced to poverty," begin an explanation of how the poor are to be treated.

Several examples are offered. The Israelites are told that, when a kinsman must sell his property, another should raise funds for its repurchase. If a kinsman falls into debt, it is forbidden to charge interest on any money or food given to him. If his situation of poverty continues and becoming enslaved is his only solution, he is to be treated as a hired laborer, not as a slave. If a poor Israelite is purchased by a resident alien (a non-Israelite), it is the obligation of his family to raise funds for his release; if he is fortunate and prospers while enslaved, he may purchase his own release. (Leviticus 25:25, 35, 39, and 47)

These regulations concerning treatment of the impoverished evolved into important discussions among Jewish commentators about the obligations of *tzedakah*. Through the centuries, ethical standards dealing with care for the needy emerge into a unique pattern of Jewish social responsibility.

For example, in discussing the meaning of the words "and if your brother should be reduced to poverty," the rabbis emphasize that helping those who have lost their property, who are without food, shelter, or clothing, or who are sick, infirm, or helpless, not only benefits the needy, but also brings happiness to the generous. Those who do *tzedakah*, says Abba ben Jeremiah in the name of Rabbi Meir, have the knowledge that their Good Inclination is ruling over their Evil Inclination. Rabbi Isi claims that those who give even a *perutah*, or "a small amount," feel fulfilled.

Several of the rabbis claim that the Torah's comment "and if your brother should be reduced to poverty" has to do with the obligation of rescuing those held by pirates or oppressors. Rabbi Huna argues that it refers to the mitzvah of visiting the sick and even estimates that one-sixtieth of a person's illness is cured by such visits.

*Zugot*

Rabbi Johanan says that the Torah means to instruct us to carry out the commandment to bury the poor with dignity and honor.

In another interpretation of reaching out to those who have fallen into poverty, Rabbi Jonah suggests that the Torah is particularly concerned about the feelings of the needy. They should not be embarrassed about their plight. By way of example, he tells about a person who had lost his money and was ashamed to ask for help. "I went to him," says Rabbi Jonah, "and told him I had news that he had inherited a fortune from a distant relative living far away. Then I offered him help, telling him that he could repay me when the inheritance was delivered. After giving him the gift, I assured him that it was not necessary for him to repay me. In that way I reduced his humiliation."

Other rabbis warn against shaming the poor with embarrassing questions. God, they warn, will punish those who are comfortable and ask the needy, "Why don't you go out and find a job, make some money, and put your own bread on the table?" Or, who say: "Look at those hips, look at those legs, look at that fat body. Such a person can work. Let him do so and take care of himself!" Such people, the rabbis observe, will bring evil upon themselves because they do not honor others as images of God. (*Leviticus Rabbah, Behar*, 36:1–16)

---

**The art of doing tzedakah**
*The greatest charity is to enable the needy to earn a living.* (Shabbat 63a)

*The person who gives charity in secret is greater than Moses.* (Baba Batra 9b)

*A torch is not diminished though it kindles a million candles. A person does not lose by giving to those in need.* (Exodus Rabbah 30:3)

*Charity knows no race or creed.* (Gittin 61a)

*If you wish to raise a person from poverty and trouble, do not think that it is enough to stand above and reach a helping hand down to him or her. It is not enough. You must go down to where the person is, down into the mud and filth. Then take hold of him or her with strong hands and pull until both of you rise up into the light.* (Solomon ben Meir ha-Levi of Karlin, 1738–

1798, as quoted in Francine Klagsbrun, *Voices of Wisdom: Jewish Ideals and Ethics for Everyday Living, Pantheon Books, New York, 1980, p. 331*)

The third-century teacher Eleazar ben Eleazar Ha-Kappar, who was known as Bar Kappara, maintains that we "are duty bound to view a poor person's body as if it were our own." In other words, we are to clothe, feed, and shelter the needy as if they were extensions of our own flesh and blood. Our standard of care for them ought to be what we would wish for ourselves. It should be given with respect for their dignity and concern for their feelings.

*Tzedakah* is not a matter only for the rich; nor is it exclusively material help. The poor are also responsible for giving *tzedakah*. Rabbi Levi explains that, "if you have nothing to give, offer consolation. Comfort the needy with kind words. Say, 'My soul goes out to you. Even though I have nothing to give you, I understand how you feel.'" (*Leviticus Rabbah* 24:1–15; see also *Sotah* 14a; *Baba Batra* 10a)

These observations by the early rabbis on the Torah's statement, "and if your brother should be reduced to poverty," define the obligations of charity within Jewish tradition. Building upon them, Moses Maimonides in his *Mishneh Torah*, written during the latter part of the twelfth century, identifies *tzedakah* "as the most important positive commandment" given by God to the Jewish people.

Agreeing with the early rabbis, Maimonides encourages generosity and sensitivity to the "cries of the needy." He counsels that human beings must learn to listen to one another, to speak to one another with sympathy, and never to insult those whose lives are broken by poverty and sickness. While the people of Israel are to care for one another because "they are bound together in a single destiny," the obligation of *tzedakah* also extends to non-Jews. "It is forbidden," writes Maimonides, "to let a poor person who asks for help go empty-handed."

Furthermore, helping a person who has fallen into trouble is not a matter of whim or sympathy. It is a *mitzvah*, an obligation, a commandment of God. The word used for "charity" in Hebrew is

*tzedakah* from the root *tz-d-k*, meaning "right," "just," "morally correct." Within Jewish tradition, *tzedakah* is a matter of doing the "right thing." That, undoubtedly, is why Maimonides emphasizes the law: "If a person has no clothing, it is your responsibility to provide clothing. If furnishings for a home are needed, give furniture. If a poor person requires help in affording a marriage celebration for a child, help with the marriage celebration. If the person is hungry, offer food. And do so without delay, without any further begging!" (*Mishneh Torah* 6–8; see also Jacob Neusner, *Tzedakah*, Rossel, Chappaqua, New York, 1982, pp. 81–106)

In summarizing the attitude of Jewish tradition toward *tzedakah*, the giving of charity, Maimonides offers a ladder of eight levels. It is now a classic expression of Jewish ethics.

### Maimonides' eight levels of tzedakah

1. *The highest degree of all is one who supports another reduced to poverty by providing a loan, or entering into a partnership, or finding work for him, so that the poor person can become self-sufficient.*
2. *Below this is giving to another so that the donor does not know the recipient, and the recipient does not know the donor.*
3. *Below this is giving to another so that the donor knows the recipient, but the recipient does not know the donor.*
4. *Below this is giving to another so that the recipient knows the donor, but the donor does not know the recipient.*
5. *Below this is giving to the poor without being asked.*
6. *Below this is giving to the poor after being asked.*
7. *Below this is giving to the poor less than is proper, but in a friendly manner.*
8. *Below this is giving, but in a grudging and unfriendly way.* (Mishneh Torah 10:7–15, based on translation by Jacob Neusner)

The single emphasis of all interpreters of the Torah's words "and if your brother should be reduced to poverty" is the obligation to offer help. If a person is in debt, you are to lend him money without interest. If it is clothing, food, or shelter that is required, you are to provide it. Commenting on the Torah's statement, Rashi notes that it is followed by the words "you shall strengthen him." These words, Rashi says, mean: "Don't let the poor fall and become impoverished so that it will be hard for them to recover. Instead, strengthen them the moment their strength and fortune fail." (See also *Torah Temimah* on Leviticus 25:35.)

Within the realm of Jewish ethics, charity is to be given immediately, generously, and always in a way that protects the dignity of those in need.

## PEREK GIMEL: *Rewards and Punishments: The Consequences of Our Choices*

Modern interpreter Rabbi Bernard J. Bamberger points out that many ancient Middle Eastern nations developed legal systems that promised great rewards for those who observed them and cruel punishments for those who violated them. Both the Sumarian *Code of Lipit-Ishtar* and the Babylonian *Code of Hammurabi* announce blessings for those who live by the law and suffering and death for those who do not.

The Torah, Bamberger maintains, does not follow either of these codes. Instead, it offers another view of the consequences of choices made by individuals and nations. While there are blessings and curses brought on by choices, the Torah also holds open "a glimmering of hope" of new opportunities for reward and happiness. In other words, we may suffer the consequences of our choices, but we are never completely doomed by them. (*The Torah: A Modern Commentary,* pp. 953–954)

In setting out the list of blessings and curses facing the Israelites, *Parashat Bechukotai* raises serious questions. First it describes the blessings that God will bring upon the people *if they follow* the commandments of Torah. They are promised prosperity and peace, safety from wild beasts, and victory over their enemies. Their land will yield abundant crops, and their population will grow. On the other hand, *if they do not follow* the commandments of Torah, they will be punished with diseases, crop failure, and the death of their flocks and children. Fear of enemies and starvation will overwhelm them. Their cities will be ruined. They will be defeated, ravaged by their enemies, and taken into exile. (Leviticus 26:3–38)

A parallel of this catalogue of blessings and curses is found in Deuteronomy 28–30.

After reading such a list of blessings and curses, one may ask: Does God actually punish those who do not observe all the laws of Torah? Is it possible to say that the people of Israel actually suffered exile, starvation, and fear because they did not all choose to live by every law in the Torah? Does Jewish tradition teach that nations and individuals are punished by God for their wrong choices, for not living according to the laws of Torah?

Contemporary commentator Baruch A. Levine notes that "two major principles of biblical religion find expression" in this section of the Torah. The first is the concept of *freewill,* that is to say, the conviction that each person has the liberty to determine whether to follow what the Torah commands or to reject it. The second concept concerns *reward and punishment.* It holds that "obedience to God's will brings reward; disobedience brings dire punishment." (*JPS Torah Commentary: Leviticus,* p. 182) These two principles not only function within the Torah, but they are also found in the writings of many of its interpreters.

In elaborating on these principles, Rabbi Hama ben Hanina maintains that all the commandments of Torah were given to human beings in order to safeguard them from their inclination to make evil choices. If one faithfully acts according to the commandments, rewards will follow. If not, one will suffer the consequences.

Rabbi Eleazar illustrates this view by claiming that God presented the Jewish people with a package from heaven, containing the Torah and a sword. "If you observe what is written in the Torah," God told the people, "then you will be saved from the sword. If you do not live according to the Torah, then you will be destroyed by the sword." (*Leviticus Rabbah* 25:5–6)

This view of reward for obedience to the commandments of Torah and punishment for disobedience is echoed in a story told by the early rabbis. It is about a man who falls from the deck of a ship into the sea. The captain throws him a line and tells him: "Grasp it tightly. Don't let go. If you do, you will lose your life." The Torah, say the rabbis, is the lifeline of the Jewish people. If they grasp it faithfully and practice its commandments, then they will live. If they let go of it, pay no attention to it, then they will perish. Their rewards and punishments have to do with the choices they make. (*Tanchuma Buber* to Numbers, p. 74)

This classic view of reward for loyalty to the Torah and punishment for disloyalty is reflected within the "Thirteen Principles of Faith" written by Moses Maimonides and included in most traditional prayer books for many centuries. The eleventh principle declares: "I believe with perfect faith that the Creator . . . rewards those who keep the commandments and punishes those who transgress them." According to Maimonides, everything depends upon the free choice of human beings. If they do good, they will be rewarded with good. If they choose evil, they will suffer painful consequences.

What about those, however, who are loyal to the Torah, who faithfully observe all commandments, but, rather than enjoying the rewards of peace of mind and material benefits, bear burdens of misery and pain? How do those who claim that God rewards all who keep the commandments and punishes all who do not explain the suffering of good people?

Some Jewish thinkers, like Rabbi Eleazar ben Simeon, who suffered persecution by the Romans, teach that human beings and nations should always see themselves as half-guilty and half-worthy, knowing that the next choice will tip the balance to either reward or punishment. Clearly, from Eleazar's point of view, those who suffer have made wrong choices—even though they fail to recognize where they have made their mistakes.

On the other hand, there are teachers who believe that the rewards and punishments are not given in this world but in heaven. Human beings are judged by God at the end of their lives. They reap the benefits of living a good life or suffer the consequences of evil decisions throughout all eternity. Because the mix of good deeds and sins is so complex, it is only God who can make an ultimate judgment. For this reason, as the medieval Jewish philosopher Joseph Albo suggests, God dispenses material and spiritual rewards and punishments not only during life on earth but also after death in heaven. (*Kiddushin* 40 a–b; *Sefer ha-Iggarim* 4:29ff.)

---

### A guarantee for the future world

*Rabbi Harold M. Schulweis points out that some of the ancient rabbis "repudiate the doctrine of reward and punishment as running counter to their sense of justice. . . . The suffering of the righteous is, in fact, a badge of honor, not a stigma of transgression." The Holy One brings suffering upon the righteous of the world in order that they may inherit the future world. (Kiddushin 40b; see "Suffering and Evil," in Abraham E. Millgram, editor,* Great Jewish Ideas, *B'nai B'rith/Bloch Publishing Company, 1964, pp. 206–207)*

### Causes of human suffering

*Rabbi Roland B. Gittelsohn does not believe in a God who sits in heaven and rewards those who live in accordance with the commandments of Torah and punishes those who do not. Instead, Rabbi Gittelsohn holds that there are four sources of suffering. "One: defiance of nature's physical laws. Two: ignorance of these physical laws. Three: defiance of nature's spiritual laws. Four: ignorance of these spiritual laws." (*Man's Best Hope, *Random House, New York, 1961, p. 127)*

### Explanation of suffering

*Suffering brings out and develops character. It supplies a field for all sorts of virtues, for resignation, faith, courage, resource, endurance. It stimulates; it purifies. (Claude G. Montefiore)*

---

For many moderns, neither the conclusion that the world and human life in it are too baffling to understand nor that God rewards and punishes in mysterious ways or in an afterlife in heaven is acceptable. How, it is asked, can we explain the suffering of innocent children who were put to their deaths in Nazi concentration camps, or the agony of "good" people who endure the torture of disease, or the cruelty and brutality of others?

Where are God's rewards and punishments in situations like these?

Rabbi Harold S. Kushner, in his book *When Bad Things Happen to Good People* (Shocken Books, New York, 1981), argues that one reason for the suffering of innocent, good people "is that our being human leaves us free to hurt each other, and God can't stop us without taking away the freedom that makes us human." In other words, human pain is not the result of God rewarding or punishing, but it is the result of human beings harming one another.

Kushner puts the matter this way: "Human beings can cheat each other, rob each other, hurt each other, and God can only look down in pity and compassion at how little we have learned over the ages about how human beings should behave. . . . When people ask 'Where was God in Auschwitz? How could He have permitted the Nazis to kill so many innocent men, women, and children?' my response is that it was not God who caused it. It was caused by human beings choosing to be cruel to their fellow men."

But what about the sickness of innocent people, the suffering of those afflicted with disease, crippled by illness? Are these God's punishments for not observing the Torah's commandments? Kushner, whose son Aaron died in his teens of a rare disease, writes: "I don't believe that God causes mental retardation in children or chooses who should suffer from muscular dystrophy. The God I believe in does not send us the problem; He gives us the strength to cope with the problem." (pp. 81–86, 127)

---

### Reward, punishment, and conscience

*The whole tradition of Judaism helps us in the understanding of right and wrong that is contained in our conscience. If we want personally to believe that by this means God punishes wrong and rewards goodness, we are fully within what Judaism teaches.*

*But is all wrong punished, all goodness rewarded? What of people of whom we feel, "They have no conscience"?*

*Perhaps they are part of the abundant evidence that God's world is as yet very far from reaching perfection and that God has given man the task of developing a universal conscience.*

(*Meyer Levin*, Beginnings in Jewish Philosophy, *Behrman House, New York, 1971, pp. 78–85*)

---

Quoting the third-century teacher Yannai, contemporary Rabbi Robert Gordis writes: "It is not in our power fully to explain either the well-being of the wicked or the suffering of the righteous." Gordis sees the universe "as a work of art, the pattern of which cannot be discerned if the spectator stands too close to the painting." He claims it is only "as one moves back a distance" that the "blotches dissolve and the design of the artist emerges in all its fullness."

Gordis's point is that human beings "are too close to the pattern of existence, too deeply involved in it, to be able to achieve the perspective that is God's alone." As a result we cannot fully comprehend the meaning of God's rewards or punishments, nor the reasons for our joys and sufferings. In the end, after all our explorations and explanations, we are left face to face with the mystery of life and with the choice to mold whatever we are given into blessings or curses, rewards or punishments. (*A Faith for Moderns,* Bloch Publishing Company, New York, 1960, chap. X)

Throughout the centuries, Jews have struggled to understand God's relationship to human beings. The study and practice of Torah became the means through which they sought to master ethical discipline, celebrate the seasons of existence, and unravel the deeper mysteries of life. For the ancient authors of Torah, obedience to the commandments was rewarded with material and spiritual benefits, disobedience was punished by deprivation and destruction.

Some later Jewish thinkers accepted this view of reward and punishment; others strongly disagreed. Instead they argue it is not clear when God rewards or punishes. Perhaps it is here on earth, perhaps in heaven—maybe on both sides of existence.

Still other Jewish commentators believe that God gave the commandments to human beings for their benefit but does not sit in heaven deciding who will suffer and who will have good fortune, who will live and who will die. Instead, the Torah's commandments help us to find strength in times of trouble and faith for the confusions and pain we endure as human beings. Our reward is in the meaning and discipline that the commandments give to our lives. If there is punishment for not observing them, it derives from the loss of wisdom and potential meaning observance may provide.

---

### Obligations of Liberal Jews

*At its June 1976 meeting, the Central Conference of American Rabbis adopted a policy statement:* Reform Judaism: A Centenary Perspective. *In describing the relationship of Reform Jews to the commandments of Jewish tradition, it notes that "Judaism emphasizes action rather than creed as the primary expression of a religious life." Jewish responsibilities for action, the statement continues, "begin with our ethical obligations but they extend to many other aspects of Jewish living, including creating a Jewish home centered on family devotion; lifelong study; private prayer and public worship; daily religious observance; keeping the Sabbath and the holy days; celebrating the major events of life; involvement with the synagogue and community; and other activities that promote the survival of the Jewish people and enhance its existence. Within each area of Jewish observance Reform Jews are called upon to confront the claims of Jewish tradition, however differently perceived, and to exercise their individual autonomy, choosing and creating on the basis of commitment and knowledge."*

---

One other issue concerning the choice of carrying out the commandments of Torah is also important. While the ancient rabbis identified 613 commandments in the Torah, they did not expect that Jews would observe all of them, or all of the rituals traced to them. Since many of the commandments have to do with the sacrifices offered at the Jerusalem Temple, Jewish teachers held that all Jews are exempt from such commandments until the Temple is rebuilt.

Furthermore, there are many cases today, as in the past, where Orthodox Jewish authorities differ in their interpretation and follow diverse practices. For example, some view the commandment "Be fruitful and multiply" as a prohibition against using contraceptives. Other Orthodox Jews disagree, believing that use of contraceptives is permitted once a husband and wife have a male and female child.

Liberal Jews, among them Reform, Conservative, and Reconstructionist Jews, freely choose on an individual basis which commandments they will observe. They are not bound by rabbinic authority, and they reject the idea that God punishes them because of their choices. Instead, liberal Judaism stresses the obligation of every Jew to examine the ethical teachings and ritual observances of Jewish tradition and to choose to put into practice those that will enrich the meaning of life, "promote the survival of the Jewish people, and enhance its existence." The personal fulfillment derived from carrying out a commandment is its own reward.

Perhaps from the time students of Torah began debating whether God actually rewards those who seek to fulfill all the commandments or punishes those who ignore them, there have been Jewish thinkers who believed that the subject was beyond human comprehension. Indeed, to this very day, the matter remains controversial. No one has the answer.

We do not know why the innocent suffer, why cruelty comes into the world, and why some who are selfish have great fortune while some who are generous endure horrors of pain. All we can do is accept the mystery of life and seek to give it meaning with our choices. It is regarding those choices that the Torah tradition can help us. By asking each time we are faced with a significant decision, "What would Jewish wisdom command us to do?" we may increase our options for "rewards" and for "blessings."

## QUESTIONS FOR STUDY AND DISCUSSION

1. What are the ethical lessons we may learn from the Torah's description of the sabbatical and jubilee years? Which of these are most important? Which are least important?
2. Do you agree with Moses Maimonides' ranking of charitable giving?
3. How would you explain why the innocent suffer?
4. Do you agree that suffering and pain result from failing to observe the commandments of Torah or that suffering actually improves character?

# Glossary of Commentaries and Interpreters

*(For further information on those entries followed by an asterisk, see Introduction II in A Torah Commentary for Our Times, Volume One: Genesis.)*

Abravanel, Don Isaac.*

Adani, David ben Amram (13th century). (See *Midrash ha-Gadol.*)

*Akedat Yitzhak.* A commentary to the Torah by Isaac ben Moses Arama. (See Arama, Isaac ben Moses.)

Alshikh, Moshe ben Adrianopolis (1508–1600). Lived and taught in Safed in the Land of Israel. His commentary to the Torah contains his Sabbath sermons.

Arama, Isaac ben Moses (1420–1494). Author of the Torah commentary *Akedat Yitzhak.* Spanish rabbi. Known for his sermons and allegorical interpretations of Torah. Defended Judaism in many public disputes with Christians and settled in Italy after the expulsion of Jews from Spain in 1492.

Ashkenazi, Eliezer ben Elijah (1513–1586). Lived in Egypt, Cyprus, Venice, Prague, and Posen. Died in Cracow. Emphasized the gift of reason and in his commentary, *Ma'aseh ha-Shem,* urged students to approach the Torah with care and independence. Worked as a rabbi, Torah interpreter, and physician. (See *Ma'aseh ha-Shem.*)

Ashkenazi, Shimon (12th century). (See *Yalkut Shimoni.*)

Ashkenazi of Yanof, Jacob ben Isaac (13th century). Author of *Tze'enah u-Re'enah.* (See *Tze'enah u-Re'enah.*)

Astruc, Anselm Solomon. (See *Midrashei Torah.*)

Attar, Chaim ibn (1696–1743). Born in Morocco and settled in Jerusalem where he opened a school. His Torah commentary, *Or ha-Chaim,* combines talmudic and mystical interpretations. (See *Or ha-Chaim.*)

*Avot* or *Pirke Avot,* "Sayings of the Fathers." A book of the *Mishnah,* comprising a collection of statements by famous rabbis.

*Avot de-Rabbi Natan* (2nd century). Compiled by Rabbi Nathan, sometimes called "Nathan the Babylonian." Based on *Pirke Avot.*

Ba'al Ha-Turim, Ya'akov (1275–1340). Born in Germany. Fled persecutions there in 1303 and settled in Spain. Author of the very important collection of Jewish law *Arba'ah Turim,* "Four Rows," the basis for the later *Shulchan Aruch,* "Set Table," by Joseph Karo. His Torah commentary known as *Ba'al ha-Turim* often includes interpretations based on the mathematical meanings of Hebrew words.

Bachya ben Asher (14th century). Lived in Saragossa and Aragon. Known for his Torah commentary.

Bachya ben Joseph ibn Pakuda (11th century). Lived in Spain as poet and author of the classic study of Jewish ethics *Hovot ha-Levavot,* "Duties of the Heart." (See *Hovot ha-Levavot.*)

Bamberger, Bernard J.*

Berlin, Naphtali Zvi Judah (1817–1893). Head of the famous yeshivah at Volozhin. Supporter of early Zionism, his Torah commentary, *Ha-Emek Davar,* is a record of his lectures on the weekly portions. (See *Ha-Emek Davar.*)

Bin Gorion, Micha Joseph (Berdyczewski) (1865–1921). Though a Russian citizen, spent most of his years in Germany. A Hebrew writer, his collection of Jewish folktales, *Mimekor Yisrael,* is considered a classic. (See *Mimekor Yisrael.*)

*Biur.* *

Buber, Martin Mordecai (1878–1965). Born in Vienna. Became renowned as a twentieth-century philosopher. With Franz Rosenzweig, translated the Bible into German. His *Moses* is a commentary on Exodus.

Caspi, Joseph ben Abba Mari (1280–1340). A philosopher and commentator who lived in France. His commentary seeks to blend reason with religious faith.

Cassuto, Umberto. An Italian historian and biblical scholar. Accepted chair of Bible Studies at Hebrew University, Jerusalem, in 1939, when Italian racial laws made continuation of his work impossible. Wrote famous commentaries on Genesis and Exodus.

*Da'at Zekenim mi-Ba'alei ha-Tosafot.* A thirteenth-century collection of Torah commentaries by students of Rashi who sought to resolve contradictions found within the talmudic discussions of the rabbis.

De Leon, Moses. (See *Zohar.*)*

*Deuteronomy Rabbah.* One of the early collections of *midrashim.* *

Dubno, Solomon. (See *Biur.*) *

*Ecclesiastes Rabbah.* One of the early collections of *midrashim.* *

Edels, Shemuel Eliezer ben Yehudah Halevi (1555–1631). One of the best known and repsected interpreters of Talmud. Born in Cracow. Also known as the *Maharsha*.

Epstein, Baruch (1860–1942). Murdered by the Nazis in the Pinsk ghetto. (See *Torah Temimah*.)

*Exodus Rabbah*. One of the early collections of *midrashim*.*

*Genesis Rabbah*. One of the early collections of *midrashim*.*

*Gittin*. A tractate of Talmud that discusses the laws of divorce.

*Guide for the Perplexed*. A philosophical discussion of the meanings of Jewish belief written by Moses Maimonides. (See Maimonides, Moses.)

Ha-Cohen, Meir Simcha (1843–1926). (See *Meshekh Hochmah*.)

*Ha-Emek Davar*. A Torah commentary written by Naphtali Zvi Judah Berlin. (See Berlin, Naphtali Zvi Judah.)

*Ha-Ketav ve-ha-Kabbalah*. A Torah commentary written by Jacob Zvi Meklenburg.*

Halevi, Aharon (1230–1300). Born in Gerona, Spain. Served as rabbi and judge in Barcelona, Saragossa, and Toledo. Lecturer in Montpellier, Provençe, France, where he died. While *Sefer ha-Hinuch* is said to have been written by him, many doubt the claim. (See *Sefer ha-Hinuch*.)

Halevi, Isaac ben Yehudah (13th century). (See *Paneah Raza*.)

Halevi, Yehudah (1080–1142?). Born in Spain. Poet, philosopher, and physician. His book *The Kuzari* contains his philosophy of Judaism. It is a dialogue between the king of the Kazars and a rabbi who convinces the king of the superiority of Judaism.

Hallo, William W.*

*Ha-Midrash ve-ha-Ma'aseh*. A commentary to Genesis and Exodus by Yehezkel ben Hillel Aryeh Leib Lipschuetz. (See Lipschuetz, Yehezkel ben Hillel Aryeh Leib.)

Heinemann, Yitzhak (1876–1957). Born in Germany. Israeli scholar and philosopher. His *Ta'amei ha-Mitzvot*, "Reasons for the Commandments," is a study of the meaning of the commandments of Jewish tradition.

Hertz, Joseph Herman.*

Hirsch, Samson Raphael.*

Hirschensohn, Chaim (1857–1935). Born in Safed. Lived most of his life in Jerusalem. Supported the work of Eliezer ben Yehuda's revival of Hebrew.

(See *Nimmukei Rashi*.)

*Hizkuni*. A Torah commentary by Hizkiyahu (Hezekiah) ben Manoah (13th century) of France.

Hoffman, David Zvi (1843–1921). A leading German rabbi. His commentary on Leviticus and Deuteronomy is based on lectures given in the 1870s, seeking to refute biblical critics who argued that the Christian New Testament was superior to the Hebrew Bible.

*Hovot ha-Levavot*, "Duties of the Heart." A classic study of Jewish ethics by Bachya ben Joseph ibn Pakuda. Concerned with the emphasis on ritual among the Jews of his times, Bachya argues that a Jew's highest responsibility is to carry out the ethical commandments of Torah. (See Bachya ben Joseph ibn Pakuda.)

*Hullin*. A tractate of Talmud that discusses laws dealing with killing animals for food.

Ibn Ezra, Abraham.*

Jacob, Benno.*

Kasher, Menachem. (See *Torah Shelemah*.)

*Kelei Yakar*. A Torah commentary written by Solomon Ephraim ben Chaim Lunchitz (1550–1619) of Lvov (Lemberg) Poland.

*Kiddushin*. A tractate of Talmud that discusses laws of marriage.

Kimchi, David (RaDaK).*

Leibowitz, Nehama.*

*Lekach Tov*. A collection of *midrashim* on the Torah and the Five Scrolls (Song of Songs, Ruth, Lamentations, Ecclesiastes, and Esther), by Tobias ben Eliezer (11th century C.E.).

Lipschuetz, Yehezkel ben Hillel Aryeh Lieb (1862–1932). Lithuanian interpreter of Torah and author of *Ha-Midrash ve-ha-Ma'aseh*. (See *Ha-Midrash ve-ha-Ma'aseh*.)

Luzzato, Moshe Chaim (1707–1746). Known also as *Ramhal*. Italian dramatist and mystic whose commentaries were popular among chasidic Jews. His textbook on how to become a righteous person, *Mesillat Yesharim* became one of the most popular books on the subject of Jewish ethics. (See *Mesillat Yesharim*.)

Luzzato, Samuel David.*

*Ma'aseh ha-Shem*. A commentary by Eliezer ben Elijah Ashkenazi published in 1583. (See Ashkenazi, Eliezer ben Elijah.)

Maimonides, Moses, Rabbi Moses ben Maimon (1135–1204). Known by the initials RaMBaM. Born in Cordova, Spain. Physician and philosopher. Wrote the *Mishneh Torah*, a code of Jewish law;

*Guide for the Perplexed,* a philosophy of Judaism; *Sefer ha-Mitzvot,* an outline of the 613 commandments of Torah; and many other interpretations of Jewish tradition. Famous as a physician. Served the leaders in the court of Egypt.

MaLBIM, Meir Lev ben Yechiel Michael.*

*Mechilta.* *

*Megillah.* A tractate of Talmud that discusses the biblical Book of Esther.

Meklenburg, Jacob Zvi. (See *Ha-Ketav ve-ha-Kabbalah.*)*

Mendelssohn, Moses.*

*Meshekh Hochmah.* A Torah commentary published in 1927. Written by Meir Simcha Ha-Cohen, rabbi of Dvinsk. Combines insights from the Talmud with a discussion of the philosophy of Judaism. (See Ha-Cohen, Meir Simcha.)

*Mesillat Yesharim, "Pathway of the Righteous."* A discussion of how one should pursue an ethical life. Written by Moshe Chaim Luzzatto (see above).

*Messengers of God.* A study of several important biblical personalities, by Elie Wiesel. (See Wiesel, Elie; also Bibliography in this book.)

*Midrash Agadah.* A collection of rabbinic interpretations. (See discussion of *midrashim.*)*

*Midrash ha-Gadol.* A collection of rabbinic interpretations dating to the first and second centuries, by David ben Amram Adani, a scholar living in Yemen. (See Adani, David ben Amram.)

*Midrash Sechel Tov.* Compiled by Menachem ben Solomon in 1139. Combines selections of *midrash* and *halachah* on every Torah portion.

*Midrash Tanchuma.* Known also as *Tanchuma Midrash Yelamedenu.* A collection said to have been collected by Rabbi Tanchuma (427–465 C.E.). Many of the *midrashim* begin with the words *Yelamedenu rabbenu,* "Let our teacher instruct us. . . ."*

*Midrashei Torah.* A Torah commentary by Anselm Solomon Astruc who was murdered in an attack on the Jewish community of Barcelona in 1391.

*Mimekor Yisrael.* A collection of folktales from Jewish tradition by Micha Joseph Bin Gorion (Berdyczewski). (See Bin Gorion.)

*Mishnah.* *

Mizrachi, Eliyahu (1440–1525). A Chief Rabbi of Turkey during the expulsion of Jews from Spain. Helped many immigrants. Wrote a commentary to Rashi's Torah interpretation.

Morgenstern, Julian.*

Nachmanides.* (See RaMBaN.)

*Nedarim.* A tractate of Talmud that discusses vows or promises.

*Nimmukei Rashi.* A commentary on Rashi's Torah interpretation by Chaim Hirschensohn. (See Hirschensohn, Chaim.)

*Numbers Rabbah.* An early collection of *midrashim.* *

*Or ha-Chaim.* A Torah commentary by Chaim ibn Attar. Combines talmudic observations with mystical interpretations. (See Attar, Chaim ibn.)

*Paneah Raza.* A Torah commentary by Isaac ben Yehudah Halevi who lived in Sens. (See Halevi, Isaac ben Yehudah.)

Peli, Pinchas Hacohen (20th century). Jerusalem-born scholar, poet, and rabbi. His "Torah Today" column in the *Jerusalem Post* seeks to present a contemporary view of the meaning of Torah.

*Pesikta de-Rav Kahana.* * A collection of *midrashim* or early rabbinic sermons based on Torah portions for holidays of the Jewish year. *Pesikta Rabbati* is similar in both content and organization.

*Pesikta Rabbati.* * (See *Pesikta de-Rav Kahana.*)

*Pirke de-Rabbi Eliezer.* * A collection of *midrashim* said to have been written by the first-century C.E. teacher Rabbi Eliezer ben Hyrkanos. Contents include mystic interpretations of creation, early human life, the giving of the Torah at Mount Sinai, comments about the Book of Esther, and the Israelite experience in the Sinai.

Plaut, W. Gunther.*

RaDaK, Rabbi David Kimchi.*

RaMBaM, Rabbi Moses ben Maimon. (See Maimonides.)

RaMBaN, Rabbi Moses ben Nachman.* (See Nachmanides.)

RaSHBaM, Rabbi Shemuel (Samuel) ben Meir.*

RaSHI, Rabbi Shelomoh (Solomon) Itzhaki.*

Reggio, Yitzhak Shemuel (1784–1855). Known also as YaSHaR. Lived in Italy. Translated the Bible into Italian. Created a Hebrew commentary that sought to harmonize science and religion.

Rosenzweig, Franz (1886–1929). German philosopher. Worked with Martin Buber in translating the Bible into German. Best known for book *The Star of Redemption,* which seeks to explore the meanings of Jewish tradition.

Sa'adia ben Joseph Ha-Gaon.* (See Introductions I and II of *A Torah Commentary for Our Times, Volume One: Genesis.*

*Sanhedrin.* A tractate of Talmud that discusses laws

regulating the courts.

Sarna, Nahum M.*

*Sefer ha-Hinuch.* Presents the 613 *mitzvot*, "commandments," found within the Torah. Divided according to weekly Torah portions. Said by some to have been written by Aharon Halevi of Barcelona. (See Halevi, Aharon.)

Sforno, Obadiah.*

*Shabbat.* A tractate of the Talmud that discusses the laws of the Sabbath.

*Sifra.** A *midrash* on Leviticus. Believed by scholars to have been written during the fourth century C.E.

*Sifre.** A *midrash* on Numbers and Deuteronomy. Believed to have been composed during the fifth century C.E.

Simeon (Shimon) ben Yochai.* (See *Zohar.*)*

Solomon, Menachem ben. (See *Midrash Sechel Tov.*)

*Sotah.* A tractate of the Talmud that discusses laws concerning a woman suspected of adultery.

Speiser, Ephraim Avigdor.*

Steinsaltz, Adin (20th century). An Israeli Talmud scholar. His book *Biblical Images* contains studies of various biblical characters.

*Ta'amei ha-Mitzvot.* (See Heinemann, Yitzhak.)

*Ta'anit.* A tractate of the Talmud that deals with the laws concerning fast days.

*Talmud.** Combines the *Mishnah* and *Gemara.* Appears in two versions: the more extensive *Talmud Bavli*, "Babylonian Talmud," a collection of discussions by the rabbis of Babylonia from the second to the fifth centuries C.E., and *Talmud Yerushalmi*, "Jerusalem Talmud," a smaller collection of discussions from the second to the fourth centuries C.E.

*Tanna Debe Eliyahu.* A *midrash* and book of Jewish philosophy and commentary believed by scholars to have been composed during the third to tenth centuries. Author unknown.

*Targum Onkelos.**

*Targum Yerushalmi.**

*Toledot Yitzhak.*

*Torah Shelemah.* A study of each Torah portion, which includes a collection of early rabbinic interpretations along with a commentary by Rabbi Menachem Kasher of Jerusalem, Israel.

*Torah Temimah.* A Torah commentary by Baruch Epstein. Includes a collection of teachings from the Talmud on each Torah portion. (See Epstein, Baruch.)

*Tosafot.* "Supplementary Discussions" of the Talmud. Collected during the twelfth and thirteenth centuries in France and Germany and added to nearly every printing of the Talmud since.

*Tzedeh Laderech.* An interpretation of Rashi's Torah commentary by Issachar Ber ben Israel-Lazar Parnas Eilenberg (1550–1623), who lived in Italy.

*Tze'enah u-Re'enah.* A well-known Yiddish paraphrase and interpretation of the Torah. First published in 1618. Written for women by Jacob ben Isaac Ashkenazi of Yanof. Divided by weekly Torah portions. One of the first texts developed to educate women. (See Ashkenazi of Yanof, Jacob ben Isaac.)

Wessely, Naftali Herz. (See *Biur.*)*

Wiesel, Elie (1928–    ). Nobel Prize-winning novelist. Author of *Messengers of God,* among other books. (See *Messengers of God.*)

*Yalkut Shimoni.* A collection of *midrashim.* Believed to be the work of Shimon Ashkenazi. (See Ashkenazi, Shimon.)

*Yevamot.* A tractate of Talmud that deals with laws concerning sisters-in-law.

*Yoma.* A tractate of Talmud that deals with laws concerning Yom Kippur.

*Zohar.**

# *Bibliography*

Abbott, Walter M.; Gilbert, Arthur; Hunt, Rolfe Lanier; and Swain, J. Carter. *The Bible Reader: An Interfaith Interpretation.* New York: Bruce Publishing Co., 1969.

Adar, Zvi. *Humanistic Values in the Bible.* New York: Reconstructionist Press, 1967.

Adler, Morris, *The Voice Still Speaks.* New York: Bloch Publishing Co., 1969.

Aharoni, Yohanan, and Avi-Yonah, Michael. *The Macmillan Bible Atlas.* New York: Macmillan, 1976.

Alter, Robert. *The Art of Biblical Narrative.* New York: Basic Books, 1981.

Asimov, Isaac. *Animals of the Bible.* Garden City, New York: Doubleday, 1978.

Avi-Yonah, Michael, and Malamat, Abraham, eds. *Views of the Biblical World.* Chicago and New York: Jordan Publications, Inc., 1959.

Bachya ben Asher. *Kad ha-Kemach.* Charles B. Chavel, trans. New York: Shilo Publishing House, Inc., 1980.

Baron, Joseph L., ed. *A Treasury of Jewish Quotations*. New York: Crown Publishers, Inc., 1956.

Ben-Gurion, David. *Israel, a Personal History*. New York: Funk and Wagnalls, Inc., and Sabra Books, 1971.

Blumenthal, David R. *God at the Center*. San Francisco: Harper and Row, 1987.

Braude, William G., and Kapstein, Israel J., trans. Author unknown. *Tanna Debe Eliyahu*. Philadelphia: Jewish Publication Society, 1981.

Buber, Martin. *Moses*. New York: Harper and Row Publishers, Inc., 1958.

Bulka, Reuven P. *Torah Therapy: Reflections on the Weekly Sedra and Special Occasions*. New York: Ktav, 1983.

Cassuto, Umberto. *A Commentary on the Book of Exodus*. Jerusalem: Magnes Press, 1951.

Chavel, Charles B., trans. *Ramban (Nachmanides) Commentary on the Torah*. New York: Shilo Publishing House, Inc., 1974.

Chiel, Arthur. *Guide to Sidrot and Haftarot*. New York: Ktav, 1971.

Chill, Abraham. *The Minhagim: The Customs and Ceremonies of Judaism, Their Origins and Rationale*. New York: Sepher-Hermon Press, 1979.

Cohen, Philip. *Rambam on the Torah*. Jerusalem: Rubin Mass Ltd. Publishers, 1985.

Culi, Ya'akov. *The Torah Anthology, Yalkut Me'am Lo'ez*. Aryeh Kaplan, trans. New York and Jerusalem: Maznaim Publishing Corp., 1977.

Danby, Herbert, trans. *The Mishnah*. London: Oxford University Press, 1933.

Deen, Edith. *All of the Women of the Bible*. New York: Harper and Brothers, 1965.

Doria, Charles, and Lenowitz, Harris, trans. and eds. *Origins, Creation Texts from the Ancient Mediterranean*. New York: Anchor Press, 1976.

Dresner, Samuel H., and Siegel, Seymour. *The Jewish Dietary Laws*. New York: Burning Bush Press, 1959.

Efron, Benjamin. *The Message of the Torah*. New York: Ktav, 1963.

Epstein, I., trans. and ed. *The Babylonian Talmud*. London: Soncino Press, 1952.

Fields, Harvey J. *Bechol Levavcha: With All Your Heart*. New York: Union of American Hebrew Congregations, 1976.

Freedman, H., and Simon, Maurice, trans. *Midrash Rabbah: Genesis,* Vols. I and II. London: Soncino Press, 1961.

Friedman, Alexander Zusia. *Wellsprings of Torah*. Compiled and edited by Nison Alpert. Gertrude Hirschler, trans. New York: Judaica Press, 1986.

Friedman, Richard Elliott. *Who Wrote the Bible?* New York: Summit Books, 1987.

Fromm, Erich. *You Shall Be as Gods*. New York: Holt, Rinehart and Winston, 1966.

Frye, Northrop. *The Great Code: The Bible and Literature*. New York: Harcourt Brace Jovanovich Publishers, 1981.

Gaster, Theodor H. *Festivals of the Jewish Year*. New York: William Morrow and Co., Inc. 1953.

Gilbert, Martin. *Jewish History Atlas*. New York: Macmillan, 1976.

Ginzberg, Louis. *Legends of the Jews*. Philadelphia: Jewish Publication Society, 1968.

Gittelsohn, Roland B. *Man's Best Hope*. New York: Random House, 1961.

Glatzer, Nahum N., ed. *Hammer on the Rock: A Midrash Reader*. New York: Schocken Books, 1962.

_____. *On the Bible: 18 Studies*. New York: Schocken Books, 1968.

Goldman, Solomon. *In the Beginning*. Philadelphia: Jewish Publication Society of America, 1949.

Gordis, Robert. *A Faith for Moderns*. New York: Bloch Publishing Co., 1960.

Graves, Robert, and Patai, Raphael. *Hebrew Myths: The Book of Genesis*. New York: Greenwich House, 1983.

Greenberg, Moshe. *Understanding Exodus*. New York: Behrman House, 1969.

Hartman, David. *A Living Covenant*. New York: The Free Press, 1985.

Herford, R. Travers. *Pirke Aboth, The Ethics of the Talmud: Sayings of the Fathers*. New York: Schocken Books, 1971.

Hertz, J.H., ed. *The Pentateuch and Haftorahs*. London: Soncino Press, 1966.

Heschel, Abraham J. *The Prophets*. Philadelphia: Jewish Publication Society, 1962.

_____. *God in Search of Man: A Philosophy of Judaism*. New York: Farrar, Straus and Cudahy, 1955.

Hirsch, Samson Raphael, trans. *The Pentateuch*. London, England: L. Honig and Sons Ltd., 1959.

_____. *Horeb: A Philosophy of Jewish Laws and Observances*. I. Grunfeld, trans. 4th ed. New York: Soncino Press, 1981.

*The Interpreter's Bible.* 12 vols. Nashville: Abingdon, 1951–1957.

Jacobson, B.S. *Meditations on the Torah.* Tel Aviv: Sinai Publishing, 1956.

Kahana, S.Z. *Heaven on Your Head.* Morris Silverman, ed. Hartford: Hartmore House, 1964.

Kaplan, Mordecai M. *Questions Jews Ask: Reconstructionist Answers.* New York: Reconstructionist Press, 1956.

_____. *The Meaning of God in Modern Jewish Religion.* New York: Reconstructionist Press, 1962.

Katz, Mordechai. *Lilmod Ul'lamade: From the Teachings of Our Sages.* New York: Jewish Education Program Publications, 1978.

Korn, Lester. *The Success Profile.* New York: Fireside, 1988.

Kushner, Harold S. *When Bad Things Happen to Good People.* New York: Schocken Books, 1981.

Lamm, Maurice. *The Jewish Way in Death and Mourning.* New York: Jonathan David Publishers, 1975.

Leibowitz, Nehama. *Studies in Bereshit.* Jerusalem: World Zionist Organization, 1980.

_____. *Studies in Shemot.* Jerusalem: World Zionist Organization, 1980.

_____. *Studies in Vayikra.* Jerusalem: World Zionist Organization, 1980.

_____. *Studies in Bemidbar.* Jerusalem: World Zionist Organization, 1980.

_____. *Studies in Devarim.* Jerusalem: World Zionist Organization, 1980.

Levin, Meyer. *Beginnings in Jewish Philosophy.* New York: Behrman House, 1971.

Levine, Baruch A. ed. *JPS Torah Commentary: Leviticus.* Philadelphia: Jewish Publication Society, 1989.

Levine, Moshe. *The Tabernacle: Its Structure and Utensils.* London: Soncino Press, 1969.

Maimonides, Moses. *The Book of Knowledge: Mishneh Torah.* Moses Hyamson, trans. Jerusalem and New York: Feldheim Publishers, 1974.

Matek, Ord. *The Bible through Stamps.* New York: Hebrew Publishing Company, 1967.

Miller, Madeline S., and Lane, J. *Harper's Encyclopedia of Bible Life.* New York: Harper and Row Publishers, Inc., 1978.

Morgenstern, Julian. *The Book of Genesis.* New York: Schocken Books, 1965.

Munk, Eli. *The Call of the Torah,* Vols. I and II. Jerusalem and New York: Feldheim Publishers, 1980.

Neusner, Jacob. *Meet Our Sages.* New York: Behrman House, 1980.

_____. *Tzedakah.* Chappaqua, New York: Rossel, 1982.

Orlinsky, Harry M., ed. *The Torah: The Five Books of Moses.* A New Translation. Philadelphia: Jewish Publication Society, 1962.

_____. *Understanding the Bible through History and Archaeology.* New York: Ktav, 1972.

Peli, Pinchas H. *Torah Today.* Washington, D.C.: B'nai B'rith Books, 1987.

_____. *Shabbat Shalom.* Washington, D.C.: B'nai B'rith Books, 1988.

Peters, Thomas J., and Waterman, Jr., Robert H. *In Search of Excellence.* New York: Harper and Row Publishers, Inc., 1982.

Pfeiffer, Robert H. *Introduction to the Old Testament.* New York: Harper and Brothers, 1941.

Phillips, Anthony. Exodus Commentary. *The Cambridge Bible Commentary: New English Bible.* Cambridge, England: Cambridge University Press, 1972.

Plaut, W. Gunther, ed. *The Torah: A Modern Commentary.* Commentaries by W. Gunther Plaut and Bernard J. Bamberger. Essays by William W. Hallo. New York: Union of American Hebrew Congregations, 1981.

_____. *The Case for the Chosen People.* New York: Doubleday, 1965.

Pritchard, James B., ed. *Ancient Near Eastern Texts Relating to the Old Testament.* Princeton, New Jersey: Princeton University Press, 1955.

Quick, James C., and Jonathan D. *Organizational Stress and Preventive Management.* New York: McGraw-Hill, 1984.

Rabbinowitz, J., trans. *Midrash Rabbah* (Genesis, Exodus, Leviticus, Numbers, Deuteronomy). London: Soncino Press, 1961.

Rabinowitz, Louis I. *Torah and Flora.* New York: Sanhedrin Press, 1977.

Rad, Gerhard von. *Deuteronomy.* Commentary and translation by Dorothea Barton. Philadelphia: Westminster Press, 1966.

Reed, Allison. *The Story of Creation.* New York: Schocken Books, 1981.

Rosenbaum, M., and Silbermann, A.M., trans. *Pentateuch with Targum Onkelos, Haphtaroth and Rashi's Commentary.* Jerusalem: Silbermann Family Publishers, 1973.

Rosenberg, David, ed. *Congregation: Contemporary*

*Writers Read the Jewish Bible*. New York: Harcourt Brace Jovanovich Publishers, 1987.

Samuel, Maurice. *Certain People of the Book*. New York: Alfred A. Knopf, Inc., 1955.

Sandmel, Samuel. *Alone Atop the Mountain: A Novel about Moses and the Exodus*. New York: Doubleday, 1973.

Sarna, Nahum M. *Understanding Genesis*. New York: Schocken Books, 1966.

Schneerson, Menachem M. *Torah Studies*. London: Lubavitch Foundation, 1986.

_____. *Likutei Sichot*. London: Lubavitch Foundation, 1975–1985.

Sheehy, Gail. *Pathfinders*. New York: William Morrow, 1981.

Silbermann, A.M., ed. *Pentateuch with Rashi Commentary*. Jerusalem: Silbermann Family Publishers, 1933.

Silver, Abba Hillel. *Moses and the Original Torah*. New York: Macmillan, 1961.

_____. *The World Crisis and Jewish Survival*. New York: Richard R. Smith, Inc., 1931.

Silverman, Hillel E. *From Week to Week*. New York: Hartmore House, 1975.

Simon, Solomon, and Morrison, David Bial. *The Rabbis' Bible*. New York: Behrman House, 1966.

Speiser, E.A., trans. *The Anchor Bible: Genesis*. New York: Doubleday, 1964.

Steinberg, Milton. *Basic Judaism*. New York: Harcourt Brace, 1947.

Steinsaltz, Adin. *The Thirteen Petalled Rose*. New York: Basic Books, 1980.

Van Doren, Mark, and Samuel, Maurice. *In the Beginning . . . Love*. Edith Samuel, ed. New York: John Day Company, 1973.

Weinstein, Jacob J. *The Place of Understanding*. New York: Bloch Publishing Co., 1959.

Wiesel, Elie. *Messengers of God*. New York: Random House, 1976.

Zakon, Miriam Stark, trans. *Tze'enah u-Re'enah: The Classic Anthology of Torah Lore and Midrashic Commentary*. Brooklyn, New York: Mesorah Publications Ltd./Hillel Press, 1983.

Zeligs, Dorothy F. *Psychoanalysis and the Bible*. New York: Bloch Publishing Co., 1974.

Zlotowitz, Meir, trans. *Bereishis*. Art Scroll Tanach Series. New York: Mesorah Publications Ltd., 1977–1981.